ITHELL COLQUHOUN

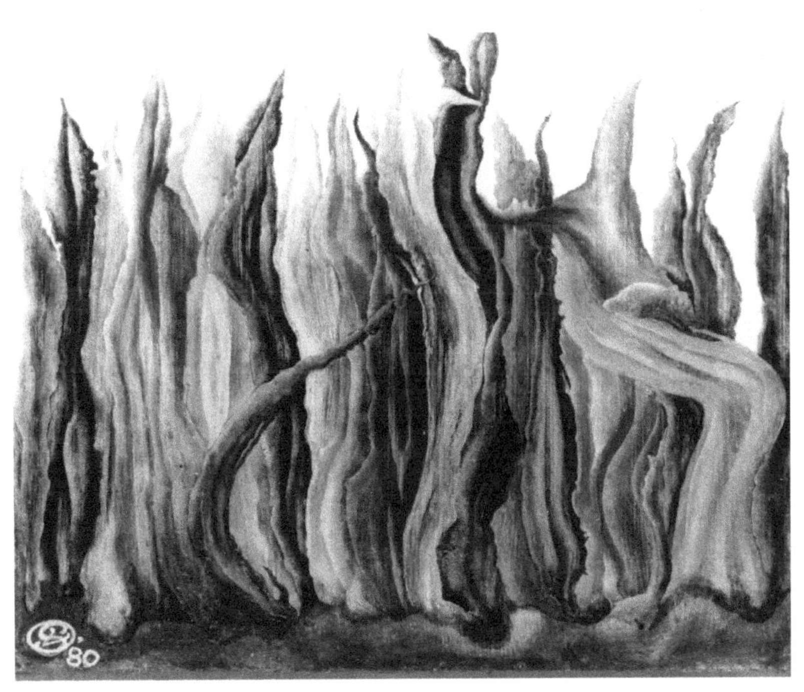

First Edition 2007
1st Impression 2016

Published by
Mandrake of Oxford
PO Box 250
OXFORD
OX1 1AP (UK)

Frontispiece : *Dark Fire* (1980, enamel on board, 24.5 x 31.8 cm)
Royal Cornwall Museum, Truro

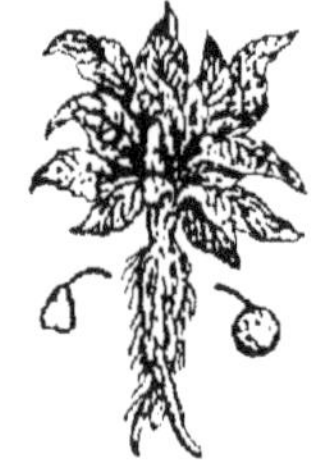

Contents

Acknowledgements

To Jane Ruddell and Jennifer Booth of the Tate Gallery archives, C.J.Pearson of the National Trust (Cornwall), Simon Buxton, John Halkes, Peter and Renate Nahum, Tony Pusey, Michel Remy, Richard Shillitoe, and Derek Stanford, who kindly provided or made available useful data or illustrations and other items.

For assistance in infomation I thank Catherine Ames, Maureen Ballard, Tehmina Bhote, Kath Boothman, Whitney Chadwick, Daniel Cohen, Marian Green, Sheila Cavell Hicks, Paul McKee, Conroy Maddox, Michael Parkin, Clare Parry, Cheryl Straffon, and Caroline Worthington.

Acknowledgements are also due to Michel Remy and Ashgate Publishing for permission to quote sundry long passages and use of the illustrations *A Visitation, Dance of the Nine Opals and Dervish* in *Surrealism in Britain*; Whitney Chadwick and Thames and Hudson for text from p.190 and use of the illustration *Bride of the Pavement* in *Women Artists and the Surrealist Movement*; Derek Stanford and Poetry Salzburg for poetry extracted from *The Memorare Sequence*; to Peter Owen for the use of text extracts from those of her books for which he still held reproduction rights; and to W.J. Brooker for valuable technical assistance in finalising the manuscript .

Eric Ratcliffe

Illustrations

CREDITS

Every attempt has been made to contact relevant copyright holders for permissions, but it is regretted that in a very few instances this was not possible.

Frontispiece © Estate of Ithell Colquhoun, photo Witt Library; **1,2**. © Cheltenham Ladies' College; **3**. © Studio Hugo, photo Tate Gallery Archive TGA 929; **4, 5**. © National Portrait Gallery, London; **6-8**. © Estate of Ithell Colquhoun, illus. Ore Publications; **9**. © Clare Parry; **10**. © Estate of Ithell Colquhoun, photo Gareth Dodd; **11**. © Clare Parry; **12**. © Estate of Elektra Mangoletsi, drawing National Portrait Gallery, London; **13**. *Gloucestershire Echo*,cutting; **14**. *Hampstead Express*, cutting; **15**.© Hulton Archives/Getty Images; **16.** © Joan Wills, illus. Parkin Gallery catalogue 1977 ('Ithell Colquhoun, Paintings and Drawings 1930-1940'); **17**. © The National Trust, photo Tate Gallery Archive TGA 929; **18**. © Estate of Ithell Colquhoun, photo Witt Library; **19**. © Estate of Ithell Colquhoun, photo Tate Gallery Archive TGA 929; **20**. © Estate of Ithell Colquhoun, photo John Halkes; **21**. © Estate of Ithell Colquhoun, photo Witt Library; **22-24**. © Estate of Ithell Colquhoun, photos Tate Gallery Archive TGA 929; **25**. © Estate of Ithell Colquhoun, illus. Leva Gallery catalogue 1974 ('Ithell Colquhoun, Surrealist Paintings and Drawings 1930-1950'); **26**. © Estate of Ithell Colquhoun, illus. from *Surrealism in Britain*, p.250, courtesy of author and publishers; **27**. © Estate of Ithell Colquhoun, photo John Halkes; **28**. © Estate of Ithell Colquhoun, photostat Tate Gallery Archive TGA 929; **29**. © Estate of Ithell Colquhoun, photo Cartwright Hall Gallery, Bradford; **30, 31**. © Estate of Ithell Colquhoun, illus. from *Surrealism in Britain*, p.246 and p.315, courtesy of author and publishers; **32**. © Tate Gallery, London; **33**. © Estate of Ithell Colquhoun, photo Witt Library; **34**. © Estate of Ithell Colquhoun, photo Royal Pavilion, Libraries and Museums, Brighton; **35**. © Hunterian Art Gallery, Univ. of Glasgow; **36**. © Estate of Ithell Colquhoun, photo Southampton City Art Gallery; **37**. © Estate of Ithell Colquhoun, illus. from *Women Artists and the Surrealist Movement*, p.128, courtesy of author and publishers; **38-43**. © Estate of Ithell Colquhoun, photos Witt Library; **44**. © Estate of Ithell Colquhoun, illus. from *Surrealism in Britain*, p.279, courtesy of author and publishers; **45-50**. © Estate of Ithell Colquhoun, photos Witt Library; **51-80**. © The National Trust; **81,82**. © Estate of Ithell Colquhoun, photos Leicester Galleries; **83**. © The Breton Gorsedd; **84**. Courtesy of Auckland City Libraries, New Zealand; **85**. © The Royal Artillery Institution; **86**. © Les Holder; author photo back cover © Karl Schmierer.

Introduction

Ithell Colquhoun was an artist of international reputation, whose best work has been well documented. Her acclaimed paintings, drawings and collages have been exhibited at many galleries and other venues. We met when, as a Guest Companion, she participated in public ceremonies of the English Druid Order; much later I visited her at Tring, in the grounds of Champneys Health Resort, where she had gone for recuperative treatment. In between I published some of her poetry with artwork relevant to her Celtic interests.(1)

Various writers have mentioned her paintings and drawings; however, she had many strings to her bow. She wrote poems which surfaced in many other places, created major texts on travel and of occult persuasion which were reviewed in the top media of the day. She published articles on or included in her texts not only her art theories on automatic processes, but also items in Hermetic and Kabbalistic traditions and on Celtic subjects.

At some time in mid-career as an artist, her occult interests grew stronger and were reflected in her work. Her refusal to abandon these lines of thought, among other resolves which characterized her active, independent outlook, led to a formal break with the London-based surrealist group to which she belonged. She had been associated with this not long after surrealism publicly reached the country (the London Surrealist Exhibition of 1936), via an international exhibition where she was an early female exponent of the art.

She was in fact bored with the restrictive political side of surrealism, and refused to conform to anti-bourgeois dictats affecting exhibition venues and other matters. Neither, it appears, had she much interest in the social climate of the hedonistic kind of more materialistic artists of the day. After her marriage to Toni del Renzio failed, she moved to Hampstead and finally found a delightful congeniality in Cornwall in which her sensitivity to nature and her Celtic interests found full expression.

The main references to her art can currently be found in books by Whitney Chadwick: *Women Artists and the Surrealist Movement*, and by Michel Remy in his comprehensive work *Surrealism in Britain* (2,3). Her four books and two poetry collections (4,5) are out of print at the time of writing.

My own feeling is that she was unique in being able to enter areas of abstract reality through an expanded consciousness, particular noteworthy in rendition of the vegetable world, objectively returning to image her experiences as co-existent with the inner life of the subject. It is a pity that my search for her work in that direction resulted in very few illustrated examples – the remainder no doubt being kept and treasured by others in collections.

The magnetism which drew her to the west country was perhaps in her maternal blood-line. Following a holiday at St. Ives in her youth, she was to return to the Cornwall area many years later, and never to permanently leave it.

Her prolific artistic output and capacity for exhibition provided a daunting task to assemble in some order many years after her death, exacerbated by the disposal of many items from her estate. Inevitably there will be omissions, but some 350 titles were found which, together with a long exhibition list, are in the Appendixes. When in Cornwall, she participated in several exhibitions at her 'local' gallery at Newlyn. Here, I feel, are omissions, as archival information could not be obtained.

I am indebted to Dr.Richard Shillitoe for provision of some basic chronological framework, which I edited and built on. A bonus was a catalogue list of works in her Paul studio prepared by Elizabeth Knowles for the National Trust in 1990, to which Ithell Colquhoun bequeathed them. This is referred to as the '1990 listing', particularly useful to define much art work not publicly exhibited in her lifetime. Ithell Colquhoun died in her beloved Lamorna Valley, with a reputation as a dedicated and skilful surrealist artist. This book gathers together, for the first time, the whole Ithell Colquhoun, with her wealth of knowledge and labours in a kaleidoscope of interests – art, poetry, writing, Celtic atmosphere, the occult and magic. I do not think that the full intensity and scope of her numerous activities have ever been realised. An offshoot of the research was an examination of her maternal blood-line (Appendix III), which includes a Surgeon-General who was a Victoria Cross holder and, much earlier, a Captain in the Sea-Fencible system devised to protect the country from Napoleonic invasion.

Lack of contact with relatives prevented possible inclusion of family information, photographs, and so on, which would have been dynamically interesting. Ithell's own writings, as seen, were minimal on matters not connected with her dedicatory interests. Her movements from place to place, dates, and connected material facts, often needed to be inferred. For the times, she was much travelled, living in Paris, Greece and Cyprus, travelling in Egypt and most European countries, including Czechoslovakia. Her work in her lifetime was shown in close to 100 exhibition centres.

The Tate Gallery archivists in post at that time provided help in the search for some art and literary effects. I hope that there are not too many omissions and errors in the various lists. Some artwork reproductions may be found wanting: these were taken from negatives or prints kindly supplied by the National Trust, intended to be used for sales or identification purposes only. Some of these were welcomed for use but naturally lack the full technique to produce professional illustrations for a text-book. Overall the artwork imagery may be found disappointing, but I did my best to secure what I could, long after the death of the artist and dispersal of valuable work to collections and galleries.

Eventually, I think, Ithell Colquhoun was well out of the shifting sands of Freudian impulse; and embraced wider and more permanent values of the inner self and states of consciousness rather in Jungian mode, allied with esoteric knowledge. The foundation archetypes, her later preoccupations with symbols of the elements, a pantheistic feeling for natural life, seemed the right way to go – to also align with the persistency of myths of the people and the land. One could note a statement by Ross Nichols in his prologue to *The Cosmic Shape* (6), when remarking on relevant basic mind patterns concerned with primitive life schemes: 'The Surrealists, while they have opened the way to a franker call upon the unconscious, wherein such patterns reside, have not taken the full liberty of their programme.'

The doors opened by automatic processes and surrealist thought can reveal much that is not part of the enduring human psyche, but a reflection of personal, primal instincts. The sexual and the desire quality of the revelations, such as emphasised in the last large surrealist exhibition, Desire Unbound, at the Tate Modern, in which Ithell was not represented, provided a visual impact of these instincts within the overall theme. In my opinion, there was a fork in the road, and Ithell Colquhoun eventually diverged to a valid path of more useful exploration.

I believe that there is an interesting large question-mark relative to the sources of painting from, say, hypnagogic starting points, to quote just one 'automatic process', both in initial acquisition of basic imagery, and sometimes in execution by uncontrolled impulse. This is not the place to discuss it further, but it lies in the confusing area of an inner world accessible at special periods which may not be illusory – the world of William Blake. I suspect that, whereas there have been many books on the subject, the fringe meeting place between this and surrealist work has received little serious attention. In this field, we need to know a lot more about ourselves, forces in the unconscious mind, multiple personalities, automatic action, and even ultimate reality before we say that the painting hand of a surrealist artist is driven by the artist's own mind in the subconscious mode.

I think it probable in those days that Ithell Colquhoun had to battle against prejudices which conferred less recognition of her as a surrealist than would be expected, as she became more learned in occult matters. But in a late essay 'Surrealism and Hermetic Poetry' (7) she compares the alchemistic search for the elixir with the aspiration of a writer sympathetic to surrealism and points out that Breton himself stressed the fact that poetry and magic were aspects of the same thing, linking him with magical tradition. Interchangeability between occult and surrealist philosophy is also analysed in *Surrealism and the Occult* (8). Colquhoun, although virtually an independent exile from the politically dominated surrealist movement, as it was then, seems much more devoted to a path of truth via occult linkage than other artists. I believe that she was one of the most loyal disciples of André Breton. As she grew older, so did her desire for peace in the environment grow, uninterrupted by noisy tourists and the background hum and rumble of the age of machinery. It was an indication that she often lived within a level of consciousness where the five-sense world and common communication was alien and had to be escaped from. It was a discipline which was to show in the tone of her textbooks and artwork.

A definitive printed catalogue of Ithell's artwork is also available from Dr. Richard Shillitoe at 19 Alexandra Crescent, Ilkley, West Yorks. LS29 9ER.

Eric Ratcliffe

I The Formative Years

Ithell Colquhoun was born in India (at Shillong, Assam) on October 9th, 1906, and named Margaret Ithell Colquhoun. She claimed to be of Irish, Scottish and Welsh descent. Her father, Henry Archibald Colebrooke Colquhoun, was in India in December 1895, appointed to the Indian Civil Service as Assistant Commissioner and Assistant to the Political Agent in Manipur, Assam. By 1912 he was Deputy Commissioner , and eventually retired from the Service in 1921 (1). Henry married the Woolwich-born Georgia Frances Ithell Manley in Assam in 1905, when he was about 35 and his spouse 32.

Appendix III contains an ancestral descent relative to Ithell's maternal line. Regarding her paternal line there is nothing substantial to record, but it is probable that it figured in important administrative posts in India. One might hazard that the 'Archibald' in her father's name was a family memory of the Archibald Colquhoun, 'a retired colonial officer who was appointed to administer the new country', in Africa, who rode with Rhodes' pioneering army to found Fort Salisbury, subsequently replaced by Dr. Jameson (2).

Nothing is known of their early married life in India, or how and where the couple met. However, each was of military descent and it might be conjectured that they met in India. Henry was the son of

Lt.-Colonel J.A.S. Colquhoun of the Royal Artillery, and Georgia's father, who had died in 1901, was an Irish Manley, retired Surgeon-General in the Royal Artillery. He was awarded the VC for bravery in rescue missions in 1864 during the Maori wars in New Zealand (3) when Assistant Surgeon.

With no back-up evidence from relatives or other sources, one needs to rely on a statement by Ithell, in an article in *The Cornishman* (4), some 55 years later, that she left India 'shortly after my first birthday'. Immediately the skein of events becomes chronologically tangled, for her father was still serving in India, and sometime in 1908 Ithell's brother Robert Sutherland was born. We need to surmise that Georgia and the infant Ithell sailed to England c.1907-8, accompanied by Henry who had taken home leave, else with a companion or alone. Perhaps even in 1909 with baby Robert as well. It does not seem an auspicious time for a long and arduous sea voyage for Georgia, either pregnant with Robert or present as a baby and is too early to consider educating her family, in England as an objective. Henry needed to complete his career, hence the split, but it was not a separation, since Ithell's parents were reported present at her 1936 exhibition at Cheltenham Art Gallery. Six years later Henry died in Cheltenham, having set up home at 'Battledown Priors', a prestigious estate development at Cheltenham, in about 1927 or slightly later.

Much-decorated with military honours, the Dublin-born father of Georgia and her mother Maria had settled at Cheltenham, probably in the 1880s. More likely, in emergency, Georgia may have decided to be with or to look after her widowed mother, who had lost a son serving with the Marines during the Boxer Rebellion in China in the same year that her husband died (1901). Whatever the circumstances, they were fortunate later for Ithell, setting the stage for a good education at Cheltenham Ladies' College, and some training at the Cheltenham School of Art. We lose sight of Georgia at a home in about 1942 where she moved from the Priors after the death of Henry.

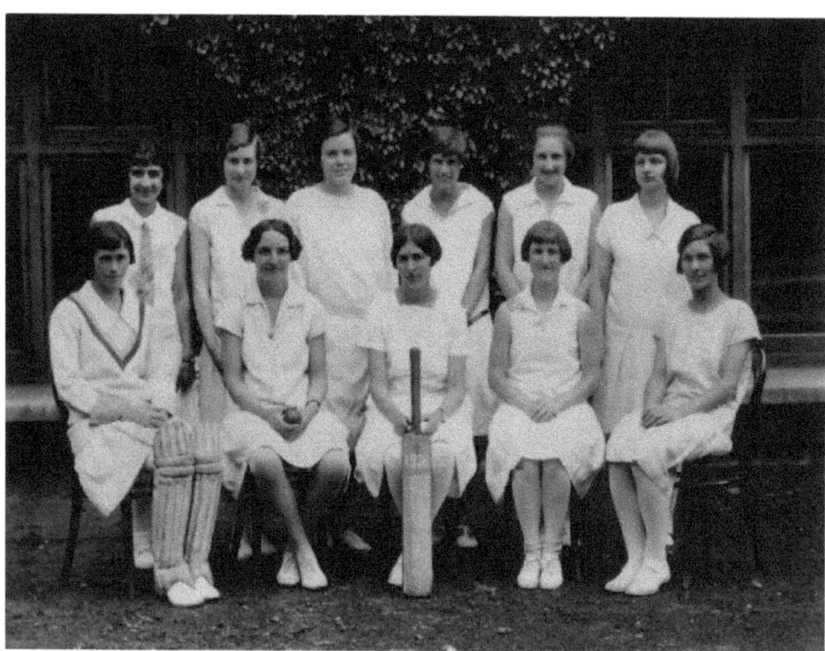

1. 'Peggy' in Cheltenham Ladies' College Cricket Team (back row, extreme right)

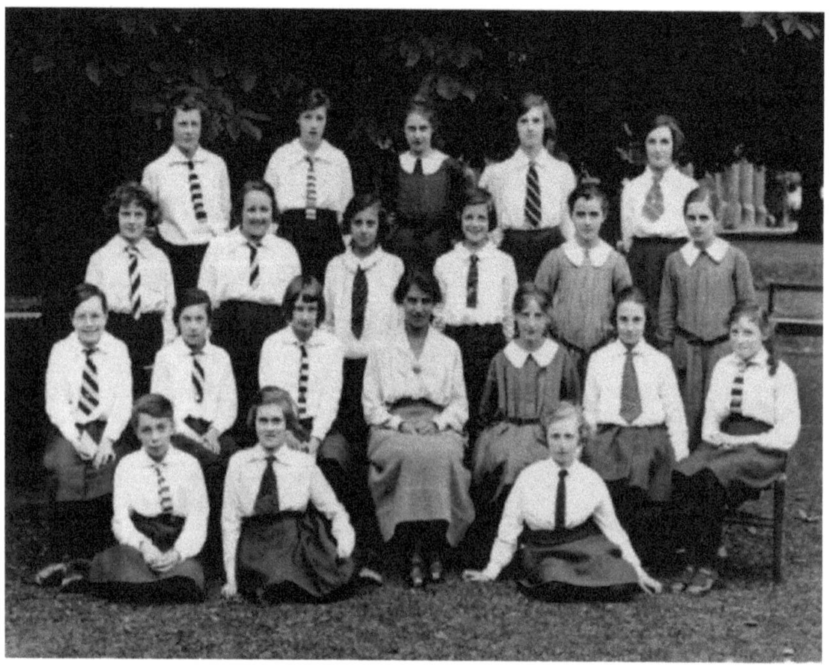

2. 'Peggy' in a junior form at Cheltenham Ladies' College, 1920 (second row, third from left)

More might have been revealed from some presumed unpublished notes of Ithell Colquhoun entitled 'Until Twelve' typed by Ithell when older, from memory or from early handwritten originals (5). The intention was autobiographical, but essential ingredients of dates and movements are tantalizingly absent. But maybe there is a little ground material here so relevant to the child from which this sensitive painter, poet and writer was to emerge. The whole of 'Until Twelve' must cover the period before admission to the Ladies' College a month short of her thirteenth birthday. It is sectioned into headings like 'First Anxiety', 'Education' &c.

The family *ayah* (nanny) was Ganga Mai:

> A face rather long, the skin noticeably darker than the teeth . . . sometimes seen for a moment, never fully apprehended. ('First Anxiety', p.1)

> A journey to-morrow and the trunks only half-packed. I began wrapping toy trains in tissue paper and fitting them into the cases as well as I could . . . A cab, a boat, a train, a cab. Diarrhoea and travel sickness next day – surely we would never arrive. Where were we going? Was everything happening at the same time everywhere? My fifth birthday at our destination. ('First Anxiety', p.17)

This puzzling journey must have been in England in 1911, three to four years after returning from India. How does some journey by train followed by boat fit the circumstances? Dangerously short of evidence, we have to suppose that the ship from India docked at Tilbury or Southampton; that the family less Henry settled temporarily a train journey away and inland from the port – and that two years later, having stabilised, they went back to the port for another, but short, sea journey. Where to? A clue may reside in a personal meeting of Ithell with Michel Remy, when Ithell said that she first went to school at Rodwell and that the name of the school was 'Thornelve'. The map showed that a Rodwell was a few miles inland from

Weymouth. One theory is that Georgia and her infant family sailed from Southampton to a port on the coast adjacent to Weymouth, in order to educate the children–perhaps there were relatives in that area, or they fancied the seaside, or they had seen an advertisement. Enquiries showed that indeed there had been a school at Rodwell, founded and running from 1890. It was called 'Thornlow' - near enough, allowing for a distortion in spelling caused by Ithell's faulty memory many decades later. But there are still difficulties in unraveling details of her education and movements prior to receiving education at Cheltenham. 'Education' in 'Until Twelve' tells that she could not read until she was eight, and that she was spared school. Was she perhaps removed from the Rodwell school and a private tutor substituted?

> Someone was employed to teach me to read, but I did not want to learn this, nor anything (except perhaps how to paint) since I already knew more than any book could tell me. I could not read at all until I was eight, and did not do so for pleasure until some two years later . . . My real education began with a morning activity which 'lessons' always interrupted – a drama, continuing from day to day, among our dolls, stuffed animals and other toys . . . if a grown-up came to listen, the automatic faculty automatically ceased, and we fell silent. We waited to be left alone . . . but at least I was spared school until the age of thirteen.
>
> ('Education', p.23)

At an early age, she crash-landed:

> Having dreamed one night that I could fly, I launched myself next day from the top of the stairs of the nursery-landing with perfect confidence in the powers of the air. I crashed painfully, and my howls lamented as much disappointment as physical harm. ('Disillusion', p.4)

There were the toys and games:

> Woollen balls knitted in brilliant patterns were tossed up to the ceiling and fell without sound or hurt: seldom we caught them before. ('Games', p.8)

> Heartrending smell of the tinsel in our square-plaited garlands! Red and gold, panoply of the regal east . . . feathers of the swan and peacock too we kept. ('Toys', p.10)

> The top has gone to sleep. The gaudy spinning bands could not be distinguished . . . The handle was of reddish wood and there were two holes pierced in its bright body, giving out a tin smell which I sniffed with delight. ('Movement', p.14)

Intimations of an artist:

> My first painting was an oval rose on a triple stem, with a bud at each side; my second was a purple sun with orange rays setting behind a green slope. ('Flowers and Light', p.15)

> At ten, I said that when I grew up, I never wanted to do anything but paint and write and study nature. Already I knew my own mind. ('The Future', p.29)

Here was a child, seemingly too intelligent to suffer the rote of primary education. She could well have been unteachable at the Rodwell school and rebelled – a 'difficult' pupil for unusual reasons. Unfortunately there is no supporting evidence to determine the actual course of events.

An interesting comment on Ithell's later thought processes is revealed below:

> At six I experienced a kind of waking coma, when my eyes would automatically fix themselves on some object, uninteresting in itself, and be glued there while my mind became a blank. This lasted for seconds, perhaps a minute. I

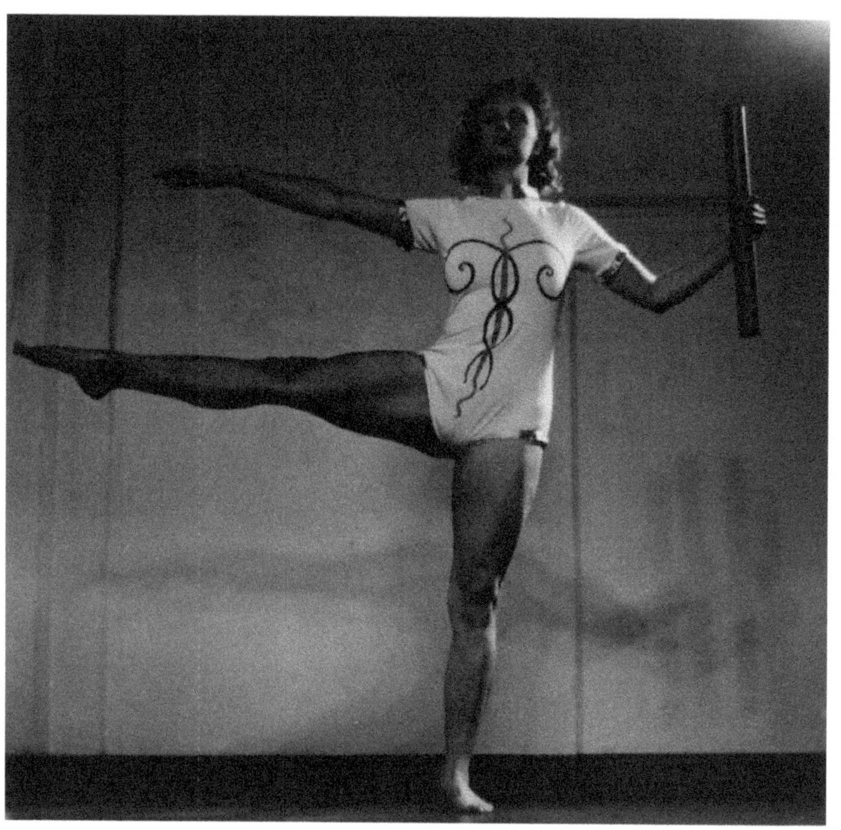

3. Dancer in Ithell Colquhoun's one-act play *The Bird of Hermes*. (Possibly Ithell herself. Note caduceus pattern on costume.)

> thought of absolutely nothing, not even the visual appearance of the object; but what was happening below the level of thought? ('Trance of the Eyes', p.24)

Hermaphroditic imagery in later paintings, or separate male and female symbolism seem foreshadowed:

> If I say that at ten years old I imagined Christ as a hermaphrodite, I shall not be believed. Yet is was so . . . I fused the red-hearted Jesus with the blue-cloaked Mary and made a god with breasts . . ('Faith', p.28)

In a few years, the family is found at Cheltenham, but nowhere in the resurrected narration of childhood experiences are there tangible clues to location. 'Fire Screens, p.18 tells us that there was a billiard room with fireplace and fire-screen on which was depicted the head of a buzzard surrounded by large feathers; from 'Mutilation', p.19 we learn that there was a park with Japanese pheasants, one golden and one silver; 'Entertainment', p.26 mentions that there was a cinema 'decorated with outline figures, a long way after Egypt . . .' It sounds like a big house in Cheltenham than a location near a Dorsetshire village school. 'Balloons', p.3 may reflect early acquaintance with cliffs in the Weymouth area, for she, brother Robert and a cousin 'went about on wheels, in chairs pushed up a steep path of asphalt through cliff gardens.' Mention of a cousin reinforces the notion that the family initially went to the Weymouth area because relatives lived there. They were also placed where, from a look-out point, 'We could see ships passing at a great distance, we could see almost as far as India.' ('Review Cellar' , p.7). 'Until Twelve' also provides evidence of Ithell's sensitivity to the plight of caged birds and delight in the natural world.

However, late information (6) partly unravels previously unknown factors during these early years, although not regarding her younger brother. Sue Monro in *The Peninsula Voice*, who doubtlessly knew Ithell in her later years in Cornwall, writes

> They [her parents] considered India a lethal place for children and were too involved with their own careers to devote themselves to child-rearing, so Ithell was dispatched to the Mother Country to be cared for by relatives. There is sadness in her voice when she talks about those early years, for although adequate provision was made for the children's material needs, there was none of the warmth and love of a close parent/child relationship. She was left to explore and discover her own creativity, it provided a solace and source of comfort in an otherwise sensitive environment. She describes herself as having been a backward child who couldn't read until her eighth year . . .

At Cheltenham, Ithell as Margaret Ithell, known as 'Peggy' was admitted to the Ladies' College in September 1919, aged 12 years and 11 months. She was a day girl, and her address (presumably parental or that of her grandmother) was 25 Park Place, Cheltenham. From there she took the London General Certificate in July 1924 and the Higher Certificate the following year, including French, German and subsidiary Latin. Distinctions were gained for French and German. An excellent achievement, one might think, for a girl who could not read until a relatively late age. The College archivist remarked that in her final year she was noted as having 'marked ability in literature' and, previous to that, was recorded as showing 'ability really good in humane subjects.'

There are no other records from the early 1920s, such as home pursuits at or near Cheltenham except a handwritten account of 'Three Memorable Dreams' probably written in retrospect (7). Like many others who have vivid dreams, she had recorded two in full; noteworthy perhaps of the backgrounds of Leckhampton and Taynton (title only); and of the appearance of sheaves of ten-foot long blades of 'marrow-grass' with sharp edges, hedges with green leaves on red stems and meadows of coloured flowers. More practically useful were the names of her brother, Robin, 'Daddy';

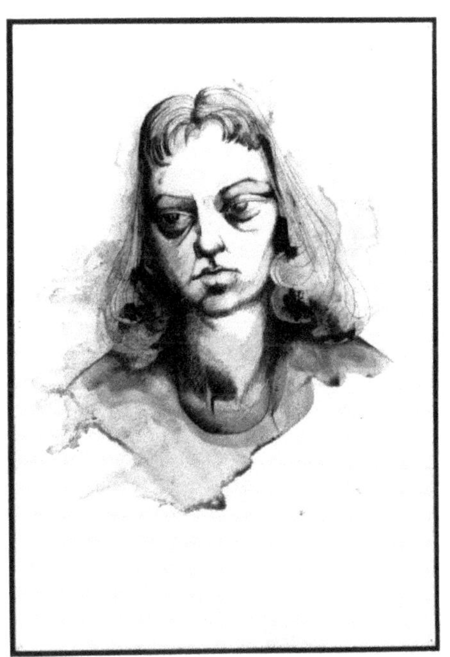

and Sylvia, Hilda Edge, and Norah Pridham, possibly friends from the College.

In October 1927, Ithell, having left the Ladies' College in 1925, and after two years at Cheltenham Art School, went on to study at the Slade School of Fine Art (London University), in Gower Street. She was true to her first impulses, doing what she had known she wanted to long ago in her childish desires, the continuation of which was to consolidate her future as a skilled artist As she said in the *Cornish Magazine* (1963, p.287):

> I started painting at the age of four or five; in fact I cannot remember a time when I was not painting.

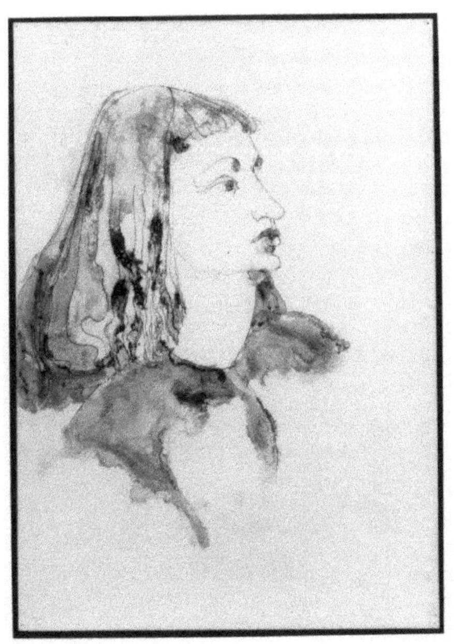

4. *Self-portrait, Ithell Colquhoun*
5. *Self-portrait, Ithell Colquhoun*

2 Early Occult Interests

Before describing Ithell Colquhoun's achievements at the Slade School, it is timely here to mention her occult interests which manifested before and during her studentship. She retained interest in the occult throughout her life and eventually became extremely knowledgeable in all branches of such matters. In the sense of initial exploration of and experiences with relevant sects and groups, some of this occurred before she completed studies with the Slade and when she was based in London. More practical interest was eventually put aside while she forged a career as an artist.

One stimulation appears to have been an accidental reading encounter of a newspaper article on Aleister Crowley's Abbey of Thelema when she was a girl at home in Cheltenham. Sometime later she read some of W.B.Yeats' early essays in which the Golden Dawn Order was mentioned. She tried to find out more but without success.

We can also go back to the period when she would be about 19, when she wrote a one-act play 'The Bird of Hermes' and probably performed in it, with others. It would seem that she was at Cheltenham Art School – there is a possible, though tentative photograph of her in dance costume in a design showing the caduceus of Hermes. Evidence of actual date and place is absent. The 1990 listing of works after her death records her costume designs for the play. ('Mask for the Phoenix', 'Mask and Wig for the Fair-Haired Girl', 'Mask and Wig for the Dark-Haired Girl'.) The Hermes Bird was another name for the alchemical Philosopher's Stone (as was the Goose of Hermogenes, which she used for the title of her later novel).

Over her lifetime she gained knowledge of the history of the Golden Dawn and its Rosicrucian-connected founders – in particular its prime mover, MacGregor Mathers, and his wife; details of membership of temples; histories of druidic and other Orders, various alchemical processes, studied serious applications of and innovations to the Tarot pack (which she always referred to as 'Taro').

Some of her earlier attempts to make entry into contemporary occult, magical and esoteric groups were unsuccessful. A conclusion can be reached that she often knew more than the 'experts'. She was no easy pupil under tutelage and never had been from her childhood.

While studying with the Slade, she used spare time to become acquainted with *The Quest*, the magazine run by G.R.S.Mead, president of the Quest Society. Such was her interest and level of writing, that her tyro contribution 'The Prose of Alchemy' was accepted for the journal. Kensington, where she lived, afforded easy opportunity to join the Quest Society and attend meetings in a Clareville Grove Studio in South Kensington. Members included Margaret Woods (Edwardian poet), Dr.Crow (Grandmaster of the Order of Holy Wisdom, whose Order she joined many years later), Dr. Gaster, Hugh Schonfield, and other scholars and writers. Edward J. Langford Garstin, whom she later discovered was a distant cousin and, unknown to her, had important connections with a remnant Temple of the Order of the Golden Dawn (as *Cancellarius* of the third *Alpha et Omega* founded by Moina Mathers after the death of her husband) was the Society secretary. Garstin had written alchemical treatises – 'Theurgy', 'The Secret Fire', and many esoteric matters in depth which were then unpublished.

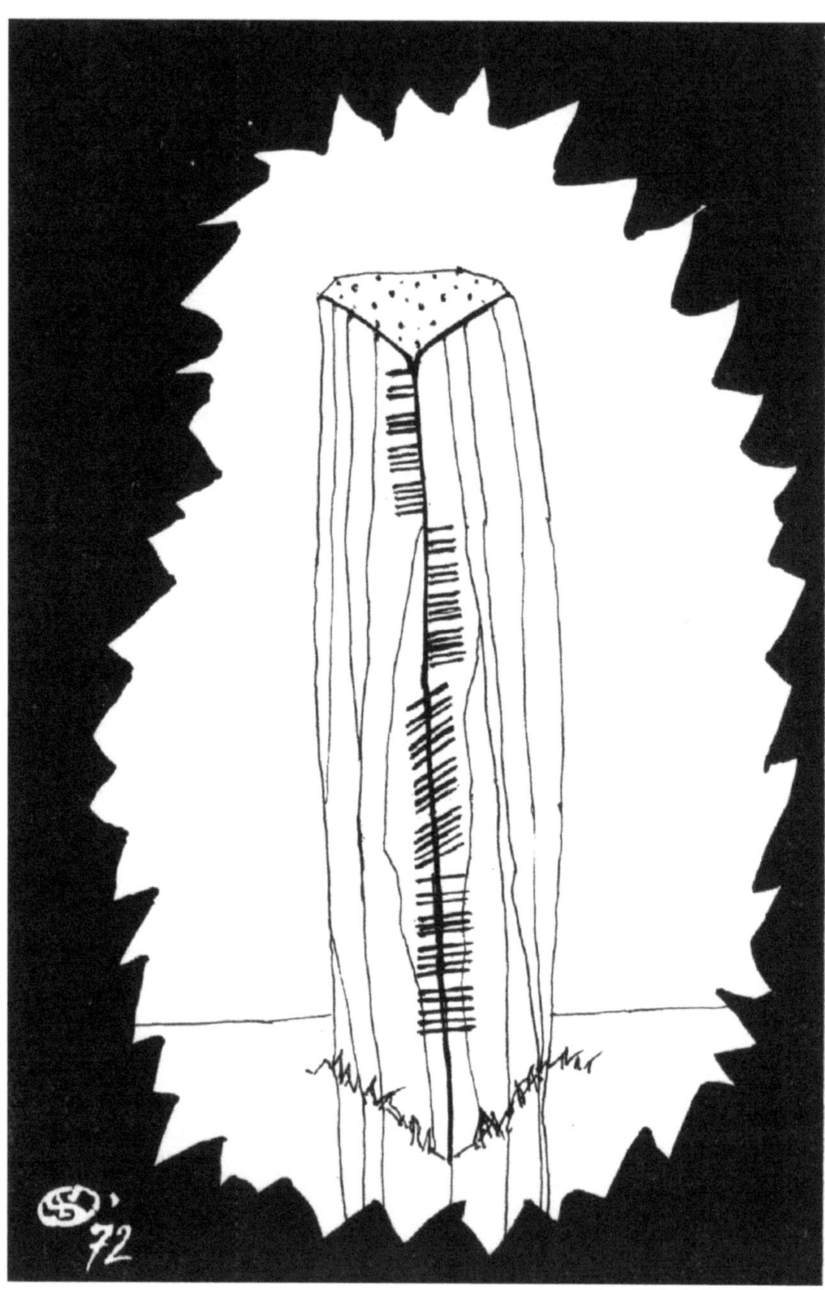

6. Ogham Stone

Edward and Ithell became good friends, in spite of the age gap. He introduced her to *The Kabbalah Unveiled* (*Kabbalah Denudata*) which Mathers had translated from the 17th-century original of Christian Knorr von Rosenroth some thirty years earlier – her first knowledge of the system. He also created an opportunity for her to know much more about occult matters, for he hinted that he and his mother were members of a 'secret society', although forbidding her to tell others in the Quest group about it. He gave Ithell a card addressed 26 Elm Park Road, London SW10, in assignation for an appointment on a particular day. Here she met Edward again and his mother, also a GD member, and they introduced her to a Mrs. Evan Weir, who provided Ithell with an application to join the Outer Order of this *Alpha et Omega* Lodge. Ithell would have reached the age of 21, which was the minimal age for applying. This temple had been run by Moina since 1919. Disarrayment in the 1900-03 period had still left a number of temples faithful to MacGregor Mathers including this (No.3). Ithell had noticed various occult paintings in Mrs. Weir's house, without knowing their origins. These had been executed by Moina, and had been transferred from the Paris temple where she and her husband had lived(1).

During the social gathering at No.26, Mrs Weir promised to forward her signed application to the 'secret chiefs' for consideration, but a week later Ithell was disappointed to receive a brief memo saying that her candidature had not been approved. The rebuff must have been a blow to Ithell and was probably based on a 'weighing up' process within the social environment of the meeting room in the house. Perhaps the opportunistic self-confidence of Ithell and eagerness to display her own theories and knowledge did not appeal to Mrs. Weir – she would be responsible for comments to whatever membership committee had to give a decision on a prospective neophyte. Ithell would have been expected to absorb and take instruction, not to offer extra knowledge – this what probably happened. It would not have occurred to her that if she had been accepted, the attendances, study, and zeal required would have

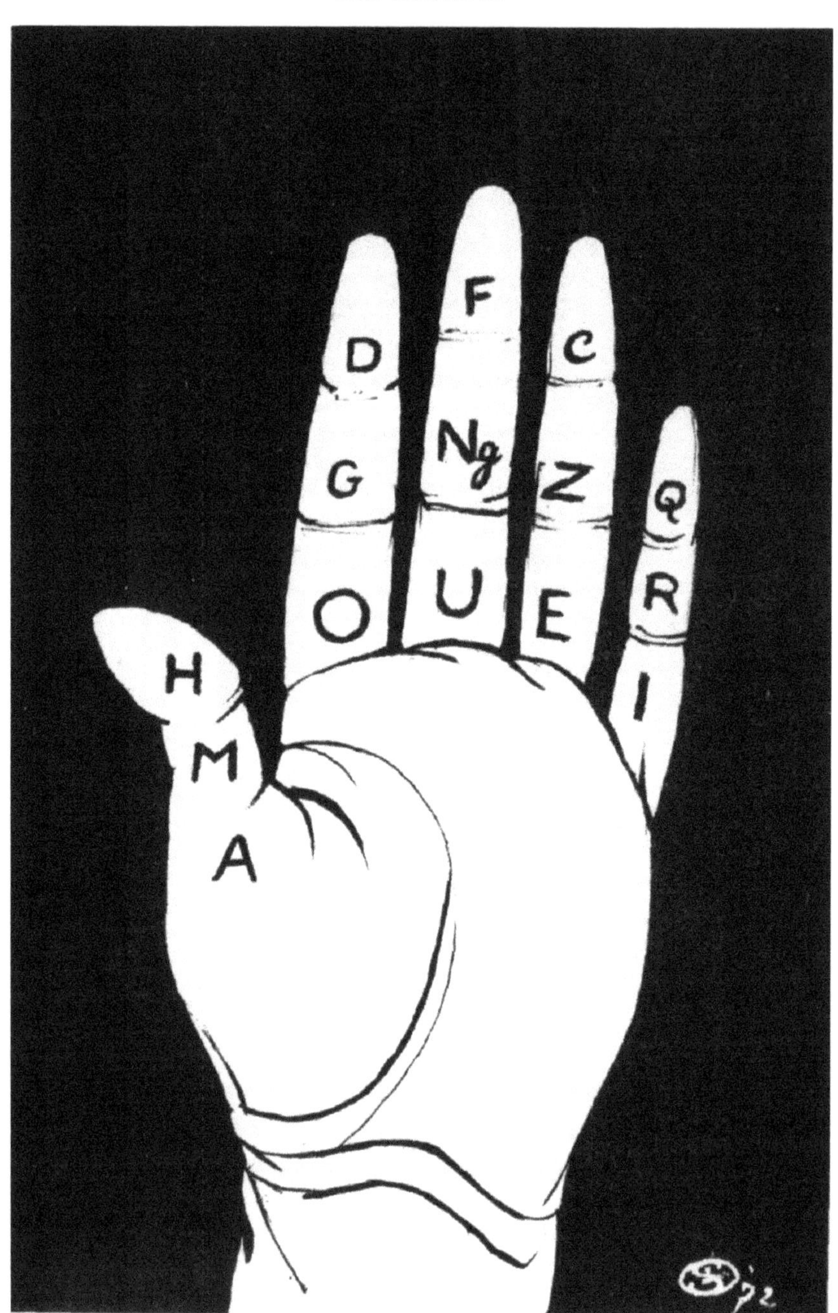

7. Beth-Luis-Nion on Hand

severely conflicted with her Slade studies. Furthermore, she already possessed potential sensitivity, a natural gift having bearing on the teaching objectives of the Order, and I believe that she would have rebelled against the rigidities of grade systems and the hieratic discipline involved. She was very much her own woman, without realising the censure involved in departure from Order thought and procedure. If the Temple administrators were looking for someone with a straight and narrow devotion to laid-down occult principles without deviation, they would not have found that person in Ithell.

In retrospect it seems a not too damaging matter that she was not accepted at that time into the Temple fold. She was already poised on the threshold of a successful art career. It could be said that it was not the right time to be involved in the Golden Dawn Order(2) to become enmeshed in the obediences of ritual.

Later, G.R.S.Mead decided to disband the Quest group, and Ithell joined the Search Society, a venture of her cousin's. George Mead went abroad on a project of which I am uncertain. In his time, as an early member of the Theosophical Society he had served as editor of the *Theosophical Review* and had been private secretary to H.P.Blavatsky. His *Quest* and the group had a long life, and the young Ezra Pound who was interested in and influenced by Mead's ideas of soul-growth, had once contributed an essay 'Psychology and the Troubadors'. So Ithell had trodden in the way of notable literary feet. After she had left the Slade to study and paint abroad, she lost touch with Edward for several years. Eventually she made much use of his ideas and essays and wrote a memoir after his death (3,4). Her later contacts with occult groups will be mentioned in later chapters. For the moment she had much else to do and an art career to carve out, which she tackled with the utmost dedication, coupled with an earnest desire to show and explain her work to others.

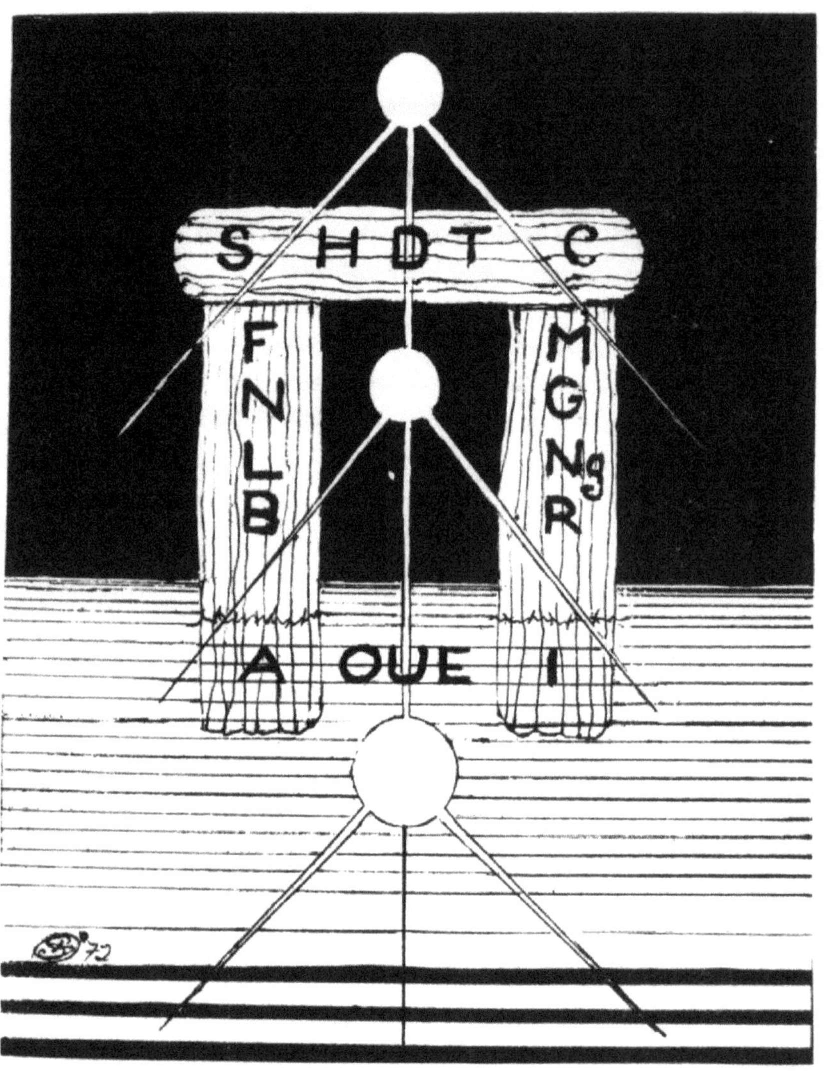

8. Beth-Luis-Nion on Trilithon

3 Into the Thirties

While studying at the Slade, to which she gained admission in October 1927, Ithell's addresses were first at 49 British Grove, W4, and later in the Adam and Eve Mews, W8. Her parents were then no longer at 25 Park Place in Cheltenham, but had moved also in about 1927 to 'Battledown Priors' in the Battledown area of the town. Battledown Estate was established east of Cheltenham in 1859, providing quality villas for the gentry (1).

Ithell obtained her Diploma in Fine Art in 1930, having been awarded the important top prize for Figure Composition in the summer of 1929 with her painting *Judith Showing the Head of Holofernes*. This was hung in the Royal Academy Exhibition of 1931. She also took a second prize for painting from life, and studied stage decoration, her work being shown in the London Goupil Gallery (2).

Complementing *Judith* , which was one of her early paintings in the then taught classical style, are *Judgement of Paris*, *Susanna and the Elders* (3), *Marlowe's Faust*, *Death of the Virgin*, and *Death of Lucretia*. Some were large-scale paintings. For some time (into the forties) she was a Member of the Society of Mural Painters, adding to her studio work various commissions.

She left the Slade School in March 1931, when 24, to study and paint abroad, and was first based in Paris. There she became acquainted with surrealism and the core part of the original manifesto of André Breton (4), and visited exhibitions showing the work of Salvador Dali. Her Paris activities also resulted in four (unknown) paintings hung in Paris salons in 1932 and 1933.

In 1976, in the Newlyn Orion catalogue of her work, she wrote:

> When I went to Paris in 1931 I read a booklet called 'What is Surrealism' by Peter Negoe – an American, I think, of whom I have never subsequently heard. I saw paintings by Salvador Dali in small mixed exhibitions. Dali had not then been excommunicated by Breton . Only in 1936 did the movement make its full impact on me.

In Paris, she was a neighbour of Paule Vézelay, the Bristol painter who had adopted a French name, noteworthy as the first Englishwoman abstract artist. In a short article 'Three Paintings by Paule Vézelay' she commented on *La Conversation Pertinente, Le Soleil : Deux Personnages et une Servante*, and *Le Bâtiment Fragile*, seen at the Salon des Surindépendants in 1932. (She was to use the first title for one of her own works at her 1936 solo exhibition at Cheltenham.) The fact that these were largely autobiographical contributed to difficulty in understanding – 'externalisation of a mood, a nameless and often evanescent emotion – a shiver, a spasm, an involuntary gesture of the mind'. Only by an intuitive leap could they be comprehended. Here was the young artist on the fringes of interest in what was to be later her own thought mode - the recording of the inner mind during the initial stilling of the reason used later to construct a painting; and the treatment of the under-conscious as a reality of human existence.

Ithell travelled to Greece later (1933), subsequently visited Tenerife (1936), and was in Corsica 1937-8. In the later years of these periods she probably returned to England to organise her exhibition work. In

9. Lamorna coastline

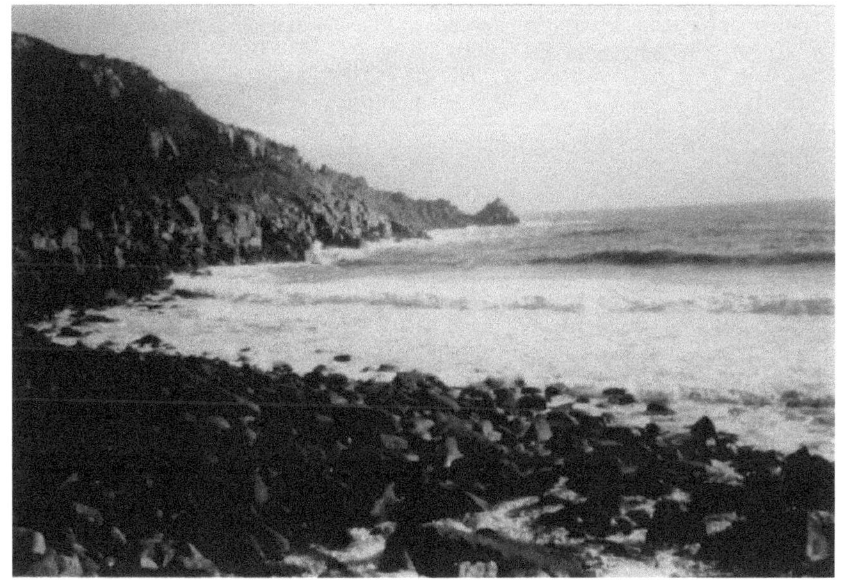

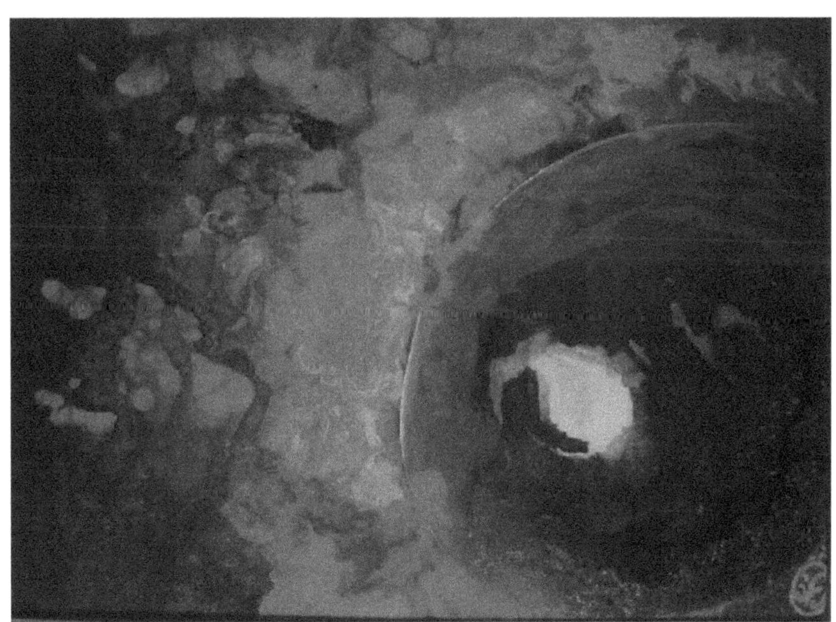

10. *A la Claire Fontaine* (1974, enamel on board, 34 x 42 cm)

Athens, she met Humfrey Payne, archeologist husband of Elizabeth Dilys Powell, later notable film critic on the staff of the *Sunday Times.* Humfrey Gilbert Garth Payne was the Director of the British Archeological School in Athens. A close friendship and much correspondence ensued (5). The meeting was eventually reflected in Ithell's ink and watercolour of 1934 – *Cartoon for 'The Man in the Doorway' – Portrait of Humfrey Payne, the Archeologist.* The study resulted in an oil painting the following year, and both works were acquired by the National Portrait Gallery. Payne died at an early age in 1936.

Ithell's work in Greece, Tenerife and Corsica obviously bore fruit with *Greek Woman*, *Ground Floor Façade, Tenerife*; *Doorway*, *Corsica*; *Lifeboat Corsica*, and *Corsican Boy*. Her periods of comparative immobility on home ground cannot be exactly determined. She was certainly featured in mixed exhibitions at the New English Art Club, at an R.S.B.A. exhibition, at a Dublin exhibition, and at the Whitechapel Art Gallery between 1931 and 1935(6). 1936 was marked by two important solo exhibitions in Cheltenham and London(7), which kick-started her career and reputation locally.

Her exhibition in her home environment of Cheltenham, which was attended by her parents, received an enthusiastic long report after a private view in February in the *Gloucestershire Echo* (8), headed by her portrait and the text 'STRIKING ONE-MAN' EXHIBITION : Cheltenham Girl's Pictures'. It was opened by the head of the Cheltenham School of Arts and Technology. Her successes at the Slade and at the Ladies' College were mentioned. There were 91 items. The point was made that they had all been executed almost within five years, and that even these constituted only about half of her work in that period.

Ithell's depictions of plants and flowers (about one-third of the exhibits), attracted attention in their finish and skill of execution. Later on there was a memorandum on *Canna* (9):

> The painting of the tropical plant *Canna* is typical of the work

> Colquhoun described as *magic-realist* or *super-realist* in style during the 1930s and 40s. It is likely that she studied this and other tropical plants at Kew Gardens shortly after leaving the Slade School in London. The painting certainly has an other-worldliness created by a very limited palette where the contrasting colours of red and green predominate. The fine glazes of colour exploit the heavy weave of the canvas and the organic form of the plant is pushed to the picture surface, leaving the buildings beyond as a vague geometric shadow.

Years later she was still using the device of large foreground surface depiction of plants, as if in other-worldly context, fronting an insignificant and prosaic background – as in *Morrab Magnolia.* More current comments on her abilities to transmute the properties of plants and flowers into attributes of magic and fantasy are also on record by Remy (10):

> At the Slade, she painted portraits, exotic plants and flowers in a vein of magic realism, using superimposed glazes of colour and choosing to draw hypertrophied forms, leaves, stems, corollas . . . Clematis, anthuriums, arums, magnolia, hibiscus and pomegranate flowers all indicate her fascination for elaborate shapes, and hint at fantastic worlds inaccessible to rational man.

From Cheltenham, her works on the above themes were transported to London, to be exhibited, with their vivid and mystical life properties, under the aegis of the Fine Art Society in their showing of exotic plant decorations. It was as if she sensed within stem and leaf, some secret vegetative world of non-material origin. Many years later, in a 1973 exhibition(11) of an accumulation of items with this theme, their qualities were re-emphasised:

> The paintings in this exhibition are of flowers and plants. But there is nothing sentimental or slight in the treatment of these poetical subjects. The flowers, executed with technical brilliance,

> convey the mystical nature of their beauty, and the plant forms have an element of uncompromising truth.

Ithell Colquhoun's 1936 year was also filled with completion of mural decorations for an extension to the District Hospital at Moreton-in-the-Marsh, Gloucestershire (12). It was memorable for her as well because she visited the International Surrealist Exhibition held at the New Burlington Galleries, London, in the summer, opened by André Breton. This was the point of introduction to the public in England of surrealism, its rebellious ideas having spread from France several years before, but hardly as a collective system until Breton's manifestos and reports and articles in literary quarterlies surfaced in Britain. But in France, the 1924 manifesto was seen to herald the founding of surrealism as a movement, followed by an exhibition at the Galerie Pierre.

Final planning for the London exhibition was effected by a committee formed by Roland Penrose, Herbert Read, and David Gascoyne. E.L.T.Mesens, the poet, musician, artist, dealer and founder of the surrealist group in Belgium, was invited and monitored the siting of 300-400 exhibits, gleaned from many European sources. Gascoyne had written an introduction to surrealism in 1935(13) and had also translated Breton's *What is Surrealism.* To aid the casual reader I have included some seminal references in the Notes.(14)

Ithell played no part in the International Exhibition, which was a great success, both in attendance and in provoking public argument after the display. The exhibition, with its international contributors in fields of painting, poetry, collages and sculpture, its 360 items, its incidents, has been adequately covered in the literature of surrealism, including the newspaper reports which were largely lacking in a proper understanding of the movement and were mostly adversely critical. Women surrealists represented included Eileen Agar, Gala Dali, Léonor Fini, Jacquelin Lamba, Sheila Legge, Grace Pailthorpe. Agar

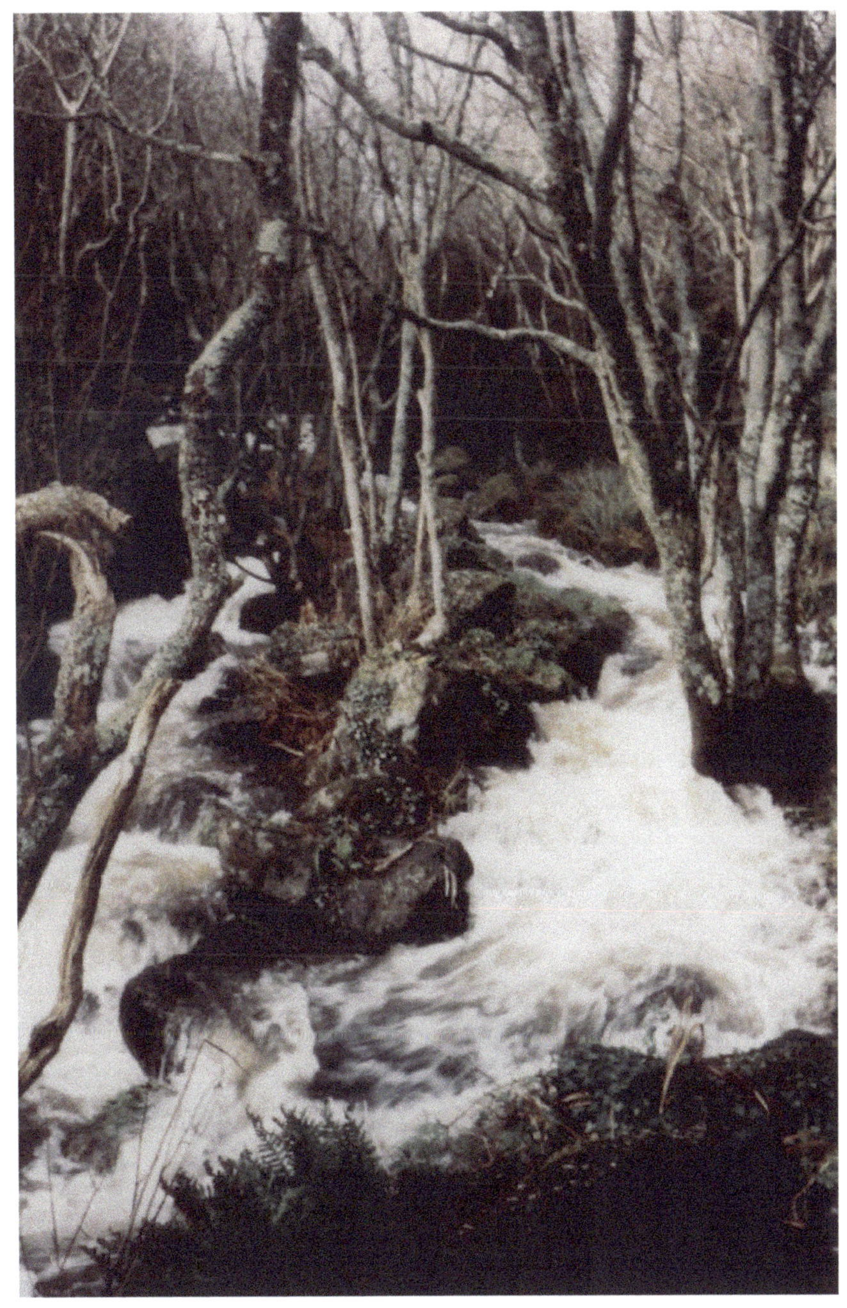

11. Lamorna stream

was a near-Slade contemporary of Ithell, but had left in 1927, the year the latter was admitted.

On her visit, Ithell heard Breton and others speak in an atmosphere momentous with strange happenings, such as Dylan Thomas offering refreshments of boiled string in teacups; and Dali clad in a heavy diving-suit with two wolfhounds on leash, who later needed urgent rescue from suffocation by unscrewing his helmet. His life may been saved by David Gascoyne who rushed out to a local ironmonger and returned with a very large spanner.

Years later she recalled the event in literature issued 1976 connected with her solo exhibition at the Newlyn Orion Galleries:

> . . . André Breton, robust and thickset, with wavy hair of a length at that time conspicuous, and others also spoke, but who could follow Dali? It seemed that he did actually evoke phantasmic presences which generated a tense atmosphere; the white cloth stretched to form a lowered ceiling vibrated as in a strong wind, though the weather was still and sultry. Dali was minute, feverish, with bones brittle as a bird's, a mop of dark hair and greenish eyes.

Dali's influence on Ithell Colquhoun's early techniques seemed to have taken root. She recalled that this

> Can also be seen (prophetically, almost) in my studies of exotic plants . . . This phase, perhaps more a 'magic realism' or 'super-realism' . . . is traceable up to the mid-1940s and beyond, but received its seal in my exhibition held under the auspices of the London Gallery in 1939 and featured in the *London Bulletin* No.17.

It is apparent that the label of 'magic realism' even in Ithell's own words, as concerned with her exotic plant studies, and descriptive of the effects of the early influence of Dali, is a useful categorization. But this 'art-world' definition tends to mask her actual genius in sensing a spiritual or magnetic life force emanating from her chosen subjects – in much the same way that the 'auras' of humans can be experienced or seen clairvoyantly by sensitives – or objectively and visually under scientific conditions. There seems a non-expansive aridity in this terminology, probably relating to 'magic' as a perceived effect of something extra, uncanny, or spiritual overlying expected naturalism or geometrical reality of the subject. It is not penetrative enough.

Thus, there is no quarrel with the following quotation, but it does not go far enough in analysis of Ithell's flower paintings and remains within accepted terminology, retaining 'magic' as a term within popular perception – a somewhat superficial approach to the subject:

> Colquhoun was first introduced to Surrealism while living in Paris in 1931 and remembers having seen several of Dali's paintings at that time . . . Captivated by his remarks [i.e. at the London Surrealist Exhibition of 1936] on paranoaic phantoms, she started to paint a series of exotic plant studies, in which a magic realism began to dominate her earlier naturalism.
>
> (*Women Artists and the Surrealist Movement*, p.126)

The International Surrealist Exhibition moved to Amsterdam two years later and thence to Mexico City in 1940. Mcanwhile, Mesens, who managed the London Gallery, and to whom Ithell had been introduced after she joined the surrealist group, included her, together with other British surrealists and artists from the Continent in his 'Living Art in England' exhibition at the gallery in early 1939. (Thc London Gallery was now owned by Roland Penrose and Anton Zwemmer, and specifically encouraged surrealistic art.) This was the first point of Ithell's official identification with the surrealists (although she had exhibited in a mixed exhibition with the group in 1937) and she has quoted her painting *Double Coco-Nut* in this respect. The painting is actually listed as early as 1936 in her solo exhibition of exotic plant decorations and was watercolour on silk. It makes use of plant fronds growing from or adjacent to a base of two kidney-shaped organic objects and a thick truncated stem, doubling as an image, with little imagination, of a cut-off penis between a pair of testicles – a far cry from her early classical work.

In the meantime, before her surrealistic debut in 'Living Art' and, it seems, a solo show in the Gallery, Ithell had effected solo exhibitions at two large London department stores – Liberty's and Whiteley's, in Heal's Mansard Gallery and the Everyman Theatre foyer, respectively, in 1937 and 1938.

Her work in the 1937-39 period included about 36 paintings, a rate of one a month, of good exhibition quality. These included one which was much exhibited and was eventually purchased by the Tate in 1977. This was *Scylla* (1938); it was reproduced in one of her obituary notices(15) captioned 'White Witchery : *Scylla*, a Daliesque vision of the artist's legs in the bath, painted by one of the last British Surrealists.' Elsewhere(16) it had been described as 'sexually charged illusionism'. A major feature is her uprisen legs as twin rocks, seaweed for pubic hair. The legs touch at the knees, leaving an opening between them and the pelvic area. A prow of a small boat is seen through the opening bordered by the inner thighs, sailing on the bath water. It is a small phallic symbol questing in the vaginal area. The point is missed or not made that the overall interpretation is the catastrophic potential of the power of the female over the male sex in a symbolic androgynous setting. It accords with the efforts of other women surrealists at that time to diminish the dominance of male artists portraying the female as a desire image.

Painted a year later, *Gouffres Amers* (1939) is also thematic in tilting at female-directed erotics by the male-dominated surrealist groups. The male figure is shown as a shipwrecked corpse or a semi-dead body, half skeleton, half flesh, cast up and beached on an inhospitable shore, with a flaccid penis exhausted of energy. One bony thigh with accentuated knee tip is phallic and the lower leg is twisted back and

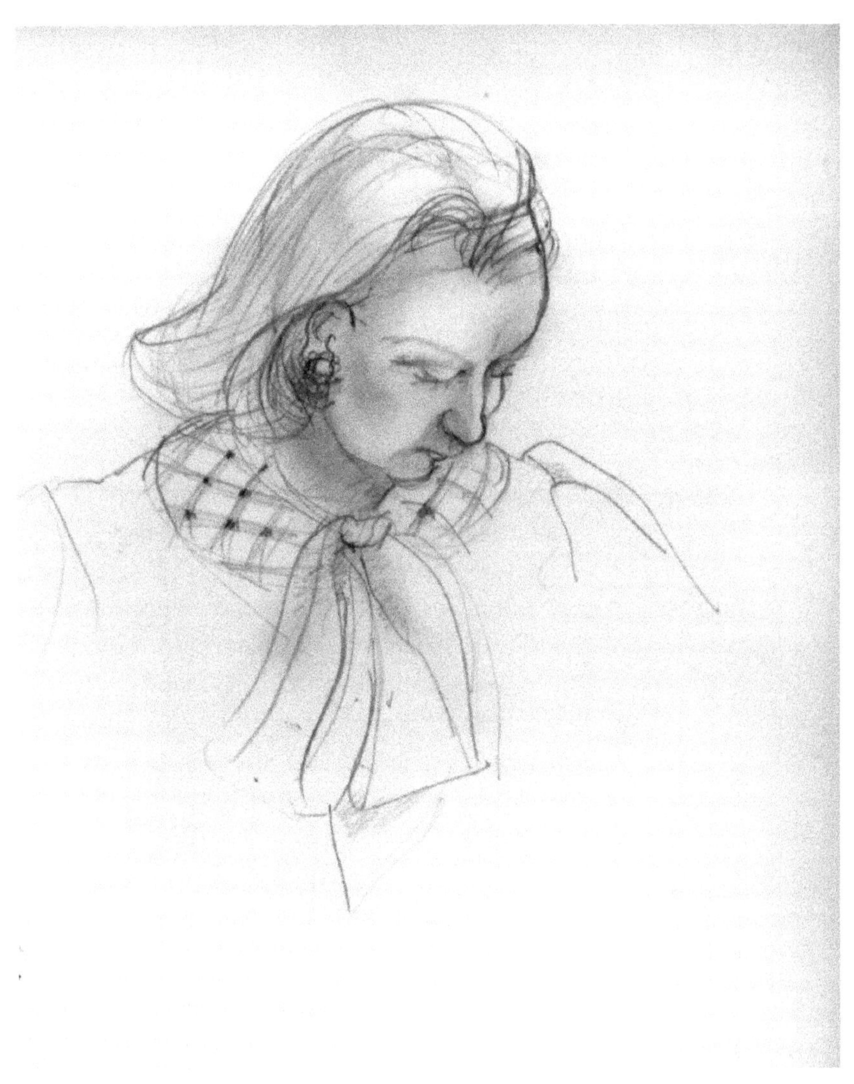

12. *Ithell Colquhoun* by Elektra Mangoletsi (1933, pencil drawing, 9 x 7 1/8 in., 229 x 181 cm)

under. The background is a menacing and jagged rock formation including what appears to be a large flinty-edged opening, possibly intended as a vaginal symbol with cutting and shredding qualities. In 1937 there is a record of an ink drawing *Drowned Sailor*, possibly, though unseen, on the same theme. Chadwick(17) has compared the scene as derived from *The Tempest*, and fixed the title as from Baudelaire's poem depicting *le navire glissant sur les gouffres amers* –' the ship slipping into the bitter whirlpool', although this seems more appropriate to *Scylla*, until it is treated as the aftermath of a whirlpool with its pathetic male discard from the pitiless waters – now calm after the 'revenge' on the mariner who ventured forth.

Leonor Fini was another artist who was taking the stance of female power and independence, in her *Cthonian Divinity Watching Over the Sleep of a Young Man.* Her nude supine, defenceless sleeping male is under the guarding control of a powerful but shadowy goddess. Fini goes further in *The Sphinx Amalburga*, where the background divinity has a stranglehold on the naked male. But whereas Colquhoun creates her theme and stands back from the creation, there is a suspicion that Fini herself is personalized in the goddess. She becomes involved in the act, but I think that Colquhoun's protest is more effective. Her males are completely done for or effectively deterred; Fini only controls them, albeit sometimes viciously. In the cases of both artists, unidirectional emotive pressures and not reasoned intellectual standpoints are more than obvious, and one must question whether there was a driving force verging on the androphobic.

Colquhoun's *Rivières Tièdes* (1939) ('Tepid Waters') was another work of the pre-war period. It depicts 'four snake-like rivulets of different colours flowing out from under the four doors of a rectilinear Spanish-looking church'.(18) As if closed-in secret happenings caused the fluxes – exoteric extensions of strange events within. In this case the date gives a clue. Official reference(19) tells us that the picture is a metaphor for the collapse of the Spanish Republic (witness the national colours represented - liquidised), and the establishment of Franco's regime. One of Ithell's best paintings.

After representation in 'Living Art in England' in 1939, Colquhoun's work appeared in some mixed exhibitions at the Peter Jones Gallery; at the Tate Gallery in its *Mural Painting in Great Britain, 1919-1939* where photographs of her murals were shown; at an Artists International Association exhibition in London; at the Ashmolean Museum in Oxford ('Younger British Painters'); and at an exhibition of 'British Surrealist and Abstract Paintings' in the Northampton Art Gallery.

In addition to participation in these six exhibitions, an important stepping-stone for her was a joint exhibition with Roland Penrose at the Mayor Gallery in Cork Street in June 1939, presented by arrangement with E.L.T.Mesens and the London Gallery. Here she exhibited fourteen paintings and two objects. The paintings included all seven of her Mediterranée series (*Le Phare*, *Beau Gosse*, *L'Helice*, *Scylla*, *L'Ancre*, *Rivières Tièdes*, and *Gouffres Amers*.) The two objects were *Death's Head and Foot* and *Heart* – carved chalk decorated with tempera. Of the above series, all except *Scylla* must have been completed in the first five months of 1939 before the Mayor exhibition!

1939, therefore, marked for Ithell a period of prodigious and unremitting energy in painting. Amazingly, she still found time in the summer to visit André Breton in France at 42 Rue Fontaine, where he lived with Jacquelin Lamba whom he had married in 1934. From biographical data published 37 years later(20) she tells us:

> The walls were 'papered' with surrealist art works, mostly of small size, including cases of tropical butterflies. Breton was interested in a group of painters who were elaborating a surrealist development they called Psychomorphology. This was an effort to tap that level of consciousness sometimes perceptible between sleeping and waking which consists of

> coloured organic (non-geometric) forms in a state of flux. Their method was little more than an intensification of the automatic processes worked by Max Ernst.

Regarding her writing, Ithell had contributed several pieces to the *London Bulletin* in 1939(21). 'What Do I Need to Paint a Picture?' was introduced with four photographs –Ithell in her studio; topless on a deserted Corsican beach; reclining in a bikini at Menton on the Côte d'Azur; and in sun-hat and white shorts at Tenerife. She liked

> . . . a resistant surface . . . as near to polished ivory as possible . . . a number, but not a large number, of opaque pigments . . . a smaller number of transparent pigments . . . a surfacing wax which I put on when the paint is dry . . . and a line to work to .. . that means a full-sized detailed drawing afterwards traced . . .

As to results:

> I aim for them to be sculptural: drawing and painting are branches of sculpture. For me, drawing is two-dimensional sculpture, painting is two-dimensional coloured sculpture. If I do any sculpture, it is coloured.

Of 'The Volcano' – Michel Remy comments:

> . . . she creates the symbolic confrontation of a 'pharos', whose message is not 'a message of reassurance' with the 'seething underground cauldron' of a volcano whose 'last eruption . . . flung millions of pieces of money into the air'. The reality in Colquhoun's works is essentially eruptive.
>
> (*Surrealism in Britain*, p.205)

In her third article of surrealist fiction 'The Echoing Bruise' are powerful hints of deed, risk, terrors, humanities, natural forces, and death's ever-presence attendant in the long run, accompanying human effort – the outwardly observed scenario is sea-sport, with the young boatman Ildebrando struggling against sea-currents to achieve, at a price, a win for his port. An echo from the treadwheel of mankind where the only solution is release to a higher level of existence to escape the life-death cycle.

> . . . look now into the heart of Ildebrando; below the proud surf lie images of the perpetual terror of earth and sea: first the twelve men he saw frozen stiff in the stranded lifeboat; then more recently the brothers from Lumio drowned in each other's clasp . . . finally the corpse he had seen half-eaten by worms at the cemetery – his ribs still echo with the horror of their tawny hue.

We close the 'thirties' on the Ithell of '39, with the year's count of at least ten paintings or drawings, five articles, six exhibitions and a visit to Paris. War against Nazi Germany was declared only a fortnight after the close of the Northampton exhibition where she was linked to Nash, Penrose, Pailthorpe, Mednikoff, Agar and other surrealist painters and had shown there three of those paintings exhibited at the Mayor – *Rivières Tièdes, L'Hélice* and *Le Phare*. The potential oncoming conflict left her work and enthusiasm unimpaired. She managed continuity at a time when surrealists world-wide became mostly split-up, ceased painting, or had to change locality or country.

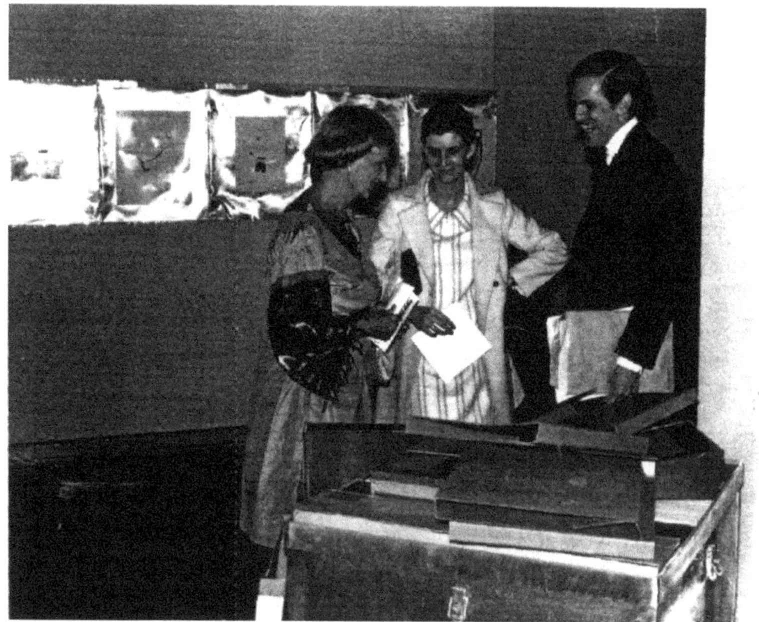

13. Ithell Colquhoun, in newspaper account of her exhibition at Cheltenham Municipal Art Gallery in 1936

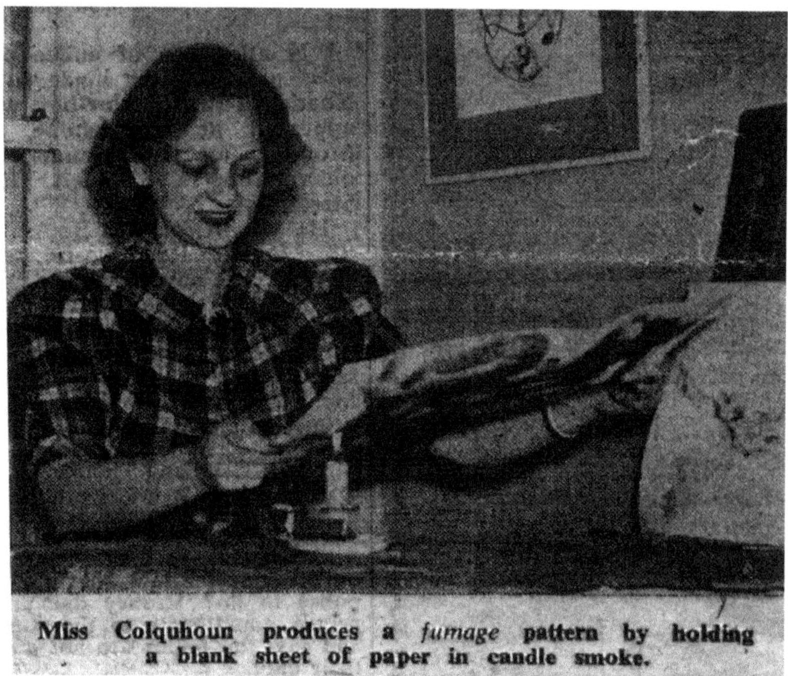

14. Demonstrating *fumage* in a television programme

4 Into the Forties

In all too short a time, after autumn 1939 and into the forties, after war was declared against Germany, the London Group split up; much surrealist activity in Britain was curtailed, former members became engaged in the war effort. For example, Eileen Agar did no serious work until 1946; Edith Rimmington, another contemporary of Ithell Colquhoun, had a much restricted output; aliens such as Max Ernst suffered internment in France, which in turn severely affected Leonora Carrington; and Léonor Fini left Paris. The *London Bulletin* paused after June 1939 and only resumed a year later with a triple issue - Mesens himself, as a Belgian, was destabilised but later managed to return to England where he did propaganda broadcasts for the B.B.C. He had already published isolated poems in the *Bulletin*, and after the war published a collection of war poems.

Many galleries closed in bomb-devastated areas, and the London Gallery stock suffered bomb damage. Art culture in public places took a not unexpected dive, particularly in London, but some travelling and regional exhibitions continued. Mainly for the Forces on leave, The Windmill Theatre in London continued entertainment,

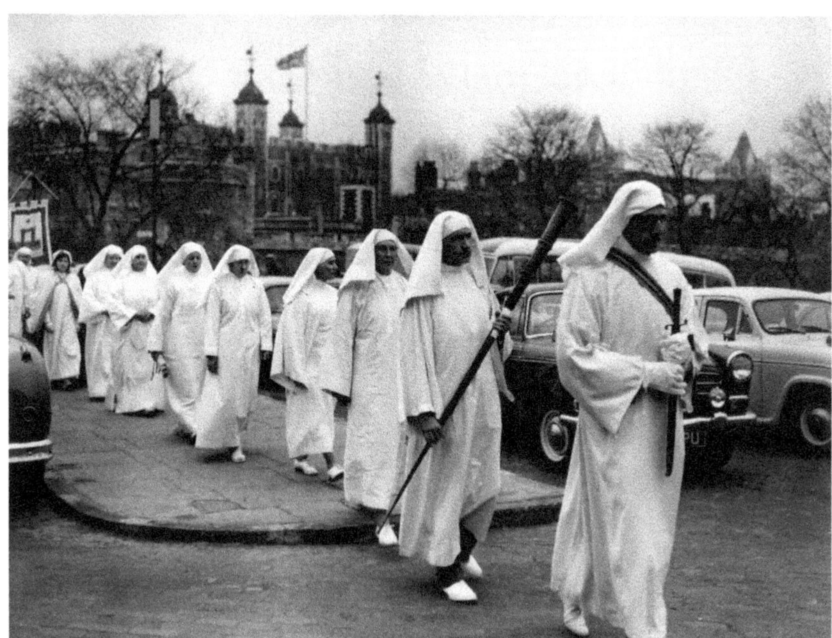

15. In druid procession, Tower Hill (7th robed figure, hands clasped)

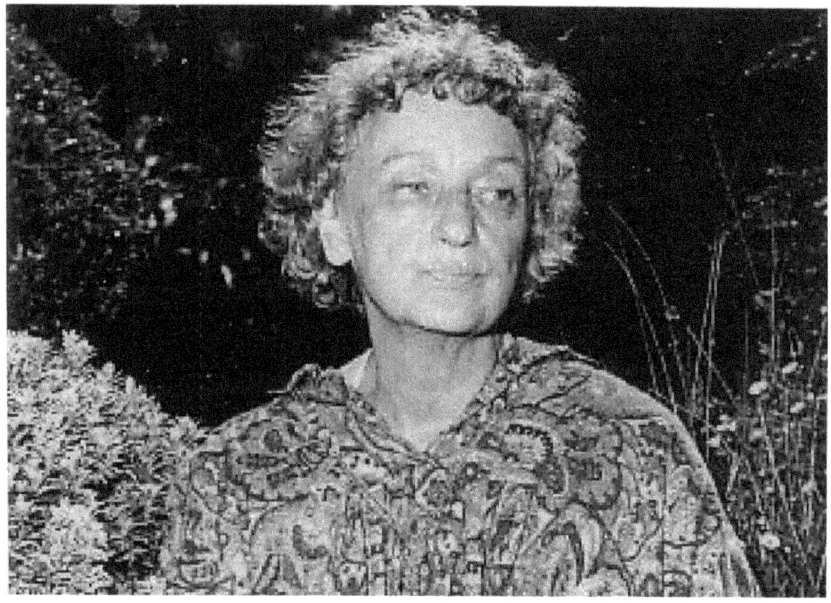

16. In her garden at Paul

with stand-up comics, leggy chorus girls, and nude 'stills' of set pieces, under restrictions of 'no movement' - oblivious of the need to preserve poses with a stiff female upper lip in the explosion-ridden area.

In the early war years, probably in 1940, Ithell had moved to a two-storey studio complex at 45a Fairfax Road, Bedford Park. In London, she contributed in that year, to an exhibition at the Leicester Galleries ('Artists of Fame and Promise'), then in Green Street, off Leicester Square, with at least her oil painting *Interior* (1939), and to an R.S.B.A. exhibition. The end of the thirties was reached in a blaze of effort, work, travel and successes. Circumstances decreed that her career as part of the important surrealist group was to be blighted at this peak time.

> In the beginning of April, 1940, Reuben Mednikoff convened a meeting of surrealists in London, at the popular meeting-place, the Barcelona Restaurant in Soho, with the objective to discuss their position in, and towards, the art world. The conclusion, which was strongly supported by Ithell Colquhoun and Eileen Agar and seems to have rallied most of those present, was that the artist should be left free in his choice of venues where to show his work . . . Mesens had not been invited.
> (*Surrealism in Britain*, p.209)

The story continues that, soon after, in April, E.L.T. Mesens issued strict guidelines on the matter, at the same venue. Obviously the word had got around, and Mednikoff had pre-empted a thorny subject. Anxious to purify the thrust of the surrealist movement, Mesens asked whether the surrealists were prepared to follow his rules. Those negatively inclined were likely to be out of favour or banned outright from the core of the movement. Whether this was the right time for a possibly divisive set of instructions to be issued, during the equally divisive hazards of the war period - or on the contrary, this aided preservation of surrealist purpose after the end of the war - is arguable. But given the necessity to oppose fascism and the strength of the French communists, the pressures at that time were obvious if art was to be committed and not viewed as individualistic enterprise. With hindsight, there was little to cement the English group after the war.

Out of the dozen or so points made by Mesens, there were three main ones, viz: (a) the boycotting of exhibitions 'springing from an artistic bourgeois spirit' ; (b) adherence to the proletarian revolution; (c) the boycott of any association, professional or other and including any secret society, except the surrealist group. Particularly, relative to (a) he asked those at the meeting if they were prepared to withdraw membership and support from the British Art Centre.(1)

This April 11th meeting was fairly well attended. Women painters included Ithell Colquhoun, Ruth Adams, Eileen Agar, Grace Pailthorpe, and Edith Rimmington, out of whom Ithell objected to all main points. There were many disagreements:

> . . . Mednikoff and Pailthorpe refused to agree with the clause which asked them not to exhibit or publish except under surrealist auspices, and they were never again to be associated with the group. Eileen Agar and Herbert Read were accepted back later . . . (*Surrealism in Britain*, p.211)

Much left Ithell out on a limb, defending her corner. We hear her side of it, more fully, 36 years later, in the biographical notes to her 1976 exhibition in Cornwall, also alluded to via the 1977 exhibition in the Parkin Gallery.(2a, 2b) Supposedly the *Bulletin* triple issue of June 1940 was then either in press or not available for her remarks at the time. Regarding the boycotting of certain exhibitions:

> It meant not exhibiting or publishing at all, since there was then no surrealist gallery or publication in Britain, and those abroad were barred by war-time conditions (The London Gallery closed in 1939 and did not reopen until 1946.)

17. *Pears* (1937, oil on board)

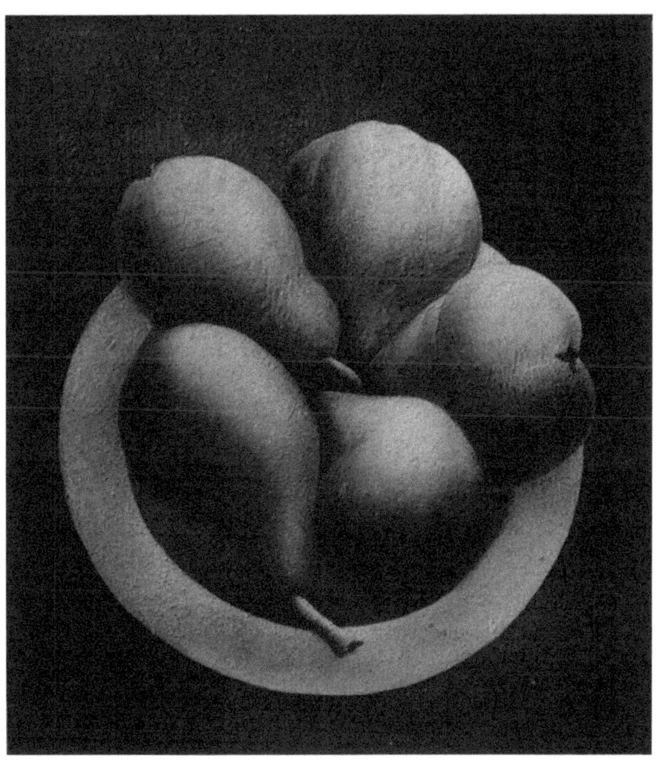

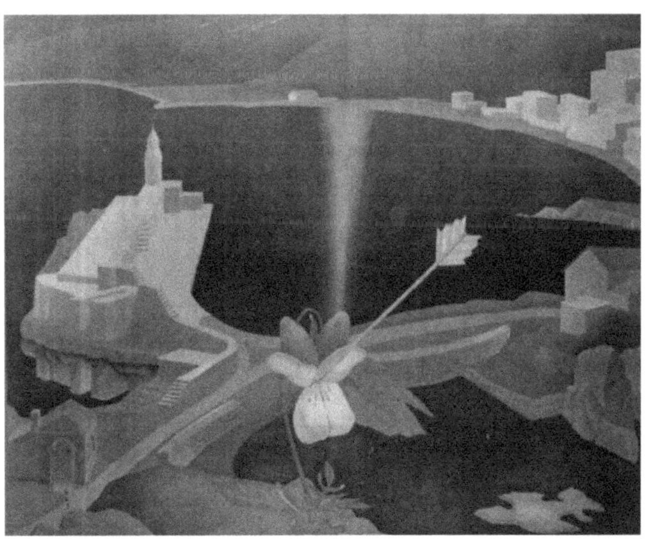

18. *Le Phare*
(1939, oil on panel, 27 x 35 in.)

Regarding Mesen's political point, we hear again from Ithell, that she had always objected to political commitments unsupported by action, and that, in any case, in wartime, the authorities would not tolerate revolutionary action.

Also. . . effective revolutionary action was a full-time job and, therefore, irreconcilable with a creative life.

Politics bored her; she wanted to get on with exploration and applications of the art to which she was dedicated. Regarding the clause that certain societies should be boycotted, except the surrealist group, one can sympathise with her state of mind, which was always questing for meanings and systems beyond the outwardly material. Ithell states:

> I said I wished to be free to continue my studies in occultism as I saw fit (It was Mesen's quirk to oppose this aspect of surrealist activity, since Breton, Dominguez, Dr.Mabille, Masson, Seligman and other continental surrealists pursued such researches without query.)

According to Ithell, objection to restriction of publication to surrealist literary vehicles by Herbert Read was later overlooked on account of his usefulness as a propagandist; and Eileen Agar, her previous supporter, who had also objected to this point, as well as to the boycott of non-surrealist associations &c, was re-instated after apologising to Mesens. Still sticking to her guns, Ithell was effectively banned from future exhibitions of the group, together with Mednikoff, Ruth Adams, and Grace Pailthorpe, who 'were deemed expendable'. It was perhaps inevitable that any challenging compromise in respect of her strong sense of independence was bound to fail. Her ultimate 'policies' were eventually to be found in nature and its mysteries, not allied to man-made groups and their art applied to worldly matters with no ultimate bases. Ithell's brand of belief in her work was beyond petty restrictions in material matters. She may not have been right in non-support of some of Mesens' wishes at this time, but if she had

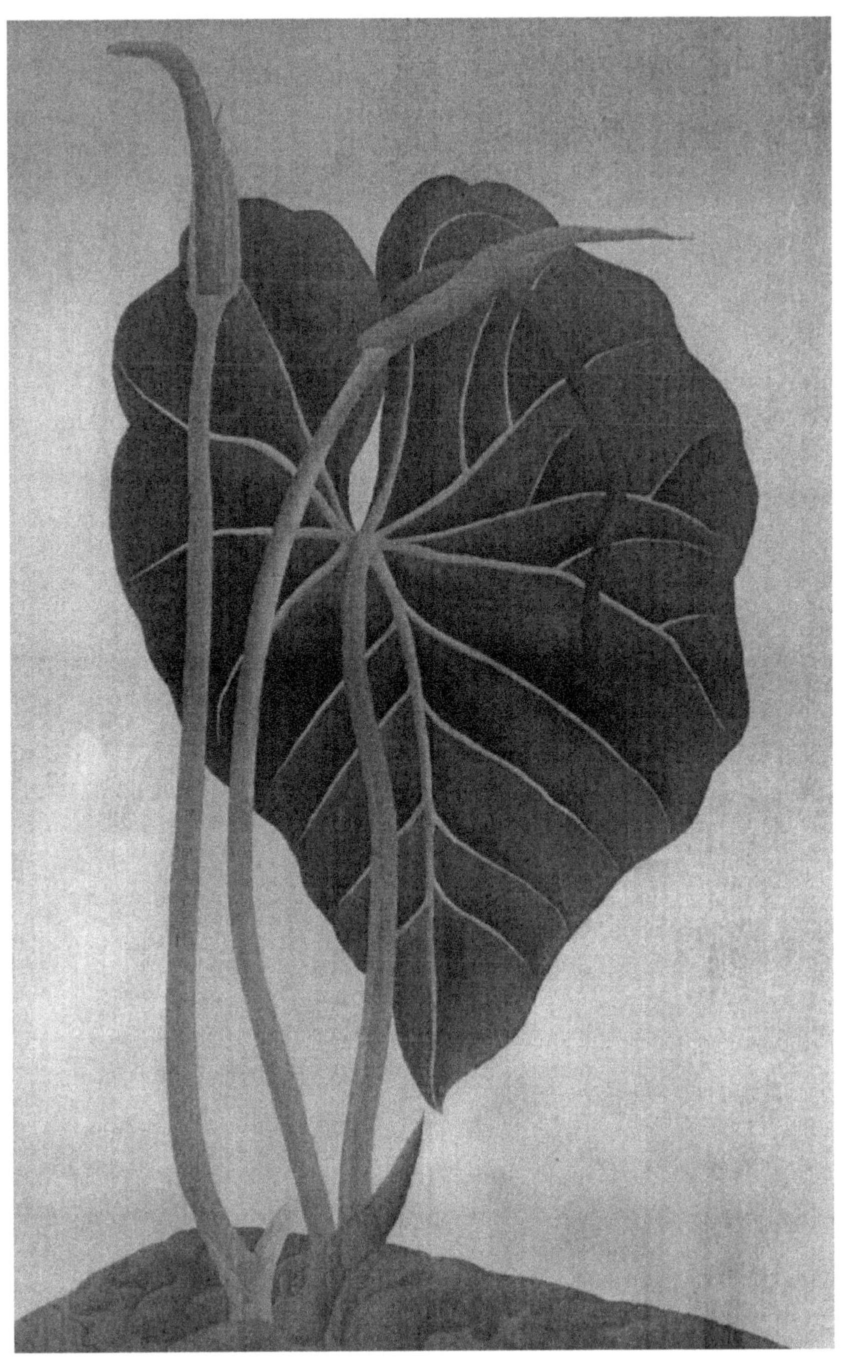

19. *Madagascar Aroid* (1936, oil on canvas)

compromised her inner feelings, self-forgiveness would have been impossible. The re-defined surrealist group was represented a few months later at the Zwemmer Gallery - work by Ithell Colquhoun and many others who were banned was therefore not shown. Michael Parkin, staunch supporter of Ithell's work, related:(3)

> This was for Ithell and others the parting of the ways from Mesens and his 'gang'. Ten years later in 1948, Ithell, thinking that bygones should be allowed by Roland Penrose to be bygones, offered a painting to the I.C.A. show *40,000 Years of Modern Art*, but it was very curtly turned down.

The painting was *Autumnal Equinox*, offered to the above exhibition in the Academy Hall, Oxford Street, below a cinema there. There was, however, a twist to the incident, since in 1949 she received a press cutting from the Turin *Gazetta Sera* picturing *Autumnal Equinox*, titled 'Figura Nella Penombra' , being carried into the gallery, a title intended for a huge bronze by Jacques Lipchitz in the I.C.A. exhibition (also featured.) In fact, Ithell had submitted her painting to a different exhibition a few weeks after the refusal. So the *Equinox*, in a measure of triumph beyond all understanding, got itself accepted on paper preposterously, if not through any unfriendly, tactless or uninterested rejection by Roland Penrose. All this she describes in the exhibition catalogue of 1976 (Newlyn Orion Galleries). Eventually the success of the Institute and other factors led to the London Gallery's financial troubles and it closed in 1950.(4)

Expulsions of Ithell Colquhoun, Ruth Adams and Grace Pailthorpe, against a wider chronological international backdrop, were only part of women surrealists' gradual disappearance from the movement for many decades. Dawn Ades has recently explored various male-female aspects in the history.(5) She has discussed some reasons for their later prominence.(6)

The artwork by Ithell for 1940 includes studies of the Nine Maidens circle in Cornwall and three works which relate to more exploration

20. *Morrab Magnolia* (1956, oil on canvas, 24 x 24 in.)

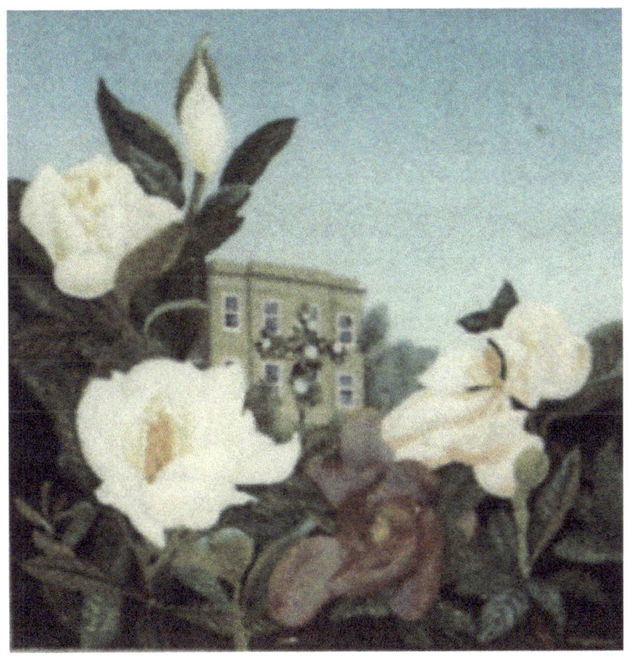

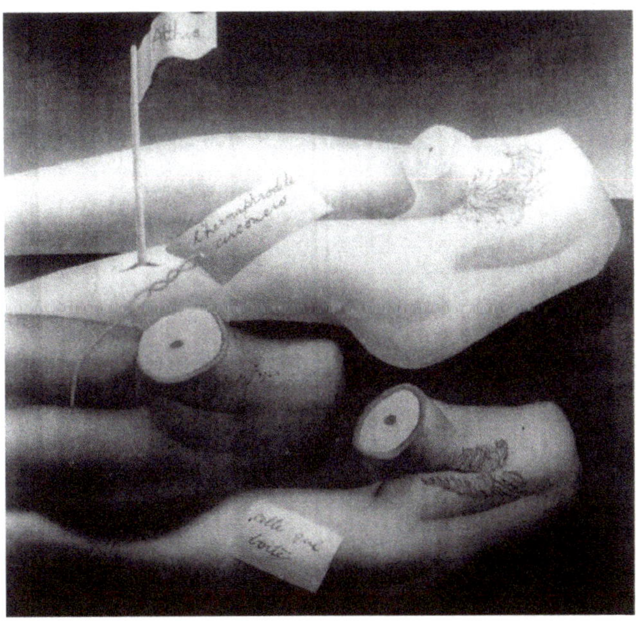

21. *The Pine Family* (1941, oil on canvas, 18 x 20 in., 46 x 50.5 cm)

out of the country – *Bronze Figure in the Desert*, *The Dunes*, *Middle East*. Her geographical circumstances in respect of the latter group, with wartime travel restrictions, are puzzling. Some kind of holiday, a relative paucity of completed work, and few 1940 exhibitions at galleries may indicate the need to recover from the events of the fateful eleventh of April. In 1941, there are just three exhibitions of work, at Harrogate, Batley, and Whitechapel galleries.

Nevertheless, in 1941, there followed completion of an important and much publicised painting, *The Pine Family*. This showed three sets of felled treelike human trunks with lower 'limbs'. Each is conspicuously featured at the joining area by a cut-off section doubling as an amputated penis. (Compare *Double Coco-Nut* of about the mid-thirties.) Also we note, via a remark of Michel Remy, that 'pine' is French slang for penis. The pairs of trunks with limbs, from top to bottom are respectively labelled 'Atthis', 'l'hermaphrodite circonsis' and 'celle qui boite'. The middle pair overlap the other two. 'Atthis' seems an inexplicable spelling choice, considering that she was a female (daughter of a king of Attica). There may be some classical quibble, that the 'h' was obligatory, or an intentional misdirection, for Colquhoun was usually precise in her language. As Attis, and male, he could have been either of Phrygian nobility or part of the country's mythology. In one version, he was a shepherd loved by Cybele, mother of the Olympian gods, and who made love to a nymph, whereupon the jealous goddess made him mad so that he castrated himself with a sharp stone. She changed him to a pine tree. A straight stick carries the flag-label Atthis', the lower end plunged into the 'flesh' of the left limb. There are various versions in the literature.(7) The emphasis on castration is heightened because, it is said, Attis himself was born from the fruit of an almond tree which fell into the lap of a river nymph, the almond tree having grown from the fallen genitals of Agdistis whom the gods attacked. This vegetation myth, with its seasonal trees and Attis for fertility symbol, parallels the Adonis/Aphrodite and Ishtar/Tammuz myths.

The portion labelled 'celle qui boite' (the one who limps) belongs to the lower pair, with the label adhering to the left limb, and has received comments.(8) I would add the Hindu myth of Shiva disguised as a naked beggar who seduces the wives of a group of sages in a pine forest, who, enraged, lay the curse of castration on him, whereupon after the offending organ drops on the ground and darkness falls over the universe. The god reveals himself and only restores the status quo on condition that they worship his linga (penis) for ever.(9) The crippled Fisher King in his Grail castle in the barren land, which can only be restored by asking the right question, is another state of loss affecting the fertility of the land.(10) There remains the middle pair labelled 'l'hermaphrodite circonsis', the label being attached by wire to a limb. This bears a prominent curve adjacent to the truncation (which is there but less prominent on the lower pair), and is interpretable as the external opening of the female genitalia. The origin of the words is discussed by Remy:

> . . . assembled from what man and woman, each of them, lacks, was the ironical nickname given by the French surrealists to the nineteenth century realist writer George Sand – a woman who had rejected her maiden name altogether and given herself a man's name vaguely inspired by her husband's. This label is literal. (*Surrealism in Britain* , p.245)

The painting is still puzzling. The general, though perhaps superficial message seems to be that identity or definition via the potency of any sexual aspect is doomed. There is no hint of hope via symbolic seasonal imagery of resurrection. The sustained driving subjective and also conscious processes of the artist are at a high, even vicious, sensitive level, planning this 'attack'. (On one level, symbolism of a forest, if not Baudelaire's more universal 'forest of symbols'.) It could be called the Colquhoun 'waste land'. (After all her dedication to her art, which was followed by the destructive impact of the Barcelona storm, it might appear that a modern waste (or wasted) 'land' had been caused, taking the place of a previously richly progressive environment.) In the painting, the components of this well of symbols juxtapose with force. The work has great economical power stemming from image reinforcement. This is less a work emotionally geared to counteracting phallic dominance than a nihilism expressed in symbolic androgynous terms.

Ithell Colquhoun, following an exhibition at the Redfern Gallery in Cork Street, exhibited this painting at the International Arts Centre in London at the end of the same year (1942), which also saw her work in a travelling exhibition 'New Movements in Art', venues for which included the City Museum, Leicester, and the London Museum.

In the meantime, a certain young man of forward-looking ideas, who was also a painter - Toni Romanov del Renzio, a Russian-born Italian who had escaped the fascist call-up and instead became involved on the republican side in the Spanish civil war, had landed in England from France in early 1940, and was engaged in reviewing the state of surrealism in England, during its shake-up by Mesens. He was, as a relative newcomer, regarded as an upstart by the newly Mesens-aligned group. However, he founded and edited from London an issue of *Arson* in 1942 - an 'Ardent Review' – 'Part One of a Surrealist Manifestation' and was highly understanding of the politics and cross-currents of the movement, in this country and internationally:

> In England, he linked up with Mesens's group and attended some of the Barcelona restaurant meetings. When force of circumstance dispersed the group, del Renzio set out to create a forum of ideas redefining the part to be played by surrealists in wartime. (*Surrealism in Britain*, p.224)

It is not clear in what circumstances Toni met Ithell. It has been conjectured that they met through Conroy Maddox. This was no doubt after Toni had seen Ithell's work at the A.I.A. exhibition and recorded dislike in no uncertain terms in *Arson*. Affection has strange ways of making itself known:

> Miss Colquhoun has finally damned herself publicly with her admission of endeavouring to do in painting what the 'New Apoplexy' is doing in literature. The rest [of room 4] consisted of sterile abstractions (including one by Miss Colquhoun) . . .
>
> (*Arson*, March 1942, p.31)

Opinions seemed to be sidetracked later. In a letter to Conroy Maddox, Toni said that he found Ithell Colquhoun 'essentially a mystic, therefore individualist, conscious of being an artist, anxious to exhibit'.(11)

Arson included a reprinted interview in New York with Breton, originating in *View*, wherein he presented his ideas on changes which might occur in art ('a new spirit will be born from the present war . . . we must learn to read with and look with and through the eyes of Eros . . .') and the orientation of surrealism at that time - that which was ending was 'the illusion of independence. I will even say of the transcendence, of the work of art . . .' Deviation from group effort was egocentric. Elsewhere, among other functions, 'the diving bell of automatism' was part of an ongoing programme. Other, and direct, contributors to the wartime *Arson* were Robert Melville, Nicolas Callas, Conroy Maddox and Giorgio de Chirico, rounded off by the editor's 'The Return to the Desolation : For My English Comrades'.

Ithell and Toni certainly had a common human *bête noire* in the attitudes of the Mesens-aligned surrealists. They fell in love, lived together in a newly acquired studio at Bedford Park, and later, on July 10th, 1943, they married at the Brentford Register Office. She was then 36 and he 28. Ithell's brother Robert, who was then a captain serving in India, sent them a wedding present.(12)

Ithell's father had died in 1942. She would have been helped to recover from a low point of anxiety relative to expulsion from the surrealists. Apart from that there is plenty of evidence that she continued painting and exhibiting independently of the Mesens-controlled group.

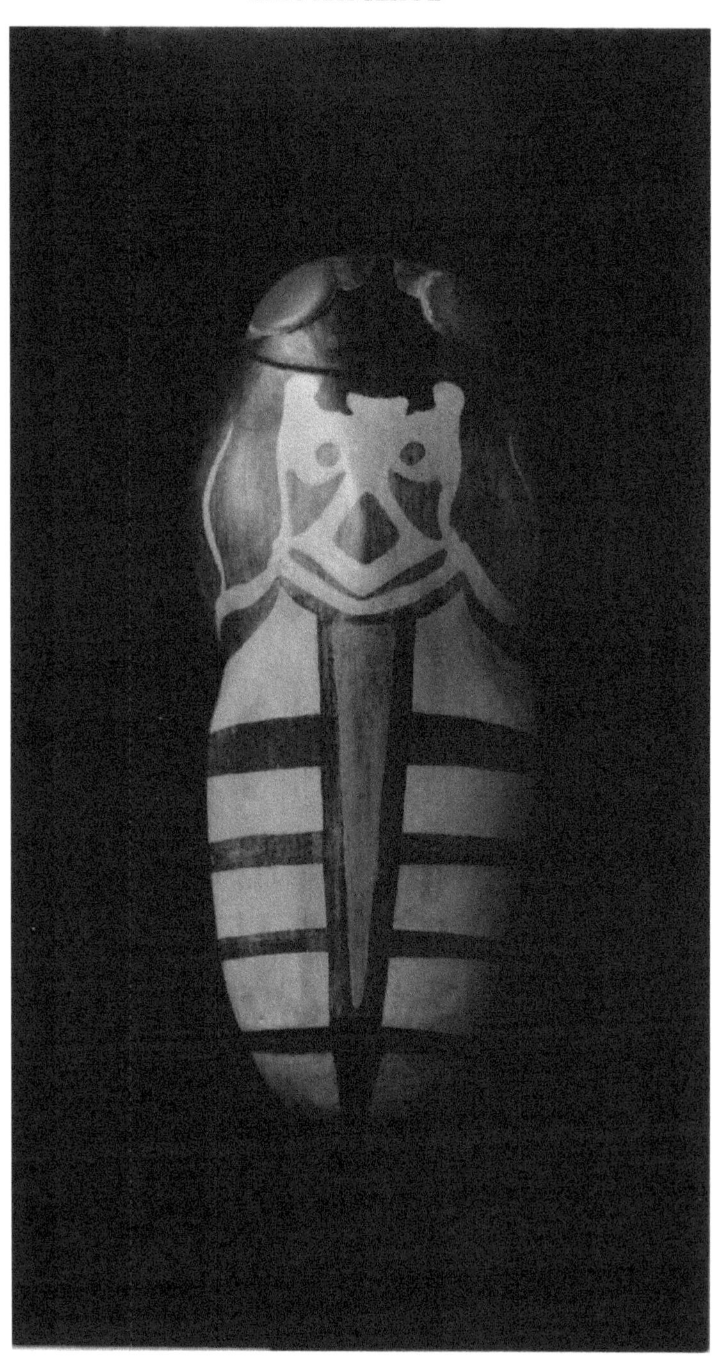

22. *Death's Head and Foot* (Object, 1938, carved chalk decorated with tempera)

Unfortunately, the marriage was to fail, ending in divorce, but initially there was a period of happiness and cooperation, when Ithell was left to feel firmer ground under her feet than she had for some time, working with a partner.

5 Bedford Park

Bedford Park, W4, was a good neighbourhood for literary, art and theatre associations within the community. It had also its quota of occultists, psychics and others concerned with fringe medicine. The garden suburb, planned as an innovation in living in 1875, had carried on its traditions and attracted a somewhat similar group of inhabitants since the days of John Yeats, painter-father of W.B. Yeats. The latter had returned there in his early 1920s and recorded activities and friends in *Autobiographies*; portions of Ian Fletcher's *W.B. Yeats and His Contemporaries* are also relevant (1).

The Bedford Park studio where Ithell and Toni lived became an open house for friends and the discussion of new ideas. There was a need for surrealist and like-minded groups to keep together as much as possible of that which had been scattered by the war, and No.45a in Fairfax Road was one of a few London meeting places which performed very useful activities in this respect.

Derek Stanford, who also lived in Bedford Park in wartime during the marriage, knew each of them. He offers a glimpse of that part of wartime Britain, as he sometimes stayed overnight after parties or when on leave from the forces. In Stanford's *Inside the Forties* (2),

23. *Heart (Object*, 1938, carved chalk decorated with tempera)

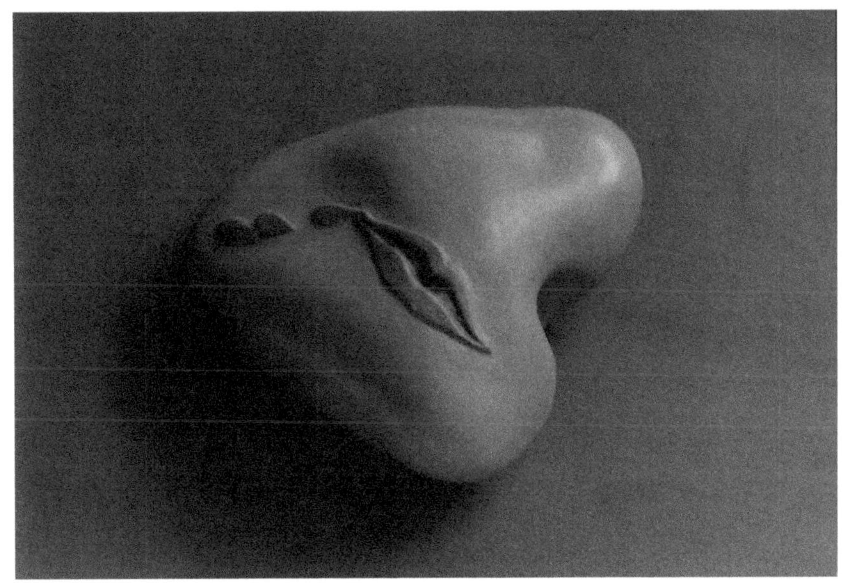

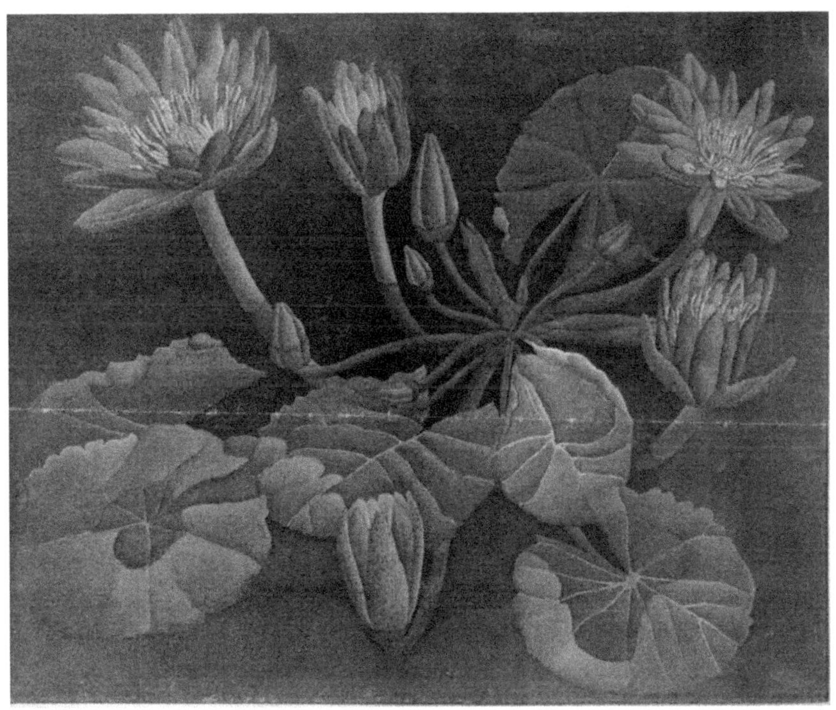

24. *Water-Lilies* (1936, oil on board)

Ithell, 'an exotic figure', who would then be in her mid-thirties, is described:

> Born in Assam and artistically the product of the Slade and Paris, she was petite, with large bright eyes in her small head with its page-boy bobbed hair. It was these eyes, with her colourful way of dressing – she would not infrequently wear a sari – which led to my forming an image of her as some twilight-hovering, pollen-sipping moth.

He has an amusing and curious picture of a night when he shacked down in a spare space in their living quarters, which were in a gallery surrounding the ground floor: there were many mobiles at ceiling level:

> Mobiles were to me then strange contraptions which I thought of as 'dingle-dangles', and flashing my torch from a mattress on the floor, I would catch these slight-stirring aerial toys as in a searchlight amid the general blackout.
>
> Nor were these the only attractions in that odd artistic hangar. One of Ithell's pictures, which I never tired of regarding, depicted a naked standing male figure. From every high point and opening of the figure radiated out in circling curves a line of circling astral force completely surrounding the man. The colouring was rainbow-bright, and the effect of the picture as a whole was both extremely sensuous and ethereal.

Of Toni, as editor of *Arson* (1942) – 'a fiery-hearted affair' judged by some of its manifesto – 'Its contributors are alight, ignited by the spontaneous combustion of the imagination's flaming spectres . . .'

Stanford remarks that, nevertheless, *Arson* carried some first-rate contributions, which included an interview with André Breton. Toni del Renzio was also a painter, but 'more of an ideas man.' In the same year, Toni had organised the surrealist show at the International

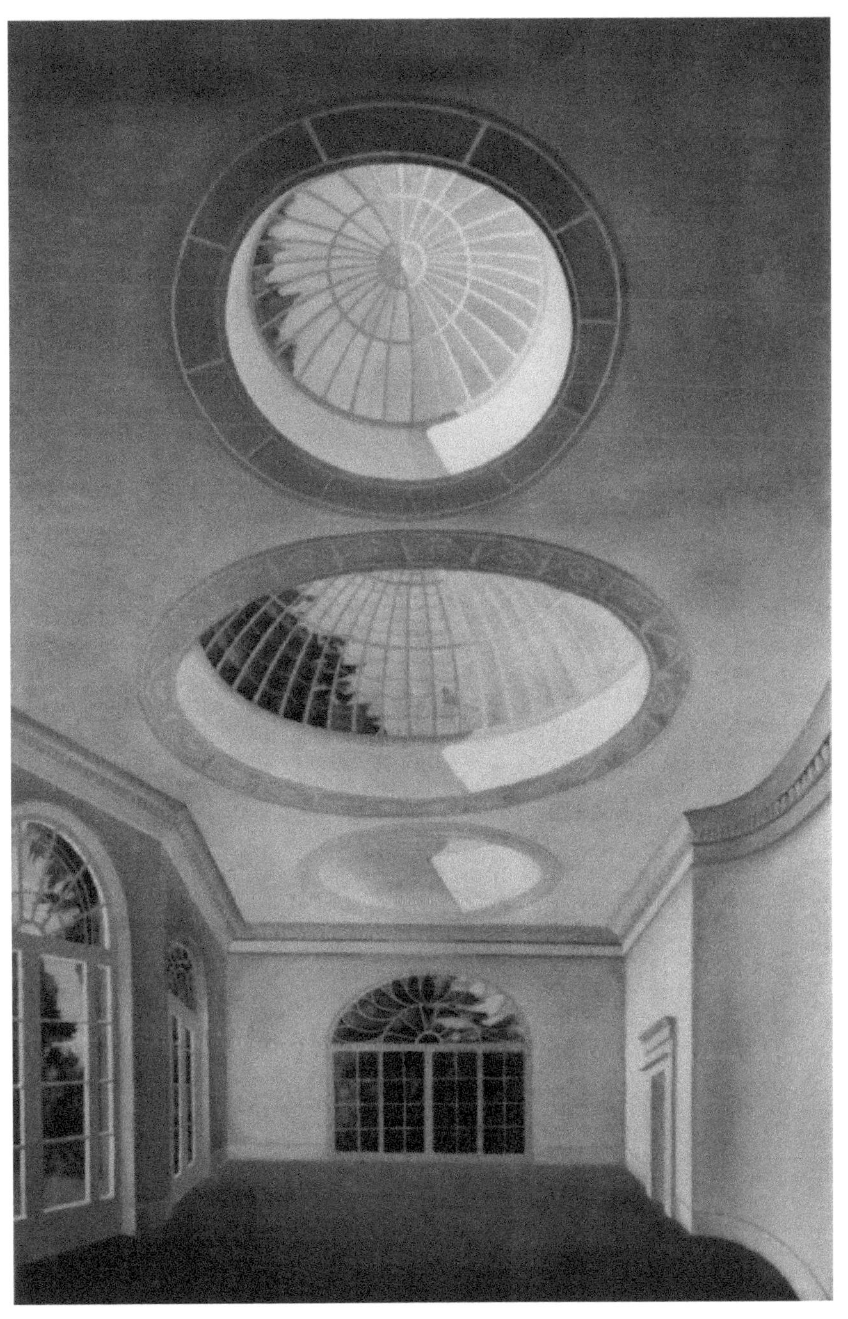

25. *Interior* (1939, oil on board, 36 x 24 in.)
Brighton and Hove Art Gallery

Arts Centre, which included some of Ithell's work. Stanford lost track of him when the couple divorced after the war:

> He was tall, well-made, and looked Gallicly fetching in a sort of matelot's striped vest which he favoured. When not being supercilious and contemptuous of English culture in general (and I very much suspect he was at least partly English), he was an interesting talker from whom I departed stimulated.

There is a knowledgeable glimpse of the welcoming atmosphere of the 'open-house' studio from Derek Stanford, in the following extract from his poem 'Homecoming' in *The Memorare Sequence*e (3):

> All-Hallows Eve. Upon the expectant air
> smell of exploded fireworks. Hard to tell
>
> fancy from fact in this gunpowder season,
> or is it odour of chrysanthemums
>
> instilling evening with autumnal pang ?
> Now shadowy men in Guy Fawkes masks go by
>
> with sacks upon their backs, a file of them:
> I tag along behind, invisible.
>
> The lighting at half-cock, we tread the streets
> in dumb patrol as in those black-out days.
>
> What was it prompted me to think of us
> as making up a funeral cortège
>
> and who or what is it we're burying ?
> Eyeing those sacks I sense their aching weight
>
> since every single shoulder drooped beneath them
> as if it felt a painful lifetime's burden
>
> but knew there was no giving up on it.
> And now in this nocturne scenario

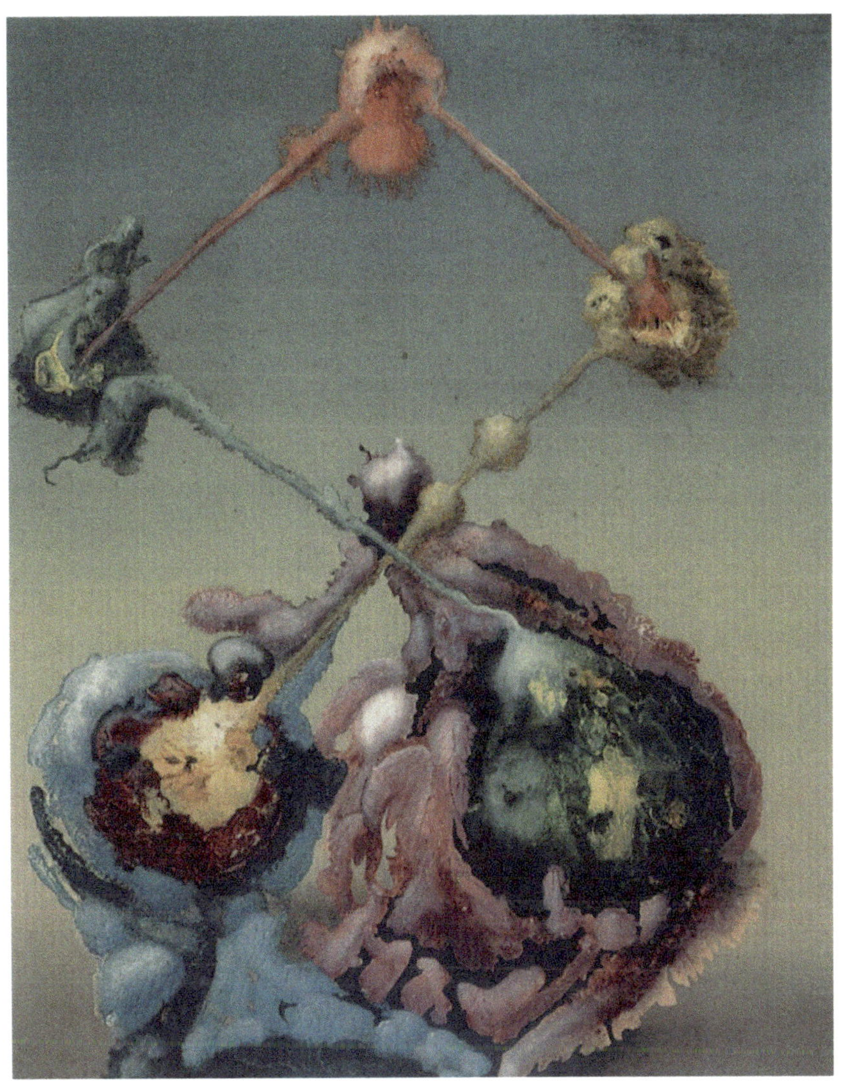

26. *A Visitation* (1945, oil on canvas, 24 x 20 in., 61 x 51 cm)

I thought I recognised our whereabouts;
a tree-lined garden suburb out of London
with bogus Queen Anne houses known to Yeats -
an artists' hide-out on the District Line

in Celtic twilight *fin-de-siècle* days.
And we were halted by a studio door

opened so often, and hospitably,
to me on week-end leave in years of war:
Aladdin's cave of wine and company,
of music, candle-light and canvases,

adding regretfully a couplet to his memories of those more youthful days:

but she who painted them has gone away
leaving her icons for posterity.

In the second part of 'Homecoming', there is humility and admiration in another extract which returns to memories of Ithell, dedicated to the 'exacting god' of her art, struggling against bad health and the deadly attack on her spirits and ideals, because of a failed marriage:

For us this studio is holy ground:
the shrine of one who worked on to the end

past rosy dawns of promise and of love,
mutinous health, a marriage on the rocks;

on through an uncompanioned solitude,
a void with nightmare voices mocking her;

her name repeated in the inner ear.
Your mind is going and your gift is gone.

Her mind survived this sick apocalypse.
You understand now why we bowed so low,

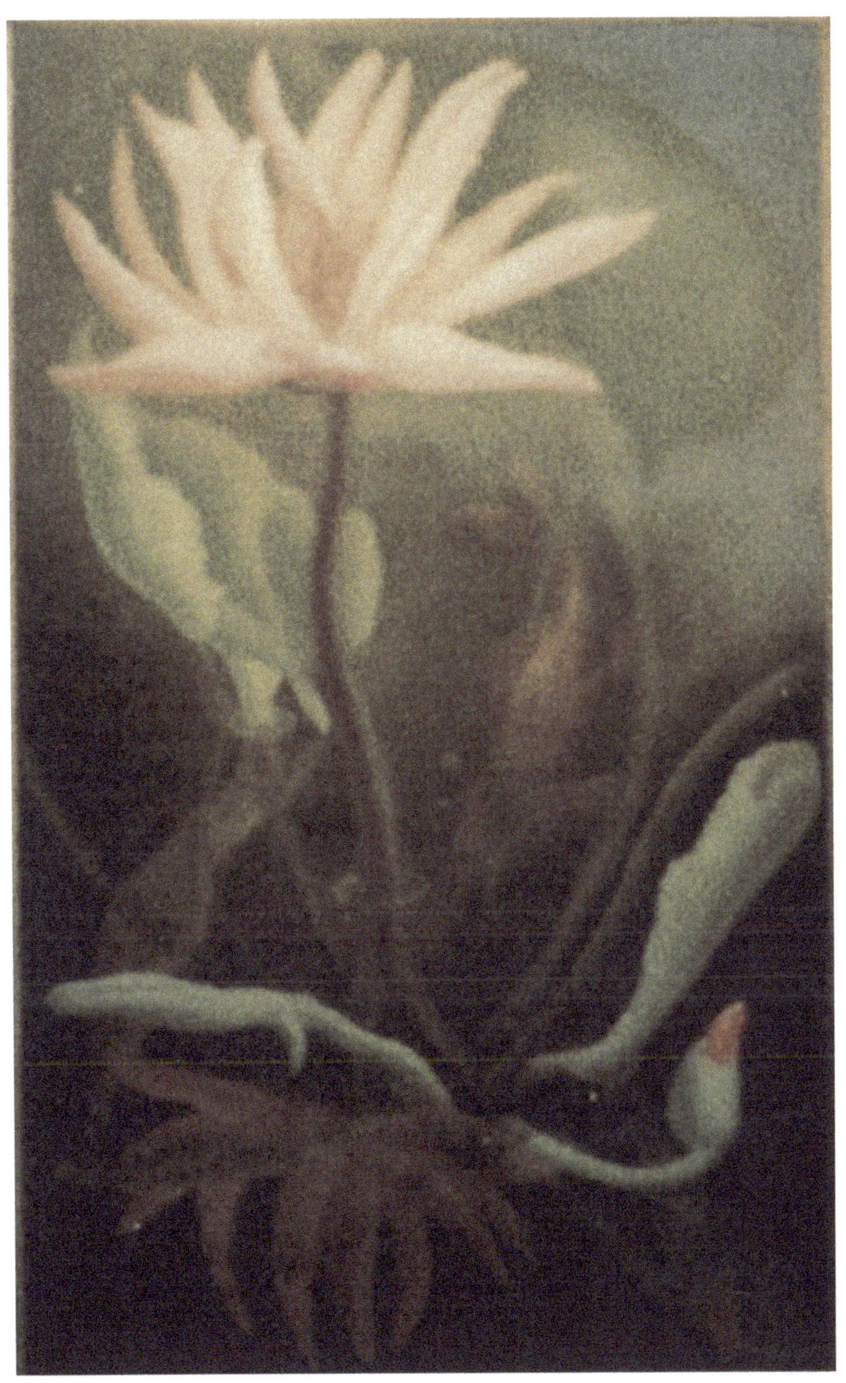

27. *Water-Flower* (1938, oil on canvas, 41 x 30 in.)

religionless, without a heavenly mansion,
we souls who chose perfection of the work

yet failed - as this one never did -
to sacrifice before the exacting god.

Therefore most blessed be her name
and may she intercede for us,

stuck in this neither-here-nor-there
lacking a coin to grease the boatman's* palm.

* i.e. Charon, the ferryman across the Styx.

Ithell completed in 1942 the mockeries of *Bride of the Pavement*, and *The Bride Carried a Bunch of Tethered Flies.*. These were obviously with her 1943 marriage in mind. I find it curious that no art critic has thus connected the paintings, though Chadwick provided notes on both, as a cynical matrimonial reference which reappears '. . . Colquhoun not only kept her distance from the Surrealist cult of love, but she also used it to fuel an imagery in which well-known Surrealist images and ideas are transformed, either visually or verbally, and their meaning once again inverted.' (*Women Artists and the Surrealist Movement*, p.129)

An important symbolic reflection on her birth and, perhaps career, in a Celto-magical mood, was *The Dance of the Nine Opals*, with its birthday allusions of October 9th, the opal being an October stone. The nine stones in a circle, in which, as in amber, are apparently entrapped human symbols - perhaps of varied attributes bestowed by her birth genes, are interlinked by power lines and with a main upspringing Earth-force. They circumscribe a straight path, maybe her passage or ideal passage through life, on the Earth's surface. The line disappears into the distance through mountainous peaks in the background. Here is actually neither period nor distance, but space-time synthesis.

Toni del Renzio continued his message and ideas with the organisation of a comprehensive section on surrealism in *New Road 1943* (4),

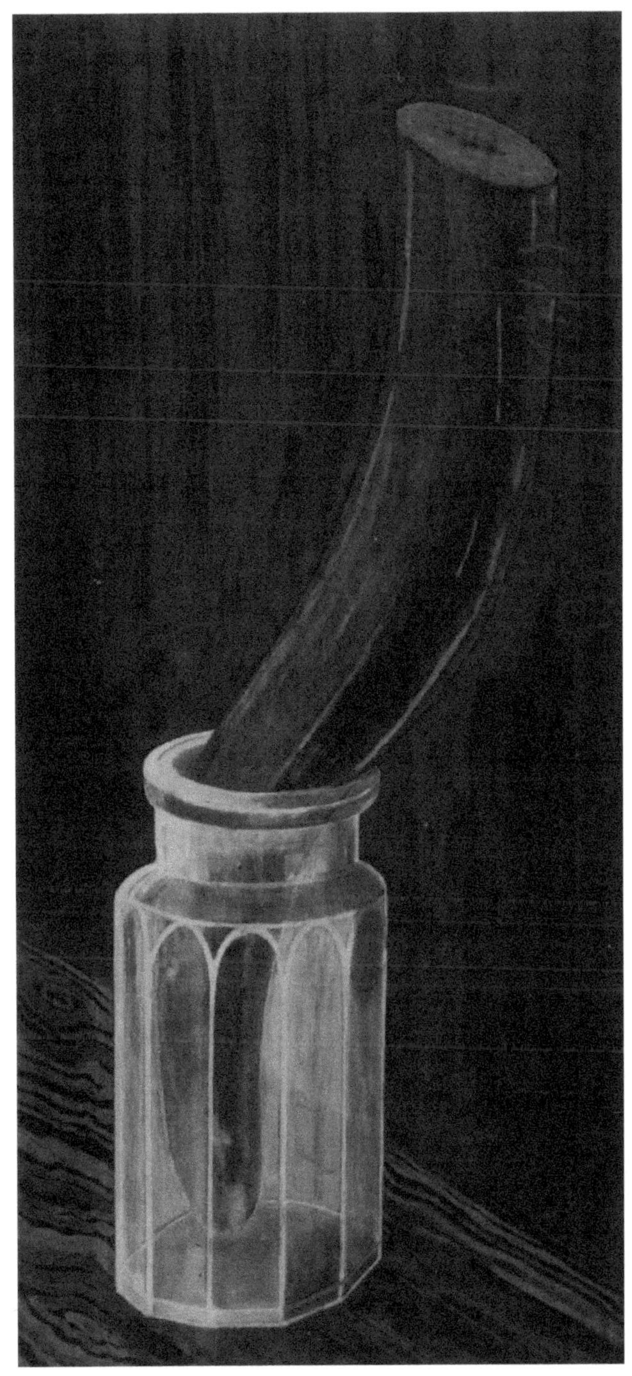

28. *Cucumber* (1939, tempera on board)

which anthology divided the work of the English surrealists from other trends. The section included articles by André Breton, Nicolas Calas, himself, and many others. Derek Stanford, in a leading critical article, drew attention to the loss of sense of direction in surrealism because the automatic process denied the right of the artist to make conscious selection. He mentioned, in this respect, the work of the 'New Apocalypse' writers who believed in the conscious employment of subconscious energy. Ithell contributed articles: 'Everything Found on Land is Found in the Sea' and 'The Water-Stone of the Wise'.(5) The former decried the style of language in scientific periodicals and gave Ithellian examples of her own (Experiments I, II, III) where both water and land occurred - a shaft in a valley containing fish-like flowers, strange flowers between Piccadilly and Oxford Street, Atlantic waves viewed from within a house in Maida Vale. In the chapter 'Sublimation' of her book *Goose of Hermogenes* will be found the first article with these three experiments – in this case referring to research literature found in her Uncle's library. The latter article is concerned with myth revealed in the region between sleeping and waking, where we will not find 'the fevered alternations of that demon-star which sponsored the birth of de Sade. . . but the hermaphrodite whole . . .' Dealing with the concept of a myth of twins - boy and girl:

> Their faculty is dream, their body-of-fate the stream of images – sensual transpositions – induced by the incandescence of their own body and mind . . . theirs is a unity conscious of its own elements . . .

Imaginatively pictured or not, if all humans were hermaphroditic, the unity would solve many legal problems and male/female disturbances! But even a surrealist could not convert this dream to worldly reality. It exists as an unconscious reality. One can no more gift a world-made material cradle for the twins on their level in the dream environment than await their deposition in a perambulator in Penzance. The brief still moment between unconsciousness in sleep and the coming into consciousness, starting the waking period, is a theoretical time platform only for such miracles.

The pushing back of the reasoning time period to the minimum for the commencement of work, yet with provision for some definite start point was at the basis of the automatic techniques of the pioneer surrealist. No doubt this too can be extended to encompass the illogical twists and turns which mark surrealist writings, for the end of each situation often provides a new surreal start-point for the beginning of the next. Only if conscious employment of subconscious energy overruns its 'fuel', or if there is long sequence moulded below the level of thought to be recovered, surely will there be direction of story or in the art. The balance between recovery and the employment must be a matter of skill on two levels.

Possibly it might be said that 'correct' usage of the conscious vis-à-vis subconscious energies was self-regulatory and varied with the writer or artist. Also in the issue was'Morgenroth', a love-poem by Toni del Renzio dedicated to Ithell, commencing 'O blood red rose of desire'. 1943 was obviously a high point in their partnership.

Breton's Manifestos were focal points for each of them. They each thought that Breton's principles had been ignored. The opposition, including Mesens, Penrose and Brunius, labelled Toni in *Horizon* as a 'spam-brained intellectual' who had smuggled himself into the surrealist wagon.(6) The subsequent literary in-fighting has been well documented. Ithell would have been unhappy at the continuing war within war. However, her personal turmoil which had begun at Mesens' Barcelona Restaurant meeting, was now increased since she had an added duty to stand by her embattled husband.

Ithell and Toni cooperated in a spate of poetry readings between 1942 and 1944, given at the International Arts Centre in London. The poems were mixed with prose, various extracts, and translations by Ithell from surrealist and other poetry. A brief selection of the wide-ranging scope of the programmes shows that they covered

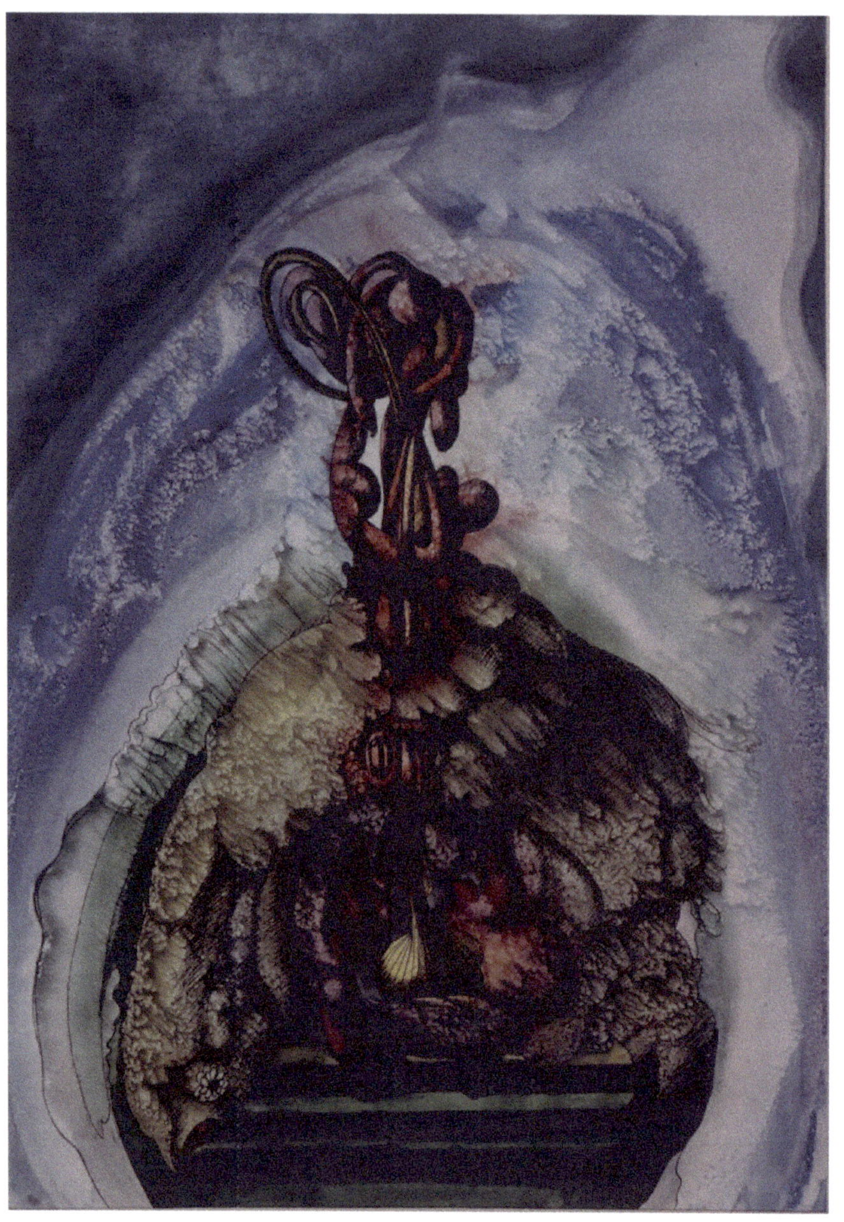

29. *St. Elmo* (c.1947, pen, black ink, gouache) Cartwright Hall Gallery, Bradford

Guillaume Apollinaire, William Blake, André Breton, Lewis Carroll, Aimé Césaire, René Char, Giorgo de Chirico, Salvador Dali, Paul Eluard, Conroy Maddox, André Masson, Valentine Penrose, Benjamin Péret, Pablo Picasso, Arthur Rimbaud, and Thomas Vaughan. Limited use was made of contributions to the *London Bulletin*, *New Directions*, and *View*. Ithell also read extracts from her *Goose of Hermogenes*, which at that time existed as unpublished MS.

The programmes appear ambitious and lengthy, and with onlyIthell and Toni reading, they might have benefited from an admixture of other mature readers. Possibly there were opportunities for unrest in the audience, which included many surrealists from Europe as well as Mesens-aligned artists from the London group. The barracking during the spring 1944 meeting is described by Ithell, taken from archival memoirs of the occasion:

> On this occasion the Mesens-mob assembled in force for barracking: they signed the Visitors' Book with such names as 'Pablo Picasso' and the 'Marquis de Sade'. Among a dozen of them were Edouard Mesens, Sibyl Mesens, Jacques Brunius, his redhead girl friend Mary . . .? Robert Baxter, Edith Rimmington-Baxter, Simon Watson-Taylor, Emmy Bridgwater, Conroy Maddox. Brunius read a newspaper ostentatiously, Mesens referred to Miss Deighton (afterwards Mrs. Alfred Torrie) as 'Madame Char-Woman', everyone interrupted, some pretending they could not hear. Miss Deighton asked them to leave and they all tramped off noisily, then the show went on.

Ithell records that Watson-Taylor published 'a spiteful and inaccurate account' of the proceedings. The firing and counter-firing in the hostilities are well confirmed elsewhere:

> These hostilities continued, when, on 14th July 1944, Toni del Renzio published 'Surrealism or else . . .', an article in *Tribune* which attacked Eluard's *Poésie et Verité 1942* and Mesen's *Third Front*, both published by London Gallery Editions, as poetry

> which can only come from 'the author's bathroom and toilets'. It also praised Aimé Césaire's poetry, recently discovered by Breton, and André Breton's speech to the students of Yale. A counter-attack in a subsequent issue of *Tribune* from Alec Smith, S.W.Taylor and J.B.Brunius followed, questioning why *Tribune* entrusted the criticism of surrealist publications to a revengeful self-appointed surrealist like Toni del Renzio, who only sought to fawn upon Breton.
>
> (*Surrealism in Britain*, p.227)

But not only the show went on, also did Ithell's creativity, though in somewhat diminished quantity. Her paintings completed during 1944-5 included *Ages of Man*, *Sea-Star* (I), *Tendrils of Sleep* (I), *Dreaming Leaps*, *E.L.A.S.*, *Garden of Adonis*, *Landscape of Nightmare*, and *A Visitation* (I).

Sea Star repeats predilection for marine imagery (e.g. *L'Ancre*, *L'Hélice*, *Gouffres Amers*, *Scylla*). A gigantic sea-seed, either in section or transparently showing the early core with inner organs which contributed to its outer skin-growth, is rooted between sea and sky. Its vast foreground presence forces itself to attention, to be accepted in all its monstrous incongruity as a sea-organism in its own right, dimensional in its water world, grown up from the waters - with the suggestion of polar roots fixed below in water and above in air. Immutable and uncannily obvious, it has some power of mental transfixation of a human viewer, and is a remarkable example of décalcomania.

So also is *A Visitation*, slightly more obviously from its symmetry, without background or introduced polarities. The upward growth of two biological energy sources (like coloured bulbs) produces a strange flowering of pushed-up essences following crossing at a central point. Readers with some kabbalistic knowledge will note that the painting has rather a glyph-like pattern analogous to the tree of life, with a risen consciousness or progression of purification from a cliphothic blackness at the base of the structure. If then Tiphereth is the crossing point, the upward paths lead to a 'Kether' image at the top. This is biological creation in symbols, the advancing stages being synonymous with advanced consciousness. Considered on a lower plant level, the topmost flowering may be said to exemplify sun-consciousness.

There is no detailed information about time and place of the break-up of the Ithell/Toni partnership, but Derek Stanford remembers them both in a newish bungalow-like building in north London; and later, Ithell on her own and very ill with asthma.

The tragic affair in the autumn of 1945, at Bayswater, of the young painter Sonia Araquistain, led to a separate creative urge in Toni (poetry), with ideas for a memorial volume; and for Ithell, the creation of *Dreaming Leaps* : *In Homage to Sonia Araquistain.* The literature and newspaper reports tell of her suicide, leaping naked from the top of her father's Bayswater house; and the event provoked many surrealists in defence of her person. The abbreviated passage below, by Michel Remy, and much more about this painting, should be read in full from his book; he is very perceptive:

> The painting is hypnotic; the movement of the fall seems to have been suddenly arrested and eternalised at its climax. Filaments of colour, garish and sombre garlands, fragments of comets. . . entanglements of intestinal ribbons of sharply contrasting colours, are suspended, like improbable peelings of a twilight sky . . . forms are reborn as in the alchemical process . . . The last three stages of the alchemical operation – exaltation, multiplication and projection – are recalled . . .
>
> (*Surrealism in Britain*, pp.278-280)

The above work should be compared with Arshile Gorky's *Waterfall* of 1943 (p.63 in Fiona Bradley's *Surrealism*). The acts of falling are somewhat similarly depicted, but differentiation of human from water needs subjective and not analytical attention, in the spirit of surrealism.

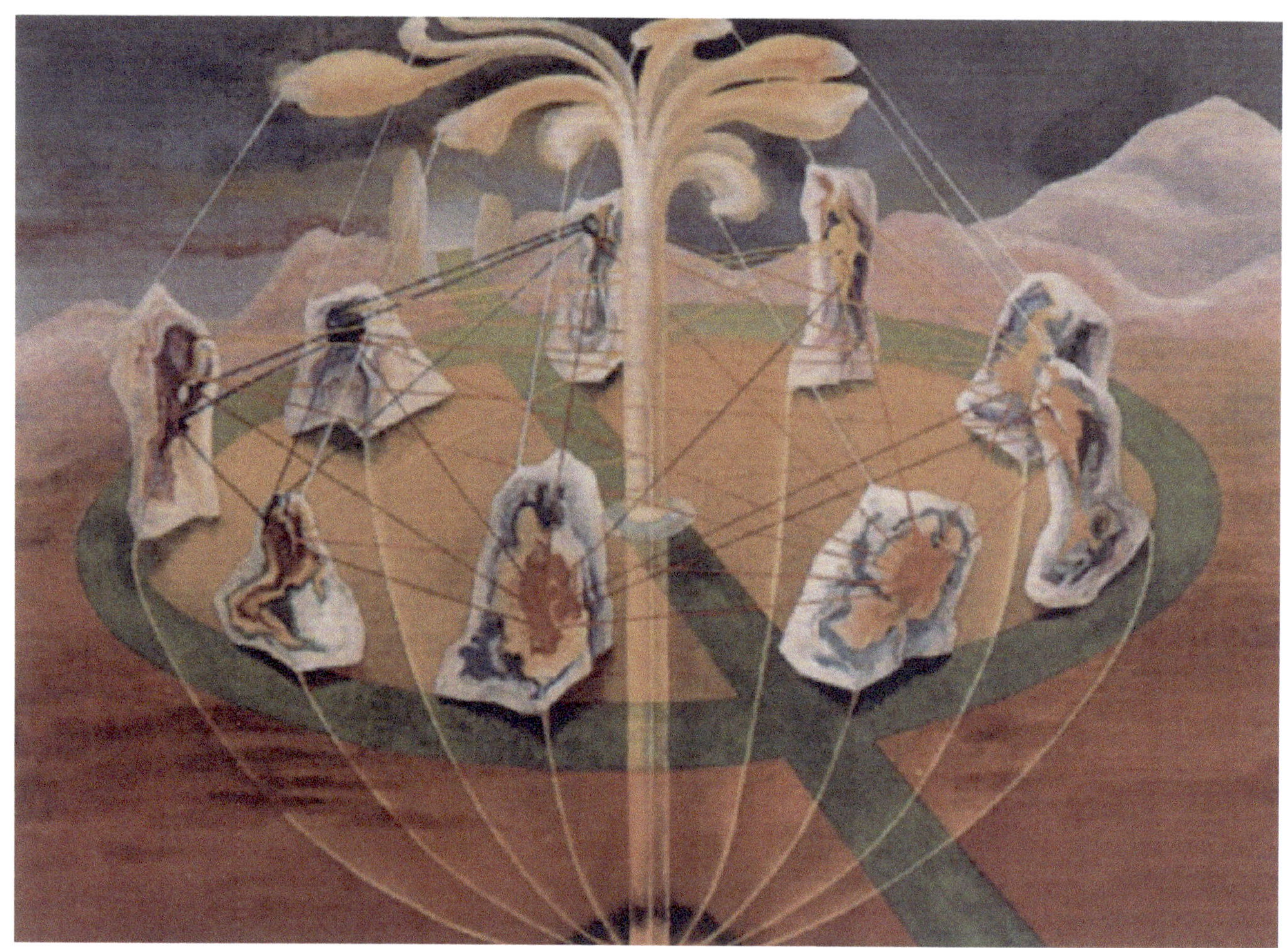

30. *Dance of the Nine Opals* (1942, oil on canvas, 22 x 28ins., 51 x 69 cm

Matthew Gale in a summary biography(7) stated that Ithell and Toni were 'acrimoniously divorced in 1947'. No doubt they had separated before then. Certainly Ithell was pictured looking happy and enthusiastic in a newspaper report in the *Hampstead Express* of August 20th in 1948, picturing her demonstrating the art of `fumage' (among other surrealistic automatic processes) for a television programme. The report stated that from 1945 she lived and worked in Parkhill Road, Hampstead, so that 1944 was probably a crisis year for the couple. From the will of Ithell's mother, Georgia, dated March 1948, Ithell was still legally named as Margaret Ithell del Renzio, but she always retained her maiden surname.

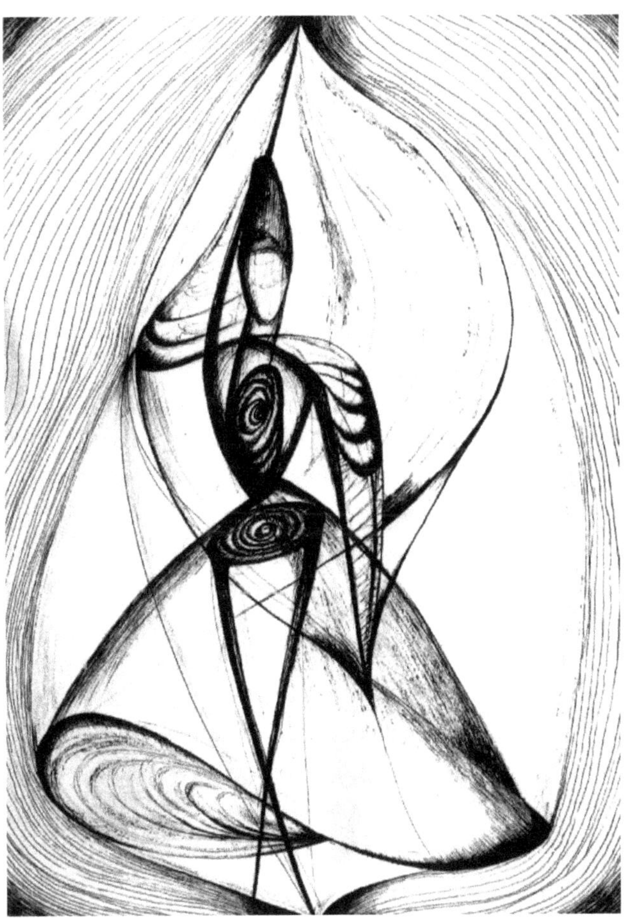

31. *Dervish* (1951, indian ink, 17 x 12¼ in., 44 x 31cm)

6 Independent Spirit

D*reaming Leaps*, regarded as one of Ithell Colquhoun's best paintings, with inspirational poetry from Toni, after the suicide, appears to be the last time that there was some link between the two, albeit accidental. She was now independent of close male support, physically and morally, and remained isolated from the surrealist group previously centred around Edouard Mesens and led by Roland Penrose. The group, in disarray after the war, was making efforts to reform, activated by some of those antagonistic to her principles, which did not help. Later, in 1947, in Paris, André Breton and Marcel Duchamp organised a comprehensive international exhibition which firmly put the post-war surrealists on stage as a 'collective myth' and contributed to a new world upspurge of interest.(1)

For Ithell, 1944 and 1945 were relatively creative low points, apart from the inspirational *Dreaming Leaps* - it was very much a transition period. Two versions of *The Visitation*, together with *Landscape of Nightmare*, in the absence of hard evidence, cannot be located as painted from any particular location. Derby Museum and Art Gallery at their 'Exhibition of Contemporary Art' held from Nov.17th to Dec.30th, 1945, showed *Death of the Vampire in a Magic Mirror*, which may have been an early study of *Death of a Vampire* (décalcomania,

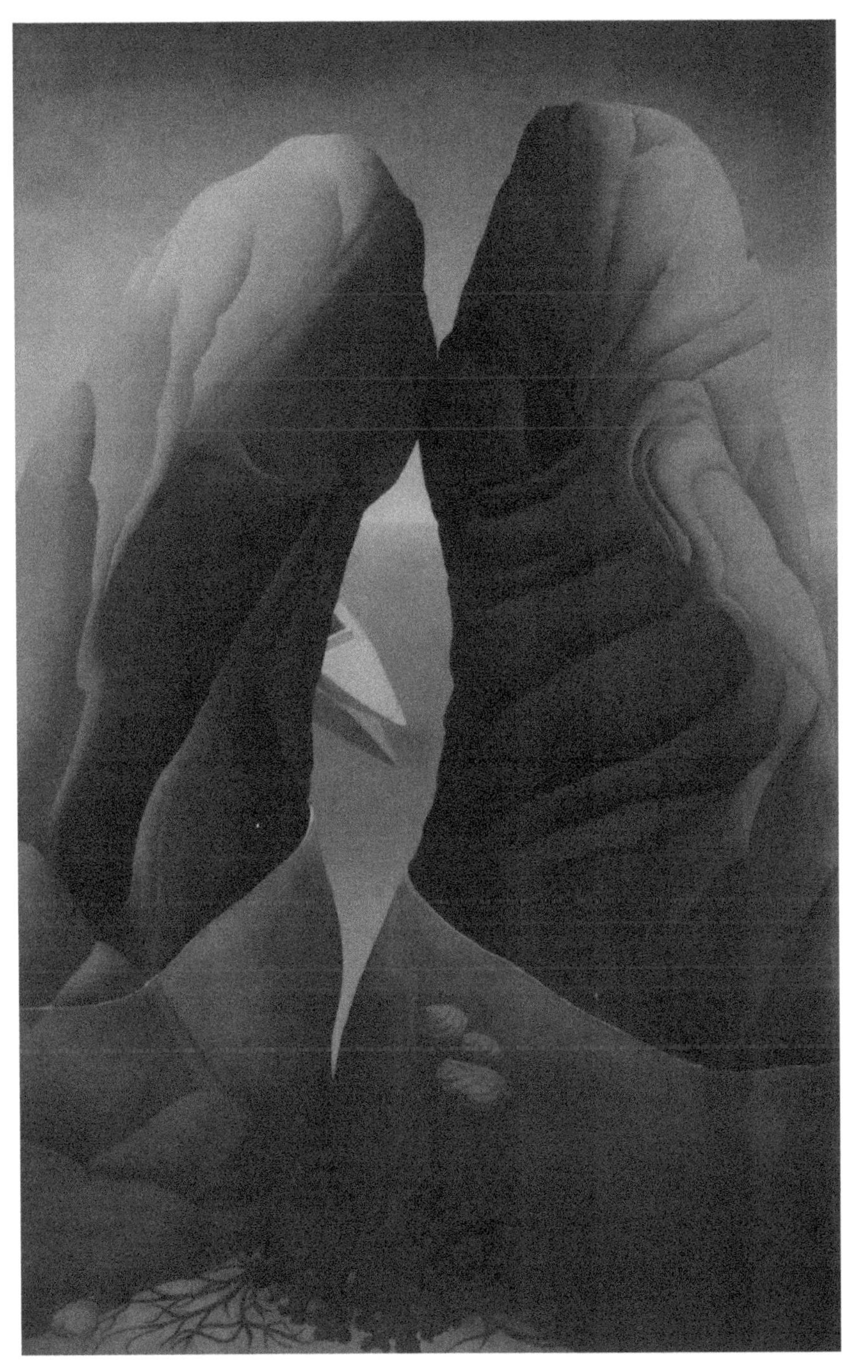

32. *Scylla* (1938, oil on board, 36 x 24 in., 91.4 x 61.0 cm) Tate Gallery

c.1960). Another product of décalcomania, *Guardian Angel*, was completed in 1946 or the following year. Using one interpretation:

> What the angel reveals . . . is an inner emptiness which turns out to be either the entrance to a grotto, the gateway into another world, a huge mouth with an enormous uvula, or two rounded transparent buttocks- or could it be the opening of a woman's genitals gaping wide apart. The eye slides between one meaning and another, dividing itself in the image of a huge ocular hole that comprises two gaping sockets. The eye and the mind are thrust towards a new threshold of perception . . .
>
> (*Surrealism in Britain*, p.313)

These statements are quite valid. It is not a simple painting to analyse, but if the implications of the title are taken into account, the violation of the female portal, i.e. the vaginal lips, seems that which is to be guarded, and the outer world is seen from the inside, as evinced by the dark over-thatch of probable pubic hair. The 'angel' seems to be embodied in what was above termed an uvula - a 'body' of great power, whose 'wings' line the opening in two symmetrical semi-circular sweeps. Subconscious processes, by their nature, are synthetic energies and can combine the several into the one, leaving the viewer to disentangle and interpret the various aspects. It appears the mark of a successful synthesis in cases of manifold explanations. It is possible and often desirable, for the human mind to receive the synthetic message and delight in it, without analysis. What is put together by keeping at bay the reasoning process can still be conveyed as a whole, but needs a receiver able to bypass analysis, much as one appreciates a musical work without interpretive analysis.

By the end of 1946, Ithell, probably getting over the break with Toni, and feeling more settled at Hampstead, in addition to the foregoing painting, completed ten other paintings, (*Alcove*, *Arbour*, *Arethusa*, *Genius Loci*, *Gorgon*, *Linked Islands*, *Linked Senses*, *The Long Journey*, *Self-Portrait*, and *The Winnowers*) the majority of which were shown in a solo exhibition at the Mayor Gallery during March 1947, which included some work of the four previous years and three new paintings completed in 1947 before the exhibition date (*Roman Sun*, *Saltimbanco*, *Attributes of the Moon*). The same gallery, in addition to this March 5th to 28th exhibition, arranged a solo show of her drawings (undated in the catalogue) on Dec.3rd to 24th, including illustrations to poems. It might be said that, with this year, her will, dedication and rapidity of execution had fully returned. She had also exhibited in mixed shows (at home in 'Hampstead Artists Past and Present' and in Paris – 'Les Surindependants', 40th exhibition) in 1946 and 1947, respectively.

In about 1948 it seems that she took a working holiday in Ireland, where she participated in the Dublin National College of Art's 'Irish Exhibition of Living Art', showing *Toy* (ink and watercolour). Her paintings *Dingle Bay* and *Kerry Landscape* were completed soon after, and most probably she recorded the events and explorations which were to result in drafting her first book, *The Crying of the Wind : Ireland*, published some years later.

The interesting work *St. Elmo* of this period (c.1947) dates from about this period. It was displayed in the 1948 spring exhibition at Cartwright Hall, Bradford, and was later bought by that gallery. Details on the reverse provide the full Hampstead address (75 Parkhill Road). The saint is also identifiable with St. Peter Gonzalez, a Spanish Dominican who, in the thirteenth century, evangelised to Portuguese and Spanish sailors, and was regarded as their 'protector' at sea. He also identifies with St. Erasmus of the third century. The luminous electrical discharge from pointed objects such as ship's mastheads was regard as a manifestation of the saint, still known as 'St. Elmo's Fire'. This painting could be interpreted as showing St. Elmo atop a masthead on the broken-off fore-part of a stricken ship, amid the turbulence of a tempest, showing the decks. However, *Linked Islands* (II), an early fifties painting (symbolising the low-tide land link between St.Agnes and Gugh in the Scillies), depicts a similar

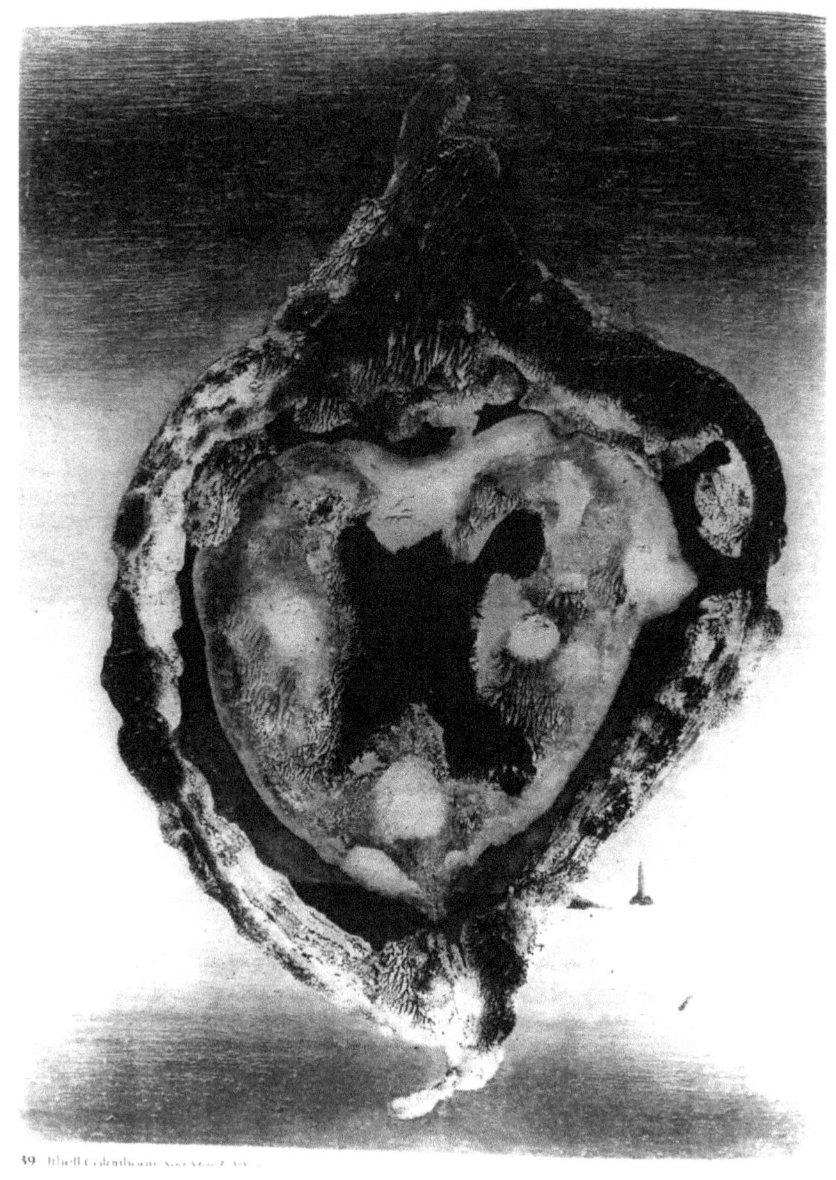

35. *Sea-Star* (I) (1943, oil on board, 14 x 10½ in., 35.5 x 26.7 cm)

'St.Elmo' figure on the shoreline of St. Agnes, in which situation the exposed decks became steps down to the sea.

Santa Warna's Wishing Well and *Santa Warna Lands* were shown at the Mayor Gallery in 1947 as undated drawings. The former can be dated to that year from a later exhibition, and it is reasonable to assume that the ubiquitous Ithell was at St. Agnes in the Scillies in that year. Her prose-poem 'The Myth of Santa Warna', the patron saint of that island, has been included later in her poetry. Probably by 1949 she was back in London, for her work was used in 'Pictures for Schools' at the Whitechapel Gallery in that year.

The end of the decade would be used also in visiting Cornwall to secure a 'hideaway' - of which more later.

It was between the late forties and the early fifties that she both wrote on automatic processes(2) and lectured on them to the Oxford Art Society, the Cambridge Art Society, and to the Working Men's College in Crowndale Road, London in 1953. Her lectures at the last venue were appreciated and reported in the *Hampstead & Highgate Record* and in *The Daub*.(3) The *Record* gave a short report of her descriptions, backed by her paintings, of the transformation of 'an ordinary stain made with coloured inks' leading to 'a painting of beauty and design'. *The Daub* commented on the practical application of her methods:

> Ithell Colquhoun with a lecture and numerous demonstrations, enlightened us and dispelled much of our initial scepticism on what was thought to be accidental picture making . . . many of her methods are recommended to students who are devoid of ideas . . . We hope to see more of Miss Colquhoun.

Another report of her demonstrating automatic processes was of the television programme of 1948. The *Hampstead Express* had reported it, with a photograph of Ithell with candle and paper, showing how a smoked pattern from 'fumage' was formed. The report also

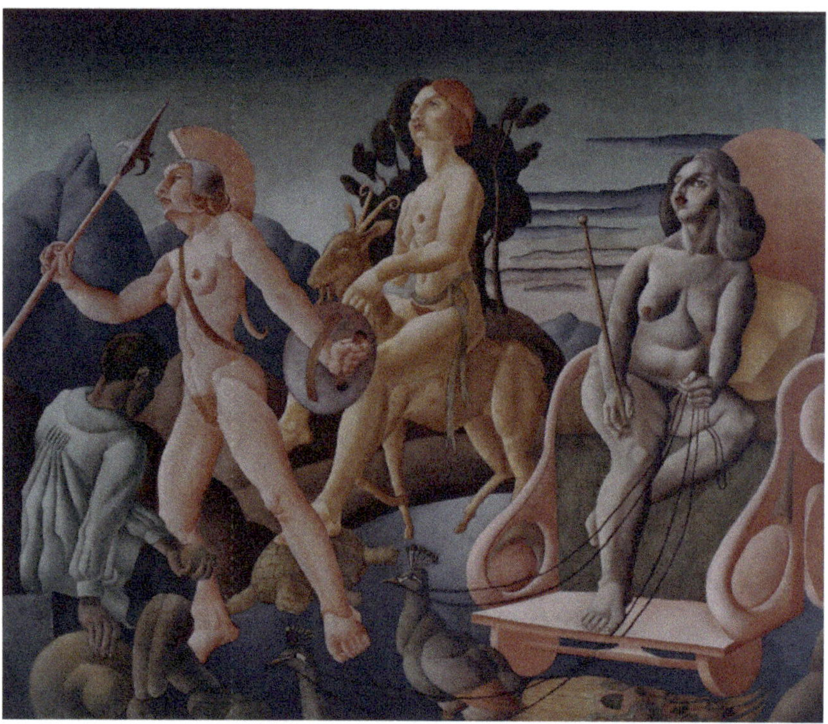

34. *The Judgement of Paris* (1930, oil on canvas, 30 x 20 in.) Brighton and Hove Art Gallery

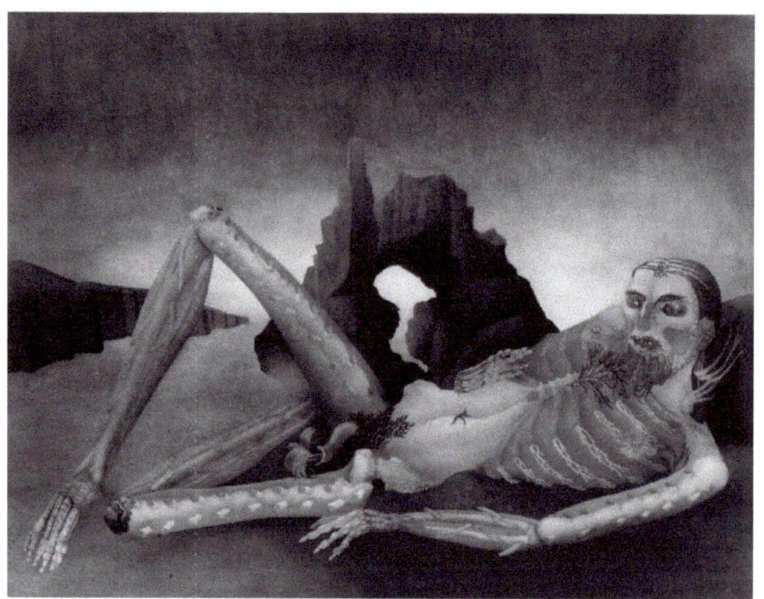

35. *Gouffres Amers* (1939, oil on canvas, 28½ x 36 in., 71.2 x 91.3 cm) Glasgow, Hunterian Art Gallery

bore a reproduction of her *Still Water* (a Hampstead Heath pond) derived from décalcomania.(4) Aside from mentioning the techniques of fumage; décalcomania (pressing paper sheets together, with ink or paint between to obtain a pattern); parsemage (sprinkling powdered charcoal or coloured chalks on the surface of a bowl of water, some of which is retrieved as a pattern by collecting it on dipped paper) - the journalistic details of the report extended to other personal matters:

> She has many other interests. One of them is alchemy - her cat is named Theophrastus Paracelsus after the mediaeval searcher for the Philosopher's Stone. She writes poetry and translates from the French, especially of Mallarmé, noted for his obscure and elaborate images. She has written a surrealistic novel. She is interested in natural history and the mystic folk lore of the countryside.

Ithell always exhibited interest in the various mechanical ways of producing basic patterns which were then used to stimulate the germ of an idea, worked on more consciously by her artistic skills. Her valuable function seems to have been the popularising of the methods, attributed to the tenets of surrealism. But more reconditely as far as education of the public was concerned, and indeed via recognition of the surrealists themselves, Austin Osman Spare, a first world-war artist who died in 1956, was a recent example of a skilled artist who had little doubt that the methods brought out the 'truth' in a work which no amount of premeditated conscious skill could achieve. His article in *Form* (5) with Frederick Carter tells us:

> The objective understanding . . . has to be attacked by the artist and a subconscious method, for correction of conscious visual accuracy, must be used.

However, as pointed out,(6) in effect the distrust of the conscious mind in favour of the all-revealing subconscious mind was replaced

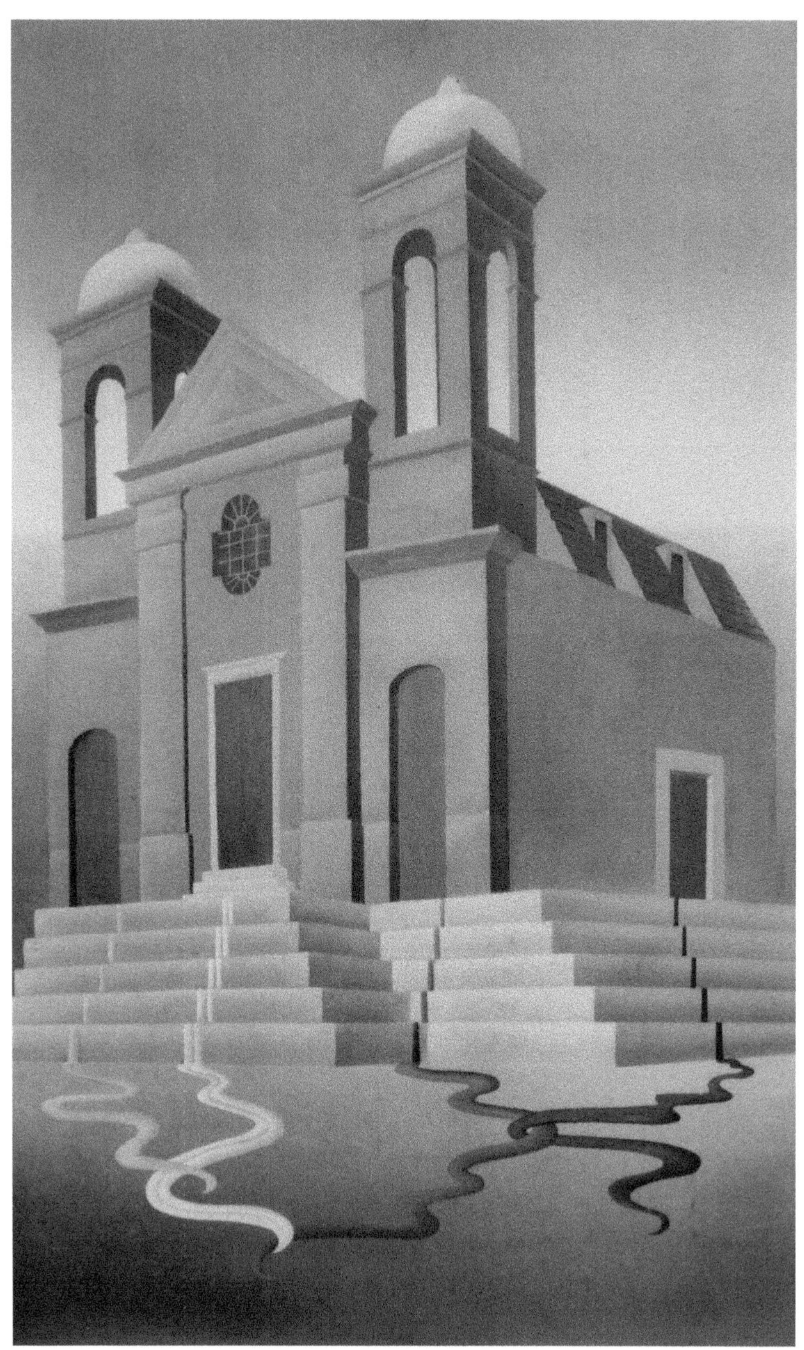

36. *Rivières Tièdes* (1939, oil on panel, 36 x 24 in., 91.1 x 61.2 cm) Southampton City Art Gallery

by the ideas of Breton in a later manifesto which treated the automatic process as a means to link the two.

Always keen to exhibit and to use publicity to advantage, Ithell somehow secured her photograph in three periodicals during May and June in 1949.(7) These show her in monster 'witchball' earrings, black mantilla headdress, with fan before face, in readiness for the Hampstead Arts Ball. Accompanying texts give brief details of her specialities in automatism in her painting. Ireland, The Scillies, painting, writing, lecturing, appearing on television, the Arts Ball. . . Ithell was obviously enjoying full independence and presumably was in reasonable health.

We note, among the proliferation of other work, the highlight that she was successful in the hanging of her *La Cathédrale Engloutie* at the Royal Academy exhibition of 1952 - a large canvas, over 4 by 6 ft, painted in the same year. This had previously hung at a Bradford exhibition and, after the Academy exhibition closed, was shown at a Women's International Art Club exhibition in London.

Ithell Colquhoun's next 'solo' was in the spring of 1953, in Cambridge, at the Heffer Gallery. Unfortunately the catalogue is missing, and only reviews remain,(8) which give no idea of the range and quantity of what was on show. The *Cambridge Daily News* commented on her *Bride of the Pavement*:

> A surrealist since 1938, Ithell Colquhoun's earlier works were of colossal flowers, but that theme is not now apparent in her work. She is engrossed in an imaginary vegetal character expressed in various ways. All her paintings of this character are beautifully executed and the detail in some is minute. Her *Bride of the Pavement* illustrates this point. It is an outstanding work showing vegetation literally growing from stone. The colouring is of exceptional delicacy . . .

This 1942 painting originated automatically by way of fumage; lack

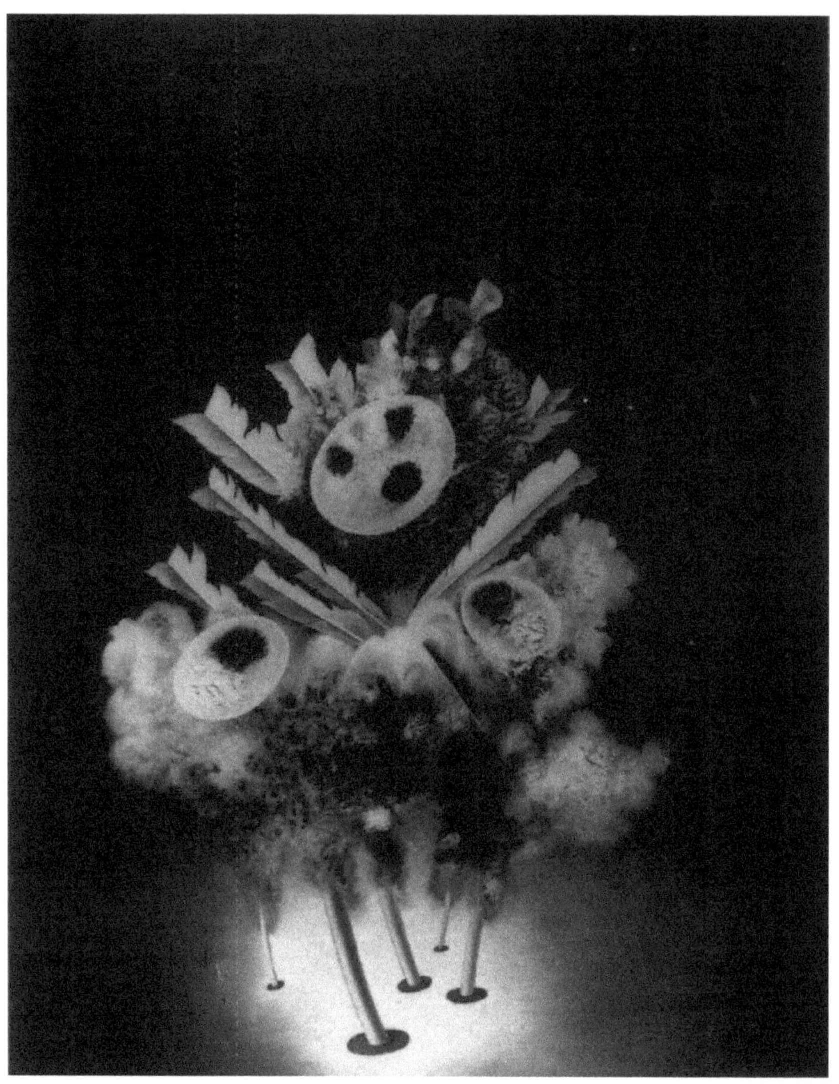

37. *Bride of the Pavement* (1942, oil on canvas, 30 x 24 in., 76 x 61 cm)

of knowledge of the circumstances in 1942 of the environment of its origination (i.e. ideas of marriage) leaves the critic to provide a superficial analysis. However, the burgeoning to life from a static state - marriage as a drawing forth of new energy from set ways, and the 'vegetal character' are valid conceptions, and a continuance of Ithell's sense of life within uncut stone and stone monuments.

The *News* also referred to the exhibited painting *The Grotto of the Sun and Moon*, which she completed in 1952 ('.... cruder work with less delicately shaded colours . . . with great depth of feeling expressed in its harsh, startling lines.') It was also shown at the Newlyn Gallery in a solo exhibition of October 1961, at Ostend in 1963, and at her solo show at Exeter in 1972. This was painted, not via automatic processes, but from a vivid dream during the war:

> The approach to the Grotto is a wide unroofed corridor or narrow courtyard, something like the entrance to one of the circular tombs of Mycenae. (One remembers that very pale Mycenaean gold, thinly beaten out.) Above the high wall at the opposite end the sky burns intensely blue. In the middle of this wall a triple archway is hollowed out, the surfaces at right-angles painted in true-fresco with deep yellow, flower-pink and slate-blue. This design is mainly abstract, but sun's rays are suggested at the top of the central arch on the wall-surface facing the spectator.
>
> Inside the arch rises a mass of dark porous substance like pumice-stone, but each of its holes is large enough to admit the passage of a ray of light. These rays seem to shine through the holes from the hidden core of the Grotto, some are paler than others, and I understand that they proceeded from the Sun and Moon. Each hole represents some crisis in the annual cycle of these luminaries; and as at Stonehenge a gap in the circle allows the Sun, rising on midsummer day, to strike a certain stone, so here the light streams through each hole in its own season ; yet

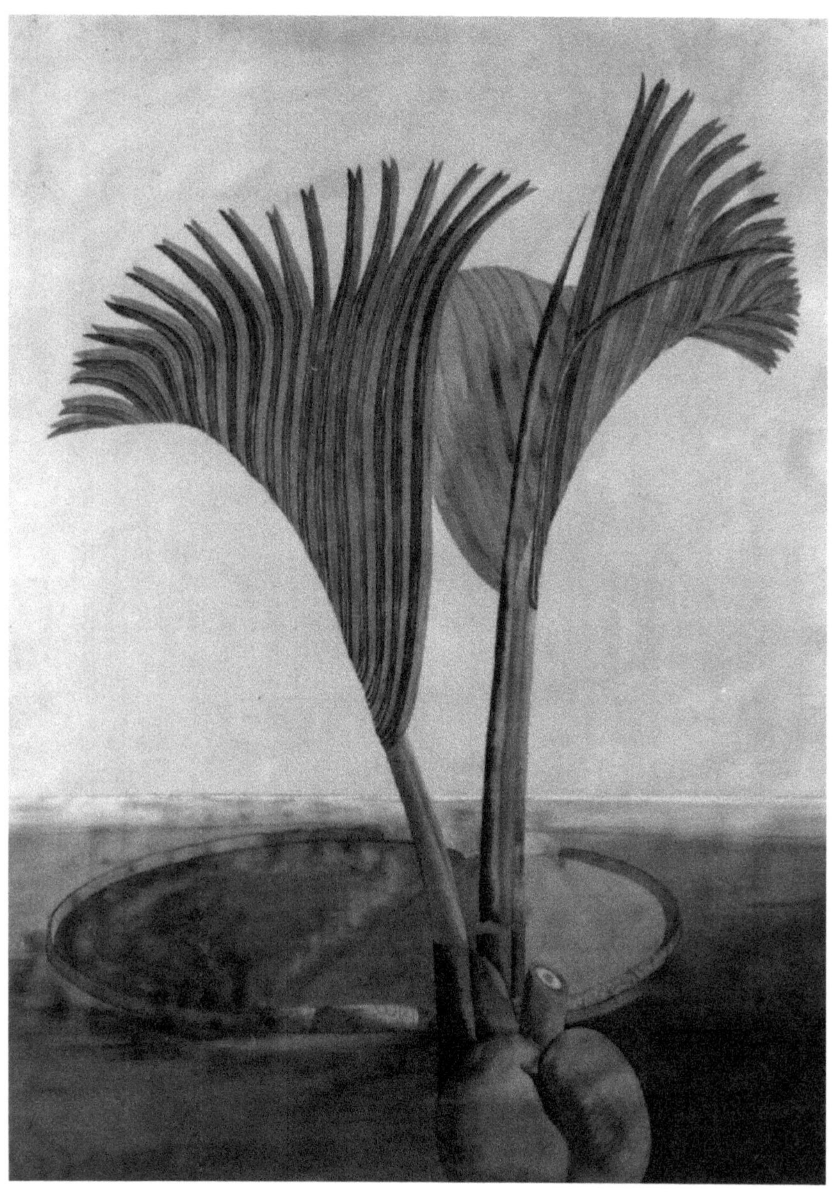

38. *Double Coco-Nut* (Early to mid-thirties, watercolour on silk)

> all appears to be happening at the same time, as though transcending time itself. A voice told me that this was 'The Grotto of the Sun and Moon, Nicaragua.'

A copy of this archived typescript, which closes with an appeal to anyone who could elucidate the dream, had been sent as a personal letter to an unknown recipient in May 1965. It suggests that the Grotto may be the sanctuary where 'the chemical rituals of the Sun and Moon' are celebrated (Ithell had been reading alchemical subjects in the sixties.)

The Cambridge *Varsity* concludes that

> . . . she is technically briliant; her brushwork is accomplished, her colour schemes daring and sophisticated, her sense of form is faultless.

As usual, the mechanical analysis is good but the ability to synthesise back into the intentions of the artist is nil:

> She is fascinated by herbage and the human kidney and both these forms figure largely in her paintings . . . 'Herbage with Kidney' or 'Kidney amid Herbage' seems to be adequate titling for most of the items on show.

Ithell Colquhoun's post-war activities in relation to place are extraordinarily difficult to define. Was she still at Hampstead to supervise sending her work to the 1953 Cambridge exhibition? The next firm date is 1959, when she is reported to have bought a cottage in Paul, Cornwall, where she lived for the remainder of her life. Between 1945 when she commenced living at Hampstead, and 1959, I have already recounted some activities, which would include a period in Ireland at the end of the forties, leading to material for her first book *The Crying of the Wind : Ireland* (1955) being assembled and drafted. There was a further post-war period of several years, most likely after the Irish trip, when she lived on and off in a hut in the

Lamorna Valley, punctuated by summer lettings, before she moved to Paul. It was in the congenial environment of Lamorna that she wrote her second book *The Living Stones : Cornwall* (1957).

In Ithell's book on Ireland, the geographical tour and itinerary are secondary to objectives relating to Irish lore and habits. Attendant chronology does not exist, composition and movements of her companions and modes of travel are sketchy, deferring to the greater interests of visits to ancient monuments and sites, with much information on attached legend, customs, old tales, local people &c. In between, she displays a very wide knowledge of plants and bird-life. The start is from Dublin, following the coast road south to Glendaloch, its mountain, lakes, graveyard, church ruins; visiting the Vale of Avoca where the Rivers Avonmore and Avonbeg meet. By the end of the excursion we have learned about deer in Irish legend - a magical tradition, the good-luck ritual of embracing the sixth-century cross of St Kevin, the ritual of dipping the hand in the water of the basin-shaped Deer Stone, and rural haunting by phantasmal forms which is shared in Dorset and Cornwall : ('They exist, that is all we can say. We share the cosmos with them'.)

Another trip is a short walk to Lucan, noting the modern desecration of a holy well, following the path to 'Sarsfield's Castle', birthplace of the Earl of Lucan - before the start of motoring west to the Connemara coast. A few pages further on, in Galway, then the seaside resort of Salthill, we follow Ithell Colquhoun's party as they climb deep into the hills of Connacht backed by the Connemara mountains. Motoring still westwards, past Oughterard, many creeks and villages are visited - Letterdyfe, Bertraghboy Bay, Roundstone are but a few features described. Further north still, there is an excursion to Croagh Patrick in west Connacht, near the coast, via Clifden and the market there - here 'resheen', a red cloth teased with honey, could still be bought, and also the 'Breedeen', a kind of tweed made by combining the bleached with the unbleached wool as weft and warp. The holy mountain or 'high hill' is a 2500-ft climb, known locally as 'The Reek' with a church at the summit. 'One climbs to the Reek . . . on Garland Sunday, the last in July.' Pilgrims start the ascent at midnight or before for the dawn masses.

Back in Galway, the island of Inishnee is visited from Bertraghboy. From the coastline is seen a pyramidal carn and half circle of wall screening a bullán (basin) scooped out of rock and filled with water. There is enchantment in the spot, the structures being decorated with 'yellow flags and with twigs of rhododendron, pittisphorum and fuschia.' Ithell associates it with a place in memory of one of the two St. Brendans.

Before the return to Dublin, there are chapters including the legendary background of islands near Roundstone and in the vicinity of Bertraghboy Bay, fairy traditions and 'palaces' (often located on the site of a neolithic or Bronze Age dwelling), Irish myth, Finvarra - fairy chieftain of Connacht, and the mystery of his Seven Daughters who gave their names to many sacred wells, many other ancient wells with their presiding spirits, &c. Later in these areas, are the experiences of the midsummer bonfires, visits to Erraloch and Cashel village.

From Dublin there is a train journey to Drogheda, sketching, discourse on the celebrated tumulus New Grange, traditionally the palace of Angus Og, Irish god of love. From Drogheda, excursions to Tara and the Fort of the Kings, the remains of the foundation of the Fort of Grainne. At the close of the journey there is an account of a visit to Dublin's Municipal Gallery.

Find profundity and originality of Ithellian thought in a theory of the land and the people in psychological terms:

> The Celtic substratum in Britain, and to a lesser extent in France, is the collective equivalent of the repressed unconscious in the individual . . . explains why the Anglo-Saxon strain, which plays the role of super-ego . . . distrusts and despises the Celtic strain, the incalculable id . . .

Of subsequent reviews,(9) *The Times Literary Supplement* review penetrated closely into the author's mind, after calling attention to the fact that she was concerned with a preoccupation with 'strata' - here, the underlying paganism of the people, and the underlying land, seemingly suffocated below modernisms of cities.

> . . . This might suggest a form of pantheism, but her views are really nearer those of the psalmist when he cries 'Send forth Thy spirit. . . and Thou shall renew the face of the earth,' or St. Hildegarde when she sings, 'From Thee the clouds move, the air flies on its way, the stony rock exudes moisture and gives forth streams, and the earth puts on its green herb.'

Concluding that *The Crying of the Wind* was 'a rare and beautiful travel book' also with an atmosphere of phantasmagoria, a final compliment is given:

> Here is the authentic touch of the Gothic novelist, and one wishes that Miss Colquhoun had both the canvas large enough and the unrestricted scope to introduce the mysterious figures that should flit across this darkling landscape.

Narrower and less understanding viewpoints were given in other periodicals. From *The Lady* :

> She wanders with no specialist urge, being glad that she is no archeologist so that she can enjoy herself among antiquities and interpret them according to her own intuitions without deference to any school of thought . . . This unusual book is decorated rather than illustrated by Miss Colquhoun's queer drawings. . .

And why should she defer? Ithell Colquhoun was her own school of thought, and her specialist urge escaped this worldly critic – that of capturing the essence of old Celtic habits and beliefs and the life within the landscape which was real on her level of consciousness, quite invisible or unreal to the insensitive person.

Reverting to describe Ithell's occult connections since her early interests: after the war, Ithell Colquhoun learned from a renewed contact with her cousin E.J. Langford Garstin that the Alpha and Omega temple of the Golden Dawn, to which she had been introduced before she went abroad to study, had been dispersed in 1939. The temple furniture had been destroyed at the instance of the 'Secret Chiefs'.

At some unknown date she was recommended to a 'free-lance psychotherapist' - a kind of healer/teacher in the person of Herbert Stone, practising as 'Meredith Starr'. Stone had been on the editorial board of Crowley's *Equinox* far back in 1912. Treatment consisted in dieting, rest and meditation at his country house. Ithell stayed for a weekend but returned unimpressed, finding the place also gloomy and cold. This was probably at East Challacombe, Devon, where Starr and his wife had established a spiritual retreat. (Starr had formed a Meher Baba Association after having as a guest that Persian mystic from India in 1931, and was probably a member of the Anthroposophical Society of Rudolph Steiner, with many contributions to *Anthroposophy*.) In spite of the background, it is obvious that Ithell was uncomfortable there in body and mind, as she explained later in *Sword of Wisdom.*

In 1952, she took a postal course as a condition for joining the Society of the Inner Light. This had been founded by 'Dion Fortune' (Violet Firth), a transmutation of her Golden Dawn magical name *Deo Non Fortuna* when in that Order. Originally the Inner Light group had been attached to the Outer Order of the Golden Dawn, in favour with Mina Mathers, head of the Alpha and Omega Lodge in England since 1928; but it continued independently later. Unfortunately, in an essay, Ithell hinted at discrepancies in Dion's *Cosmic Doctrine*. This led to her being prohibited from continuing the course. Ithell protested against this treatment, and a further course stage was allowed. After this she was still not found suitable for initiation into the Society's membership. It was an extraordinary and humiliating result of her studies; her immediate tutor had considered her one of his best pupils. It was then suggested that she re-start the course. Naturally, she refused to do this. It is apparent that she was always likely to meet difficulties on the path of fitting in with the established practice and ritual of occult groups. Her wide-ranging theoretical knowledge, and very strong inclination for independent thought to reach her own conclusions, must have led to questioning at every stage of an occult system. Her mind would not tolerate or accept external statements until these could be perceived to fit her ideas; and this was often made plain to others, instead of keeping quiet. Inevitably she was misinterpreted or opposed by those without adequate patience or, indeed, the knowledge, to cover such details as she posed.

The biographical section of *Sword of Wisdom*, shows that she was intrigued with references to 'Secret Chiefs' or their equivalents, who remain anonymous but are basically posited as being behind the scene but in control. Discussion of these covers eight pages, revealing her cache of knowledge on the subject. It was not that she was an unbeliever in certain powerful invisible influences: she herself had experienced similar phenomena, but was doubtful and suspicious of their personifications in the context of the occult system.

> The Society of the Inner Light did not call Them Secret Chiefs, preferring the Theosophical term Masters: the Correspondence Course made frequent allusion to Them under this name and students following it were enjoined to make a salutation to Them every day at noon . . . Is such a concept as that of Secret Chiefs necessary to account for the experiences I underwent? Would it not be enough to posit some psycho-physical power (I have already called it the Power of Y) as not yet understood . . . on the occasions when I felt its force it was set into motion by or through people who could lay claim to some link, close or distant, with the Secret Chiefs of the GD.
>
> (*Sword of Wisdom: McGregor Mathers and The 'Golden Dawn'*, p.32)

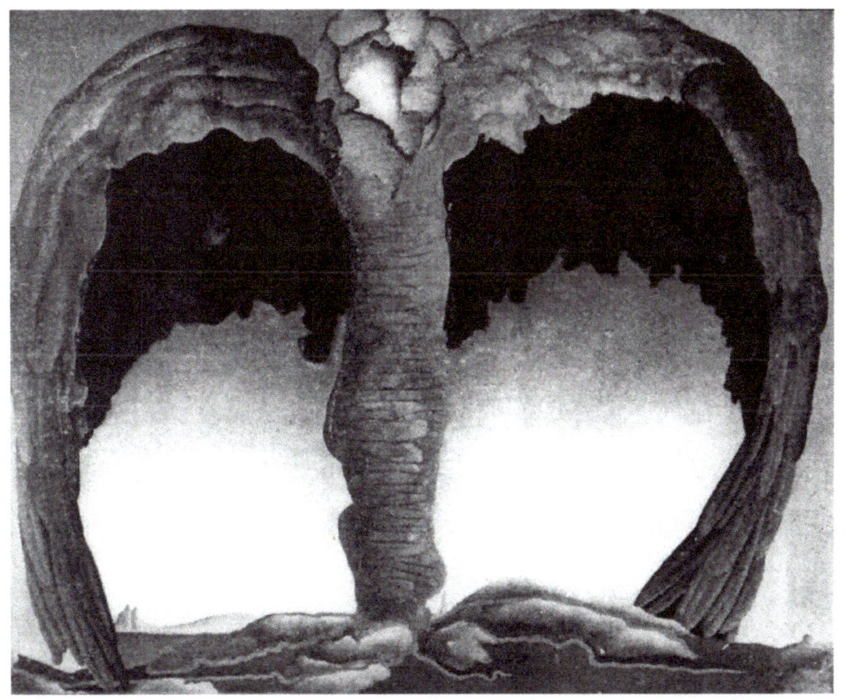

39. *Guardian Angel* (1947, tempera, 12½ x 14½ in., 32 x 36.5 cm)

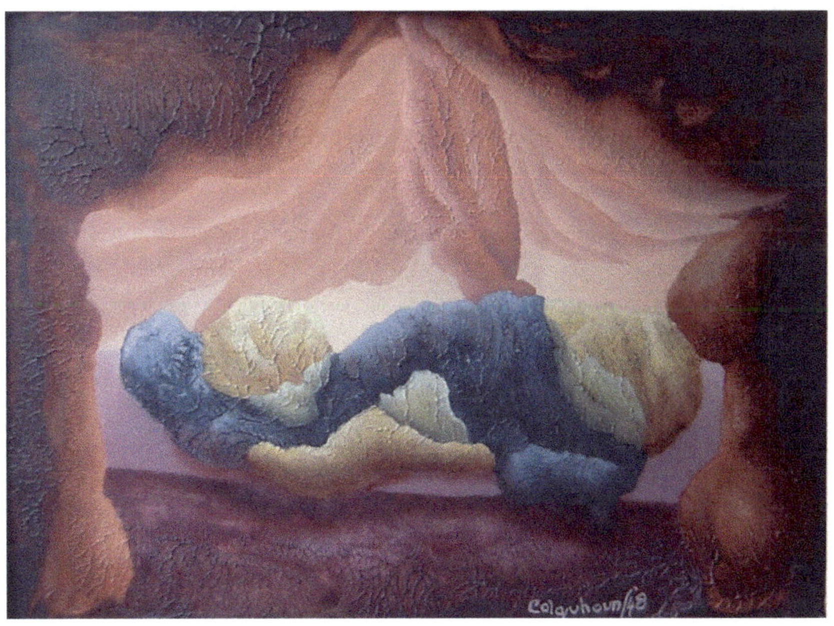

40. *The Long Journey (*1946, oil on board, 8½ x 13¼ in.)

However, when Kenneth Grant, a few years later after assuming his contested control as outer head of the O.T.O. (Order of the Temple of the Orient) from Aleister Crowley, who died in 1947, founded the Nu-Isis Lodge in the mid-fifties, Ithell, who had succeeded to membership of the O.T.O. in the early fifties, entered it as *Soror Splendidior Vitro* (10). The lodge closed in 1962. It is not known how long Ithell retained membership in it, but it may be that she temporarily reverted from her main tasks of producing paintings, for it seems that between 1953 and 1959 the numbers were minimal; no record of any at all was found for 1957, 1958 or 1959. (This is also confirmed from an unpublished draft checklist of work compiled by Richard Shillitoe.) The lodge was concerned with magical ritual and apparently attempted to communicate with discarnate entities, or dwellers beyond the outer planetary fringe, in which the oracular and mediumistic virtues of women were valued.

I am informed that one of her literary efforts was a biography of Crowley, unpublished and apparently of poor quality.(11) This may have been the draft that she offered to Neville Spearman Ltd., which was not accepted. She also wrote a self-published essay on Crowley.(12) Later she met his son Ataturk whose mother was Pat McAlpine, and apparently unpublished essays by her exist on son and mother. A selection of her unpublished work, scripts &c are referenced in Appendix IIC.

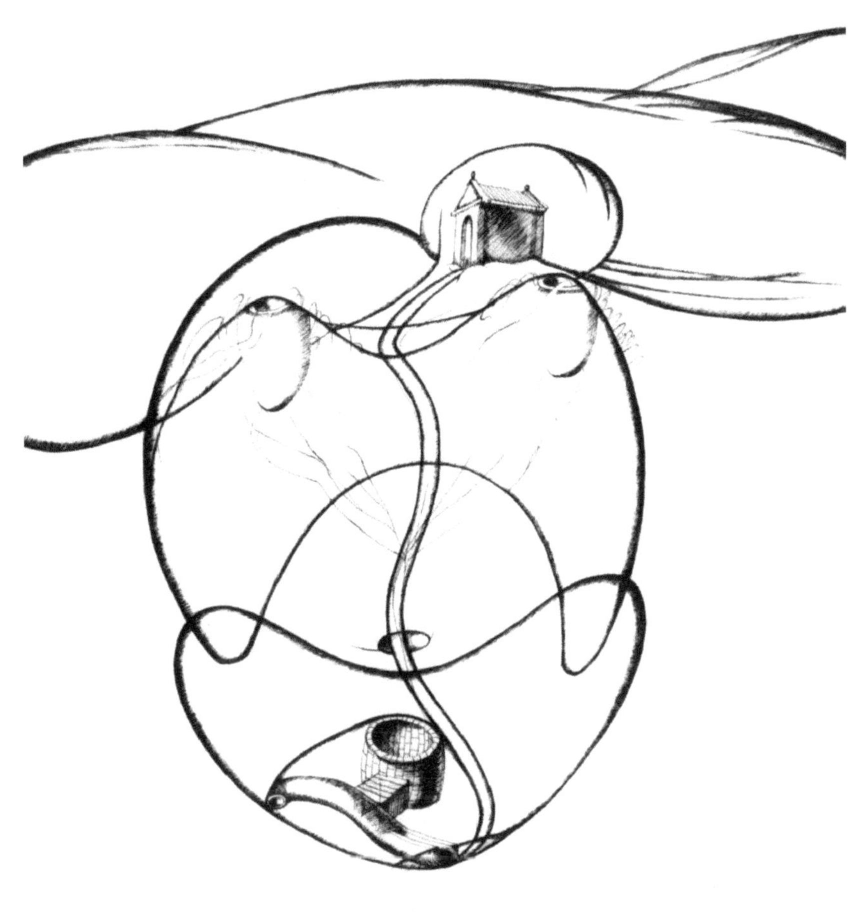

41. *Interior Landscape* (1947, ink drawing, 41.5 x 31.5 cm) Royal Cornwall Museum, Truro

7 Cornwall (arrival)

It was probably a reactionary sense of entrapment within her own environment and the need for an escape path, not from painting, but so that her spirit could re-find sufficient strength to continue in dedication to her art, that prompted Ithell to seek out Cornwall. Within her book *The Living Stones : Cornwall*, which contains many personal details, is the backing statement:

> When the war was over and I could partially escape from my own entangled life, it was to this region, this 'end of the land' with its occasional sight of the unattained past, that I was drawn.

We sense the need to put behind her the blitz, failed marriage, and possibly anxiety that she could not keep up her high standards and total dedication without renewing her batteries. Hampstead was not the natural world she yearned for; and now that she was out of mainstream surrealism and attached publicity, there was need to rethink and re-organise her life. She was also asthmatic, but any physical condition at this time is not obviously stated as the reason for uprooting herself.

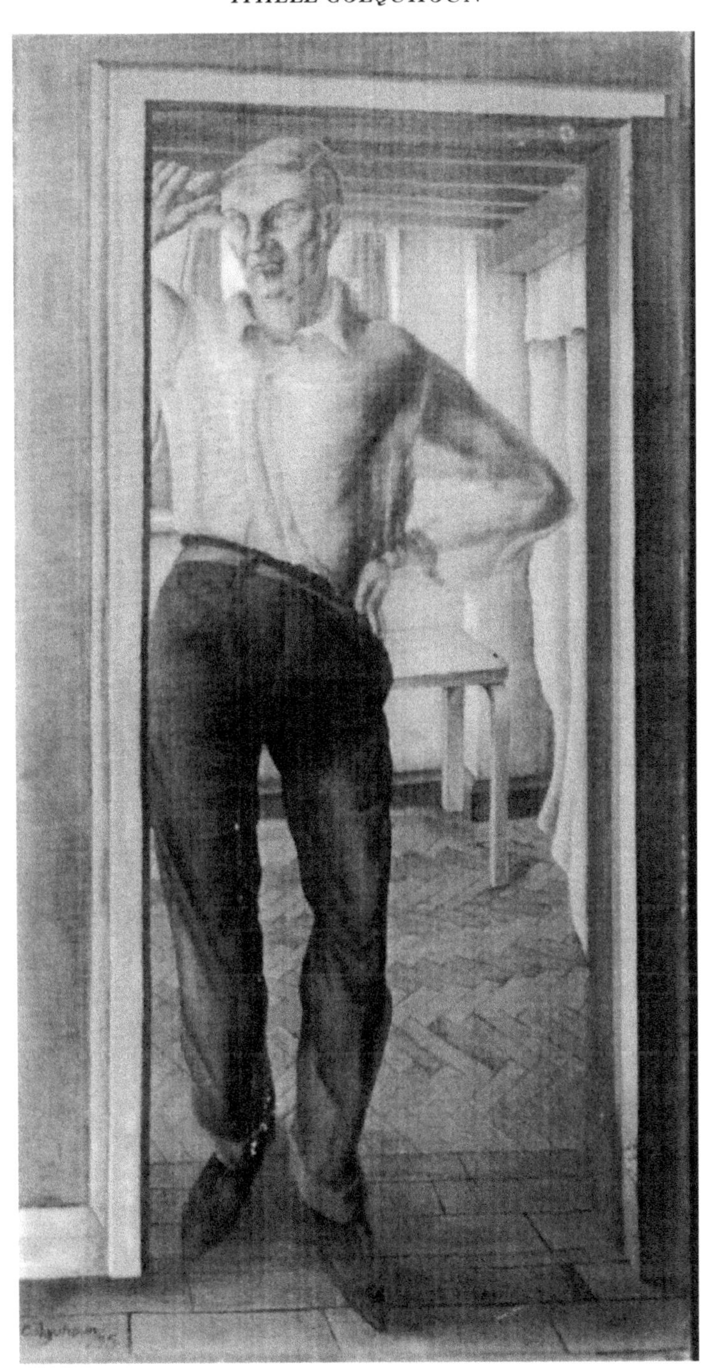

42. *Humphry Gilbert Garth Payne* (1935, oil on canvas, 27 x 14 in., 68.5 x 35.5 cm) National Portrait Gallery

> There is some balsamic quality in the air which never fails to bring healing; after years of the blitz I felt that here I could find some humble refuge from the claustrophobic fright of cities. I determined that I would never be so trapped again.
>
> (*The Living Stones*, p.13)

The attraction of Cornwall also dated from memories of St. Ives from a holiday when at Cheltenham College, and a visit to Mousehole during the blitz. It led later to frequent holiday trips to a refuge discovered in the Lamorna valley when she was in her early forties, from where she found the inspiration for *The Living Stones*. Eventually she would take up permanent residence in the county, and thence to write more and paint more. The exultation and excitement of her senses in having found an area where she felt both at peace and exhilarated, and could draw freely upon an invisible power-house of energy within the landscape, which she actually felt and could uplift her spirits, is obvious in this part-biographical travel book on Cornwall.

There are no available records for a chronology of events, but it was May, at the end of the forties, and that must be good enough for the start of Ithell's Cornish 'spring' of her new blossoming, when she negotiated for and obtained a 50-year lease of an unrepaired 'hut' of corrugated iron raised on granite piles in the Lamorna valley. This had apparently been an artist's studio, with an extensive (but leaking) skylight. It did possess an old iron stove with a chimney pipe exiting through the roof, but was without gas, electricity, running water or toilet facilities. Stung to action to renovate what she could see was exactly fitting for her needs, she made practical arrangements.

Repair and redecoration followed, with skylight, guttering and stove receiving treatment. A fence was erected to screen the property from Lamorna Lane, Calor gas was installed for cooking and lighting. The exterior was made white, the roof treated with red oxide and the interior painted with white gloss. Lack of running water was solved by taking it from a small stream which conveniently ran at the back.

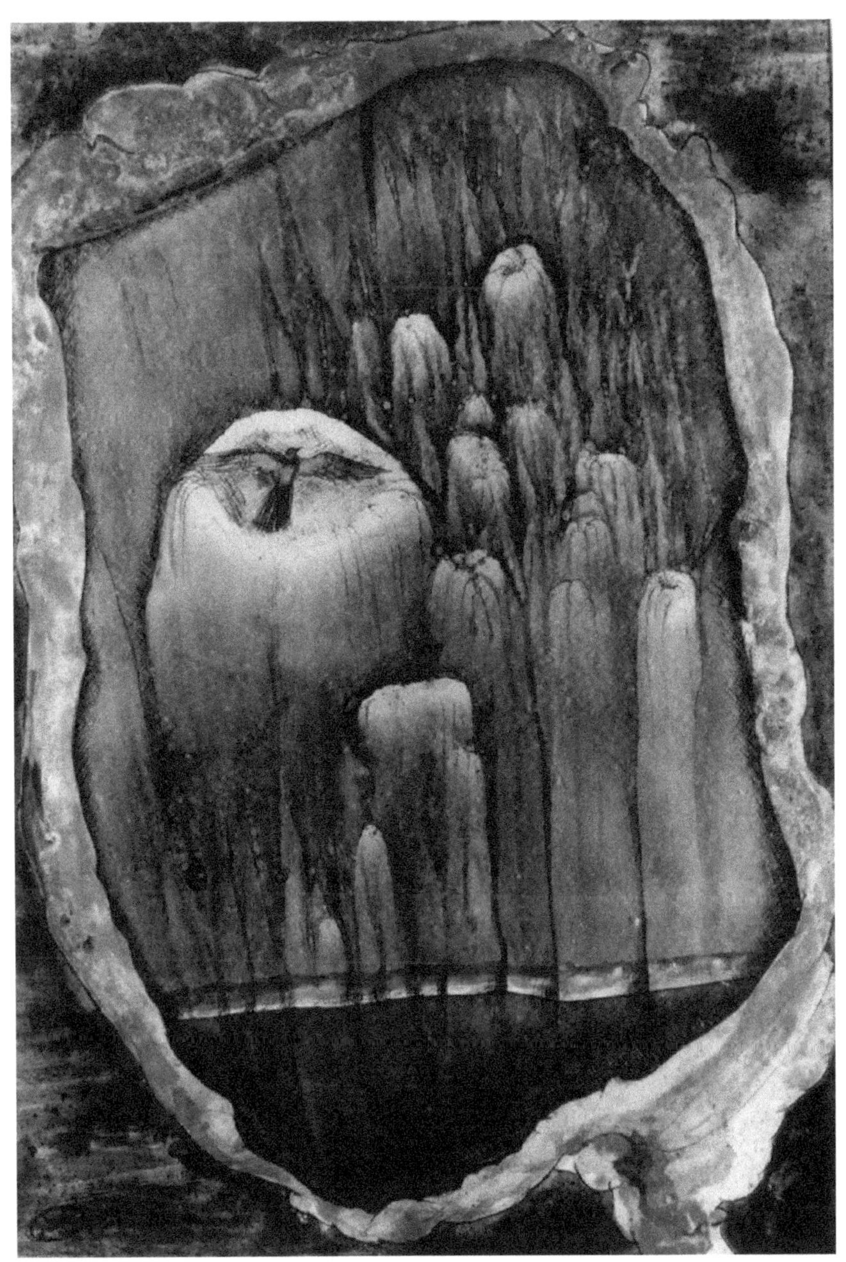

43. *Death of a Vampire* (c.1960, ink and gouache, 37.5 x 26 cm) Royal Cornwall Museum, Truro

Here, later, in the warmer weather she could indulge her love for the sun's heat in bathing nude in a naturally screened environment. She duly named the property 'Vow Cave Studio', after a locally named hollow feature under a nearby capstone at the site of Castallak Carn.

> The corner window looked up towards the rock of the carn, grey above the croft land and crowning the eastern slope of the valley. Here, difficult to find unless you know where to look, lies hidden the huge capstone with a slight hollow below it which is called the 'Vow Cave'. The name is tautological, as the first word means 'cave' as much as the second, being none other than the Cornish *vugha*, a cave.
>
> (*The Living Stones*, p.19)

Sanitation was a problem, required by officialdom to be installed to complete the offices, after which she could relax a little to enjoy the property. This was solved by purchase of a shed from a neighbour, and obtaining 'Elsan' fittings from a certain Monica Baldwin a walk away. Monica had been a nun for about thirty years, but was now celebrating or just experiencing a less cloistered life in what used to be a store for gunpowder for use of quarry blasting. She was also the author of an unpublished manuscript 'I Leap Over the Wall'. She was a niece of Stanley Baldwin, ex-Premier, and her manuscript title was the Baldwin family motto, having another edge to its meaning in her hands! Ithell exchanged its reading for her then unpublished MS 'Goose of Hermogenes' with some trepidation, but their friendship survived, although the Virgin and Pan did not mix very well. The Baldwin motto was originally 'By the help of God I shall leap over the wall', first adopted by Thomas Baldwin, steward to the Earl of Shrewsbury who guarded Mary Queen of Scots. Thomas replied to a coded letter from one of Mary's secretaries which asked what was to be her fate, but the correspondence was intercepted by the spy Walsingam, leading to Thomas being sent to the Tower who eventually metaphorically did leap over the wall of the Tower on release.

The 'Goose' was to wait until 1961 before publisher Peter Owen took it on, whereas Monica's autobiographical manuscript was a book by 1949 and created a sensation - the family name had been somewhat tarnished by her monastic leap; the motto had never been meant to support mural exit from the sanctity of nunneries. Ithell had found her when she was ready to move on and was making arrangements to sell and go to Ireland. The meeting of the two writers has been described in an undated article by Christine Rhone (1):

> Colquhoun was right; Baldwin was not ready for 'Goose of Hermogenes', an alchemical allegory hinging on the transition from Solar to Lunar knowledge. In the climactic scene the female protagonist, under the influence of strong drugs administered by her uncle, has ritual sex with the horned god, pictured as a standing pillar in a garden. Baldwin and Colquhoun remained on good terms and later corresponded, but the gap in experience prevented deeper friendship. Baldwin was hardly able to stomach the sight of bare legs.
>
> (Extract from 'The Nun and the Alchemist of Lamorna Cove')

Ithell let her Vow Cave 'studio' for summer break periods, while retaining a London home at 197, Randolph Avenue, Hampstead, but she visited it in all seasons. (Since she was living in a Paul cottage in 1959 and had the London address at least until 1965, she was in that period apparently involved with three properties). She derived intense pleasure from observing the flowers and the birds and nature in general. Hers was no casual eye, and the natural features of the valley and cove became part of her. Illness and depression could also be tolerated, so much was she in love with all that Lamorna had to offer:

> Life at 'Vow Cave' is not all flowers, one can be depressed; friends may prove as changeable as the weather, phantoms become too palpable – yet adversity is not only tolerable but

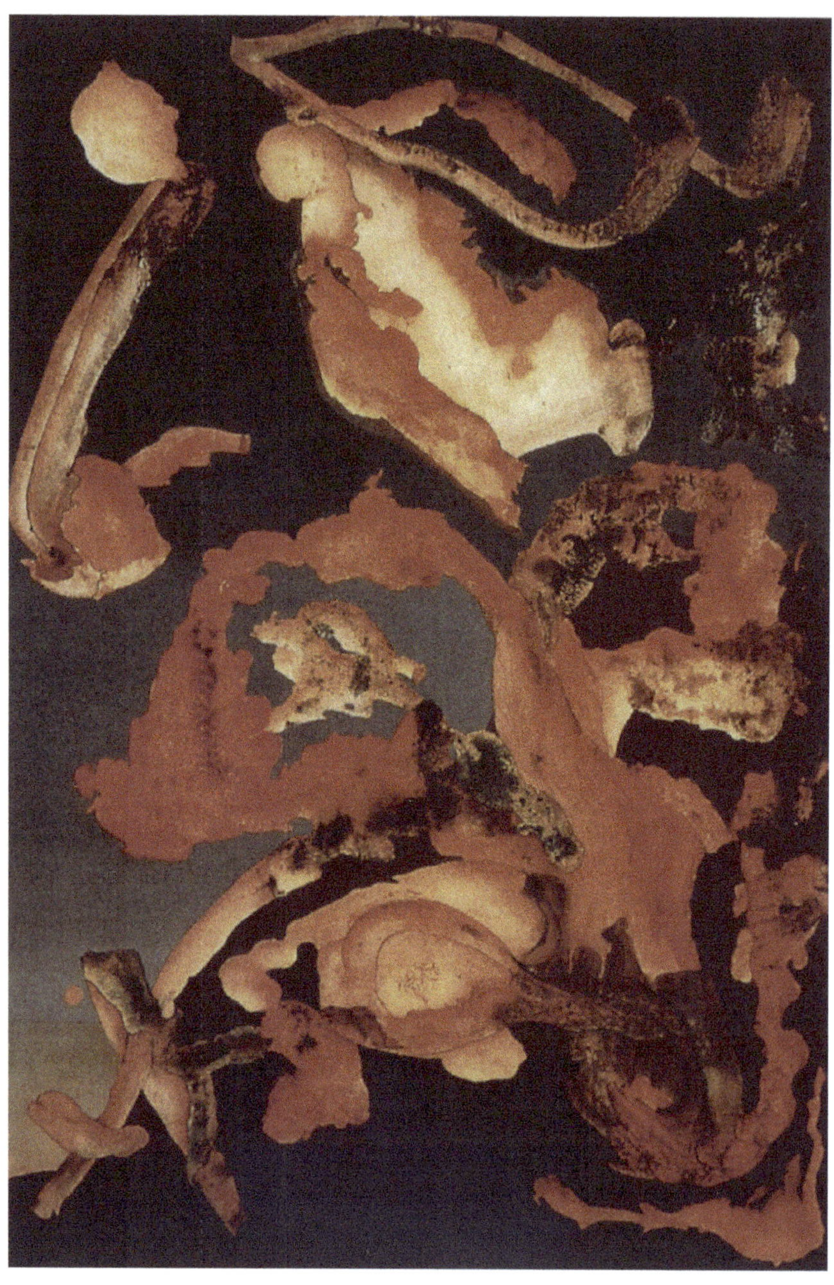

44. *Dreaming Leaps: in Homage to Sonia Araquistain* (1945, oil on paper, 31 x 21½ in, 80.0 x 55.10 cm)

> intoxicating. Cornwall never lets one down, whatever it may seem to be doing; Lamorna can do anything to me and I will not only put up with it but enjoy it. Friends in London have suspected a romance to account for its attraction, but the truth is stranger than gossip. I am identified with every leaf and pebble, and any threatened hurt to the wilderness of the valley seems to me a rape.
>
> (*The Living Stones*, p.25)

The flowers, the birds of the valley - they were part of her and she part of them when at Lamorna - the family of long-tailed tits flitting down the valley, the whistle of the goldcrest, the bullfinches, the greenfinch's cadence 'that sounds like a chain of burnished brass, the colour of its own wing-bars', bluebell, campion, stitchwort, navelwort, October ivy blossom, scylla and sea pink along the cliffs - she has noted them and delighted in them with an artist's enjoyment in the life and detail of the natural world. Here was 'such a vivid quality of life that one can enjoy what in London would merely exasperate.'

Ithell was a natural 'sensitive' who had an acute sense of life force, psychic power or ancient meaning or message stored in some granite masses, in old stone crosses, stone circles, menhirs, dolmens &c in this former territory of the Dumnonii which stretched to well beyond the eastern boundaries of Devon from west Cornwall. In her book, a quotation from the *Song of Amergin* – 'Who but I can unfold the secrets of the unhewn dolmen', precedes her frontispiece drawing of an old stone cross in the churchyard of St. Buryan. Around such relatively modern commemorative items such as the immense granite cross in the centre of Carn Brea, or an attenuated pyramidal war-memorial crowning Tregonning Hill, she found none of this ancient power, contrasting their nil modern effect with stones surrounding ancient wells and old stone crosses. She performed the needful rites of passing herself through the ring stones of the Mên-an-Tol near Lanyon and the Tolven Stone in the Helford river area. In the first case

> I crawled from east to west through the ring-like stone set on edge in the centre of the monument as a cure for rheumatism, and was disappointed wih the result, not knowing that in order to be effective the rite should be performed in a state of nudity.
>
> (*The Living Stones*, p.59)

Of the Cornish saints, she is curious about St. Uny, said to have come as a missionary from Ireland. She instinctively sensed from the atmosphere of the places associated with this saint that she was a nymph of wells and springs. The Christian overlay has no doubt preserved the name or something like it, but the original pagan side of the legend is elusive. She says that, in churches connected with St. Uny at Lelant and Redruth, 'he' is a monk, and that there is a Chapel Uny near Sancreed. Found in a hollow to one side of the Redruth church, she mentions St. Uny's well.

Ithell describes features of the annual *Gorsedd* of the Cornish Bards, which omit initiation in the classes of Ovates and Druids, unlike the Welsh and Brittany-based groups and the British Order of Bards, Ovates and Druids (OBOD) formed under the leadership of poet and savant Ross Nichols in 1964 by schism from the longer-established Druid Order. She describes a *Gorsedd* at Boscawen, as it was in 1950. The long procession of blue-robed bards included 'the Lady':

> The *Arlodhes a Gernow*, the 'Lady of Cornwall', a Ceres-figure in robes of red and yellow and attended by two yellow-clad children, is led forward by the Sword-bearer to make an offering of corn and summer fruit which is received by the Grand Bard. There follows the singing, to the accompaniment of the Celtic harp of *Arta Ef a Dhe*, a poem whose burthen is the legend that King Arthur did not die but tarries like Merlin in an enchanted doze, whence he will wake and return to lead his people. And is it not time that he did so?
>
> (*The Living Stones*, pp. 75-6)

After a few years, Ithell started to look elsewhere in Cornwall for a permanent future home, eventually found in Paul, as previously mentioned - her sharp sense of hearing, accentuated by the isolation was such that she could almost 'hear the grass grow', and she was sensitive to the encroachment of the noise of machinery penetrating to the valley. Another factor was her health. Perhaps on doctor's advice she eventually severed the London link (2).

She regarded as a sinister development, the craving of most people for a background of noise to whatever they were doing - for indiscriminate listeners, 'the hideous drone acts upon them simply as an aural drug.' In the summer season, Vow Cave and other buildings situated directly on the Lamorna lane were open to noise penetration, when previously an idyllic peace had prevailed – 'Noise, dust, litter make such places all but uninhabitable, and certainly far from ideal for concentrating on creative work.' Her own sensitivity to sounds extended to the clanging of the bell-buoy outside Porthgwarra, carried by the wind and other far-off disturbances. Sometimes sound effects were more mysterious, as she related in *The Living Stones* :

> . . . not all can be tracked down to a common-sense cause. More than once at Vow Cave I have heard a flutter of notes in an unfamiliar mode that struck the ear for a few seconds. . . on the last occasion I left the hut and stood listening in the road . . . I could hear the teasing notes rise and fall in an evanescent Celtic melody. . . sounding directly out of the atmosphere.

She never did find an explanation, unless, 'as old stories tell, it were from instruments accompanying a dance or procession of the fairy host . . . I am not the first to experience such at Lamorna'.

There were compensations, as Ithell began to search for a suitable base, to live in peace and quiet, away from the trippers. She came to know parts of Cornwall beyond Penwith, a boundary which otherwise would not have been crossed, so content had she been with her original choice of Lamorna. She found many interesting diversions for her fertile mind - the Helston furry dance and fair, and the Padstow spring dance of the hobby horse, which to outsiders were just queer country customs were, for her, serious attachments to the land and necessities for the survival of Cornish traditions. One of her forays ended in the discovery of a Society for the Promotion of Optimism, founded by a Barney Camfield, himself a member of the Guild of Pastoral Psychology. She was intrigued by his methods:

> In making a diagnosis, Barney uses the methods of Luscher and Koch: he asks the prospective patient to choose four colours out of a possible eight and to draw a sketch of a tree; also to give the usual details as to birth-date required by astrologers. For some of the interpretations of this astrological data, he calls upon Delphica Huntress, a friend living in a nearby village who was a pupil of Jung's astrologer, Leo French. From all this material, together with an example of the handwriting, he builds up a picture of the patient.
>
> (*The Living Stones*, p.129)

Ithell often attended the S.P.O. group meetings in Penzance after she had re-settled.

One of her visits was to Germoe and the ancient church dedicated to St. Germoe. In the churchyard she found the saint's 'chair' built into the graveyard wall ('a triple seat divided by granite pillars and topped by a canopy with two arches.'). However, this dated from the fifteenth century, whereas the Irish saint came over in the fifth. The detective in Ithell found the saint's well elusive, having been covered in and the coping stones used elsewhere:

> Such was the too frequent ill-treatment of baptismal wells which had been used by the Celtic Church in Britain before an indoor font replaced them; and in this respect Wales has been as remiss as Cornwall.
>
> (*The Living Stones,* pp.147-8)

There is a short detail by Robert Hunt (3) of the story of the sighting of a fairy fair in Germoe, in Bal Lane. Fairies figure in many old Cornish stories, and Ithell's interest was shown in correspondence with the Fairy Investigation Society. She mentions two fairy wells, one owned by a 'Madgy Figgy', possibly a generic term for a fairy or kindred character, and a 'Pin Well'. Children would christen their dolls each Good Friday by saying the name and dropping a bent pin in the water.

It was in the peace and quietude of her nest in the Lamorna Valley that *The Living Stones : Cornwall* was completed, and the book was published before she moved to Paul. Therein was material condensation of genuine empathy with the landscape, always for her an absorbing and sometimes spiritual experience. Reviews were forthcoming from well beyond Britain (4). Curiously, two leading national newspapers were critical of her writings, in comparison with normal or standard viewpoints of Cornwall and its inhabitants, and were unable to absorb the co-existence of Ithell's Cornish world with their own ideas of it. Critics are often concerned with 'actualities' which they understand as reality. But generally speaking, artists' or sensitives' perceptions realise many levels, whereas a `worldly' critic will treat his or her perception as the only truth, and excludes other levels.

Thus, from the *Daily Telegraph* of July 12th, 1957 under the head 'Cornish Twilight' is a one-sided remark:

> Ithell Colquhoun has written a scrappy book, penetrating in its sentimentality beyond the bounds of ordinary country living and dwelling to a picturesque twilight where superstition, folklore, sects and archaeology mingle in half-serious, half-humorous communion . . . Miss Colquhoun has toyed with too many dreams . . .

and *The Times Literary Supplement*, also of July 12th, vainly trying to

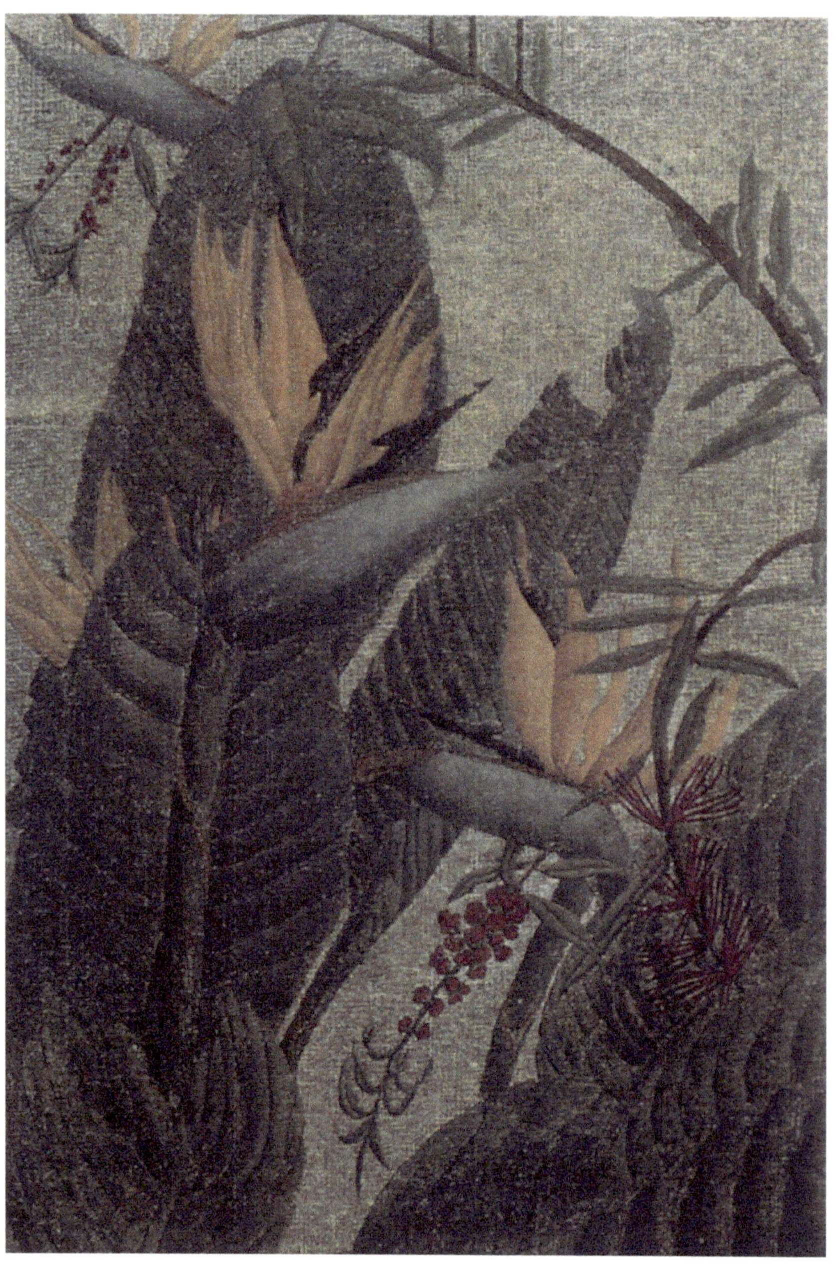

45. *Crane-Flowers* (1935, oil on canvas, 17½ x 14 in., 44.4 x 35.5 cm)

grasp the nettle of advanced perception ('Cornish Intangibles') is not much better:

> It will be realised that Miss Colquhoun is a resolute individualist . . . journeying with her through Cornwall would be an experience for the more matter-of-fact Cornishman. He would be surprised by the significances she unearths, by her determined sensitivity . . .

Both critics have troubles with a very wonderful book which perceives Cornwall in a mode not of their choice. After all, the title should have pre-served to modify their outlook. It was partly about *living* stones, not tourist-slanted items or the perceptions of the indigenous population. For once, this was no run-of-the-mill travel book, and deserved better understanding. There was redemption, however, from Neville Braybrooke in *Assisi* of the following month:

> . . . beautifully written, is *The Living Stones* . . . her descriptions, with their close attention to colour and every shade, recall an artists' notebook.

Perhaps we should not be disturbed by some materialistic comments. Many things, not only beauty, are in the eyes or minds of the beholders; they would need to be on Ithell's level to appreciate them.

On the occult side, as well as her entry into the O.T.O and participation in the Nu-Isis temple of Grant mentioned in the previous chapter, she had begun to take interest in details of The Order of the Holy Wisdom, and there are a series of letters dated around 1953 from Dr. William Bernard Crow, the Grand Master, with whom she had been acquainted in earlier years at the Quest Society. Most letters were addressed to her either at Hampstead or at Vow Cave (5), outlining the foundation and teachings of his Order, and replying to her questions. The Order had connections with branches of the Old Catholic Church and there were various ramifications, including the

Institute of Arcane Studies, not in the scope of this general biography to pursue. Dr. Crow himself many years earlier had been invited to join the Golden Dawn by Ithell's cousin, now dead, but had chosen not to apply.

8 Cornwall (activities 1959-1971)

The search for another dwelling in peaceful surroundings, more substantial and larger than the Vow Cave studio, had ended at Paul, inland from Mousehole, with a purchase of Polgrean Cottage in Green Lane, in 1959, which she subsequently renamed 'Stone Cross Cottage'. From this base, Ithell Colquhoun remained operative for almost 30 years, with visits to old friends in Bedford Park or Hampstead, exhibiting in Cornwall or abroad, painting, writing and exploring more of the areas she had empathy with and loved.

Back in London there was recognition of her talents as a prominent Hampstead painter ('Hampstead Artists, 1900-1960') in a town-hall display in 1960. In the following year the nearby Newlyn Art Gallery held a retrospective show of her work.

Some paintings dated within the first ten years or so, when at Paul, included *Temptation of St. Anthony* (1962), *Stalactite* (1962), *Potentate* (1963), *The Seasons* (1963), *Serpent of Genesis* (1966), *Primordial Slime* (1966), *Woodland Ride* (1966), *Rose of the Palace of Fire* (1969), *Night Storm at Sea* (1969), *Colours of the Sea* (1969), *De Profundis* (1969), *Volcanic Landscape* (1969), *Rocky Island* (1969), and *Break-up of a Space Rocket* (1969). But there were upwards of 60 exhibited works to the

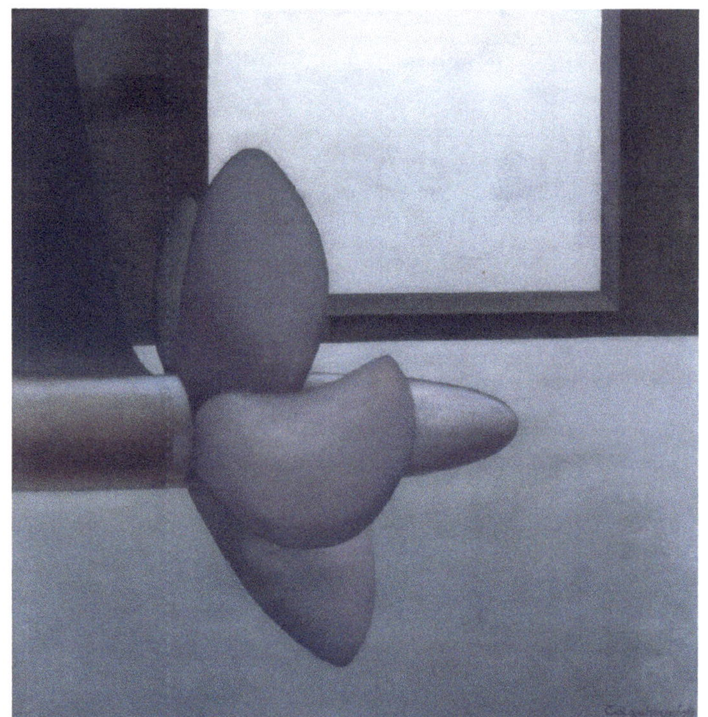

46. *L'Hélice* (1939, oil and tempera on canvas, 22 x 22 in., 56 x 56 cm)

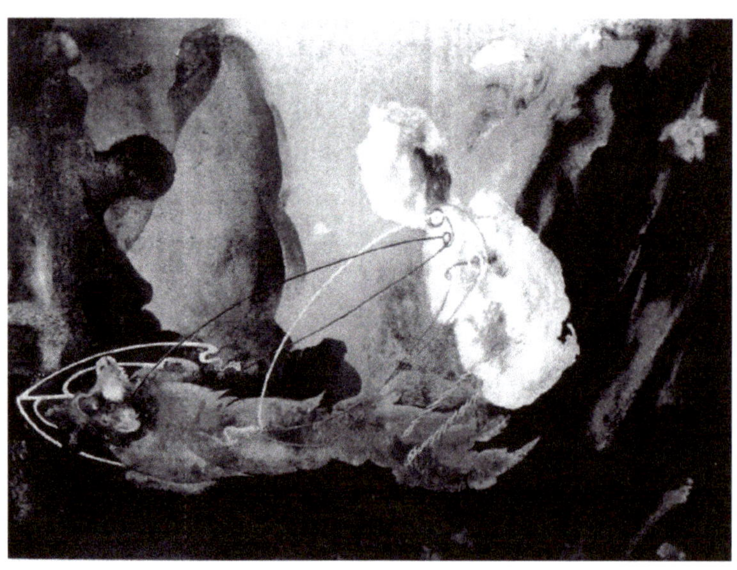

47. Cardinal Points (1940, oil on canvas, 14 x 20 in.)

end of 1969, once the move had taken place, and probably many more which were not shown.

Ithell was no longer identifiable in painting with a female high ground of rejection of obsessive male-eroticism and male personal importance in treatment of women as accessories to their desires. She had proved her point and, self-liberated, now tended to embrace Jungian concepts and occult philosophy, creating less sexual symbolism in her work with physical connotations

In fact, aided by her interests in fairy-folk and the like, and her feelings for life force, she painted situations or created relevant symbols embracing non-material entities at a level of consciousness beyond the physical senses. Examples are *Oil-and-Water Nymph* (1964), *Marsh-Spectre* (1966), *Haunted Hedge* (1970), *Marsh-Spirit* (1971), *Dryad : Willow* (1971), *Dryad* : *Silver Fir* (1971), *Elemental* (1971). She had this strong belief in the presence of supra-human entities, even as abstract personification via the later painting *Volcano Spirit* (1971) - part of her fascination with sub-earth forces (see also 'The Volcano', the surrealist prose story she wrote for the *Bulletin* (1)).

This perceptive and very sensitive feeling for spiritual counterparts in nature, manifested in her early flower and vegetation paintings as sense of life-force. These were aspects of a level of reality beyond normal consciousness, which she sensed, and which were no imaginative affairs for the sake of artistic impression. She was in touch with, if not belonging to, the Fairy Investigation Society. An archival memo shows that she made notes on and drawings of angels. Invisible presences were more than just passing interests.

Since 1959, Ithell tells, she exhibited with Aubin Pasque's Fantasmagie international group exhibitions 'all over Europe', quoting 1967-8 when touring in Czechoslovakia just before the coup (2). In the early sixties, with the group, she had exhibited at Liege and Ostend.

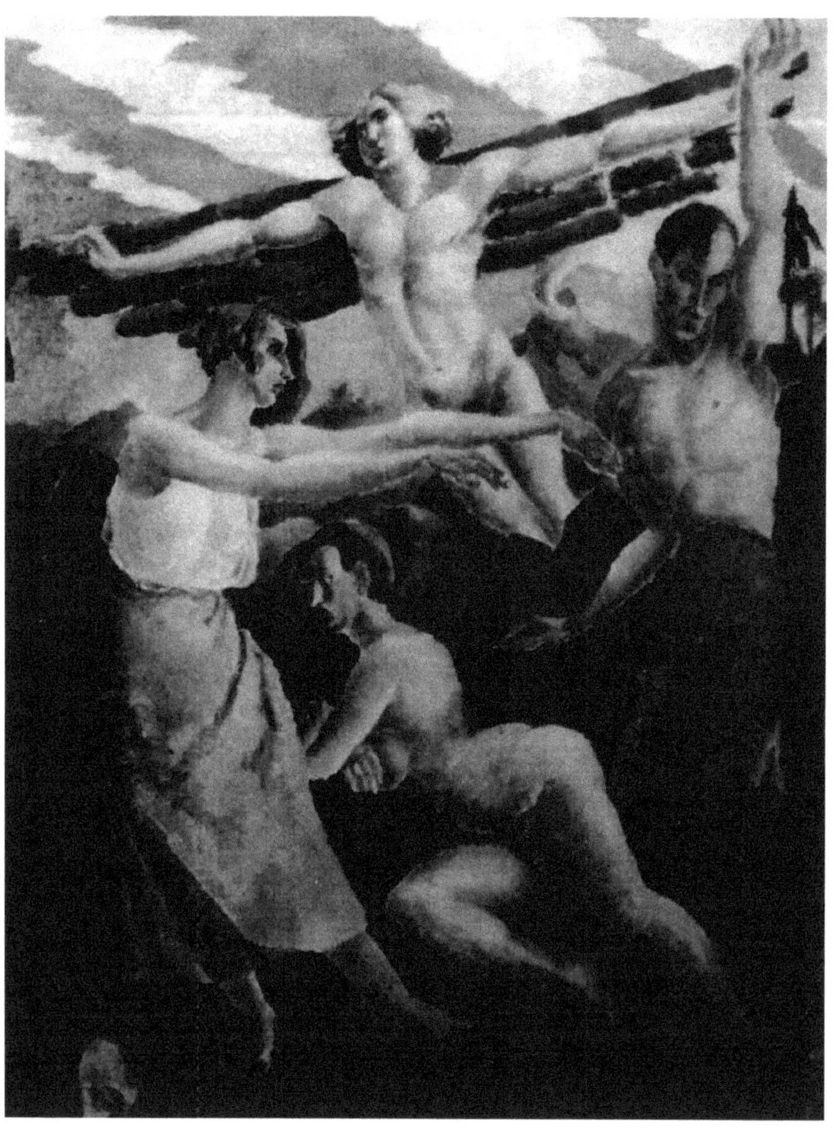

48. *The Four Elements* (c.1929, oil on board, 28 x 22 in., 71 x 56 cm)

1969 was a year of expansion for activities abroad. In that year, with Fantasmagie, she exhibited *Rose of the Palace of Fire*, *Break-up of a Space-Rocket*, and *Rocky Island* in West Berlin and paintings at Apeldoorn in Holland. Subsequently she was invited to put on solo exhibitions at Wilmersdorf andHamburg. There is a short notice with her photograph at Wilmersdorf where she displayed 25 oil paintings. A showcase of her literary work was also on view (3). At Hamburg she displayed collages and constructions, including the striking *Byzantine Cross* composed of dinner-tins.

Ithell was now also producing these three-dimensional montages of 'Merz' collages, using rubbish and found objects from her environment, the art form evolved by Kurt Schwitters in 1919 during the Dada movement. Some of these sixties collages - *Byzantine Cross* (1964), *Celtic Cross* (1966) and *Family Group* (1967) were shown at her important solo Exeter exhibition (4), which also displayed later collages constructed between 1970 and 1972 titled *Portrait of a Dignitary*, *Sun-Child*, *Ripples*, *Open Entrance*, and *Middle Eastern Landscape*. She had met the German artist during the war when in Hampstead - one of the many artist refugees from the Nazis, who had come to England via Norway. He engaged himself in England in building up a giant three-dimensional construction, but died before finishing it, in 1948. At the end of the war, he had a one-man exhibition at the London Gallery. Ithell contributed memoranda on Schwitters and the collages (5).

The text of *Goose of Hermogenes*, mentioned in the previous chapter in connection with Monica Baldwin, when in MS form, was eventually published by Peter Owen in 1961 after Ithell had been about two years in her new cottage, although the manuscript had remained unpublished for the previous ten years - a strange esoteric novel which, although a short 115 pages, has been said to be 'the most sustained surrealist text in the English language'. It is also one of the most difficult to summarise - a précis of lengthy surrealistic prose is usually inadequate or impossible and some expansion is inevitable. Surface

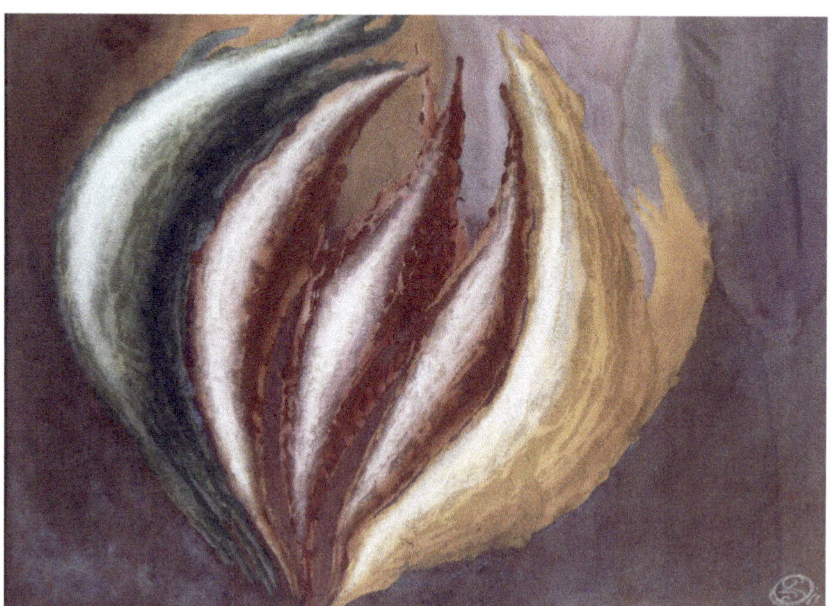

49. *Rose of the Palace of Fire* (1969, oil and watercolour on paper, laid down on board, 27¾ x 38¾ in., 70.5 x 99.0 cm)

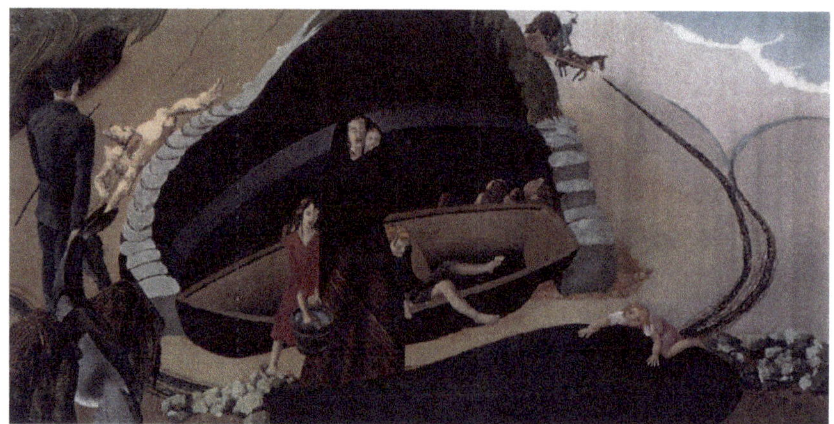

50. *The Dunes* (c.1940, oil on canvas, 18 x 36 in., 45.7 x 91.4 cm)

events or adventures as told are never to be taken at face value, and the whole is allegorical. The 'reality' in the book is mainly that of this allegorical description in the under-conscious mind of the narrator. The dream-imagery, set in an alchemical framework of chapter heads and sometimes open to interpretation of position of events on the kabbalistic tree of life, is skilfully kept enough below the surface to just show the nominal 'tip of the iceberg' which gives up the materialistic morsels to maintain the reader's interest and lead him to reflect inwardly. It is indeed 'surreal' by Breton's standards. Perhaps interpretation is less important than perception of the gateways opened to the imagination by the author - a signifier of purpose achieved.

The opening quotation from 'Eirenaeus Philalethes' (6) partly explains the title:

> It is our doorkeeper, our balm, our honey, oil, urine, maydew, mother, egg, secret furnace, true fire, venemous dragon, theriac, ardent wine, Green Lion, Bird of Hermes, Goose of Hermogenes, two-edged sword in the hand of the cherub that guards the Tree of Life. (*Metamorphosis of Metals*, 1668)

These are all names of symbols or matter present in stages in obtaining the philosophers' stone, the elixir, the achievement of which, by arduous laboratory work and meditation led the philosopher to achieve the highest spiritual level in parallel with the highest state of a metal - alchemical gold. The stone is potentially present within the processes, which represent both spiritual advancement and ultimate refinement of the laboratory material. Hermogenes, meaning one 'born of Hermes', was a Carthaginian philosopher-painter. He was an unbeliever in the perfection of a created world, the later sinfulness of which was attributed to sin being passed on from Adam which needed atonement. He was also anti-Christian gnosticism which implied, through emanation theory, that material objects emanated from a Spirit, and sinful beings from a holy Being. His answer was that God and Matter co-existed in the first place, and that the former had power to control the latter. That which was evil resisted God; that which was good yielded. Tertullian, also a Carthaginian and an early Church Father, strongly opposed his philosophy in a long treatise and likened his heretical ideas to his bad painting!

It can be seen, however, that here is a parallel to the alchemist working on the chaotic state of matter to produce the stone. Stages of the Opus were used as titles for chapters in the *Goose*. There were conflicting opinions about the number of stages needed in the 'Great Work'. Ithell's nomenclature for chapter heads follows twelve stages (7), and is taken from Basil Valentine's Twelve Keys. They are: 'Calcination', 'Solution', 'Separation', 'Conjunction', 'Putrefaction', 'Congelation' [coagulation], 'Cibation', 'Sublimation', 'Fermentation', 'Exaltation', 'Multiplication', and 'Projection'. Actually, the Tenth Key, which includes symbols denoting the third conjunction of sun and moon, also features the words 'I am born of Hermogenes, Hyperion elected me' (8). The stage is that of solar rebirth and the goose can be a solar symbol.

Treating the *Goose* as a bald narrative of dreamlike quality, the mainland-based heroine is invited by her uncle to visit his island, where she explores his land and mansion (particularly his study, which is both museum and library). There are strange happenings during a long walk to an ancient manor cum-farmhouse inhabited by her mother, two sisters and half-brother. She visits a 'green light district' in a tree where her mother manages the clientele. Later she returns to her uncle's land and has erotic experiences in sleep state where the dream is concerned with some monastic rite arranged by her uncle. She then re-explores his museum, returns to the mainland in a coracle. There follows a visit to her father in a house. He is naked, then puts on clothes and disappears from them:

> 'He does not know that he is dead,' I thought. 'Shall I have to tell him ?' But this was not necessary.

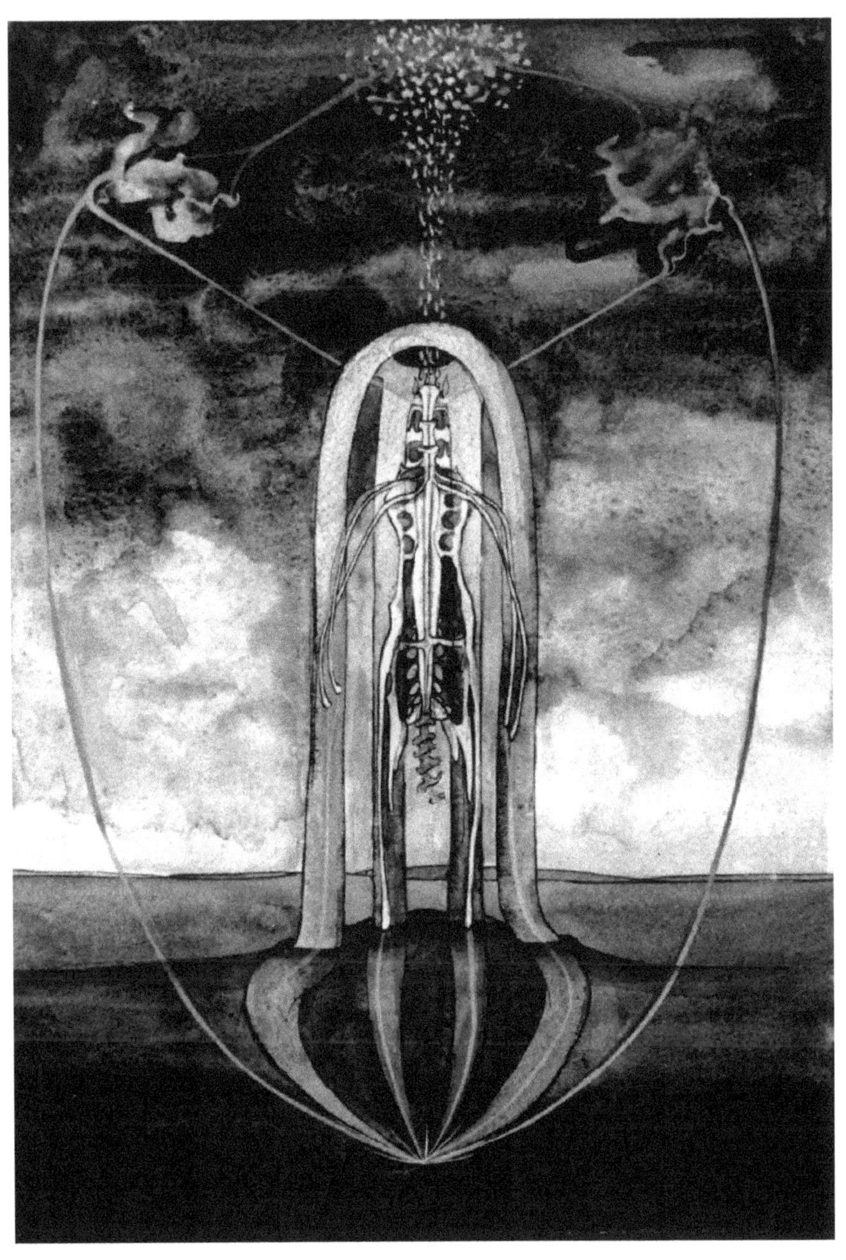

51. *Mausoleum* (undated, watercolour and ink, 30.1 x 21.7 cm)

> 'Where are the furnishings?' he asked.'Why all this emptiness?'
>
> 'Don't you realise, father,' I replied gently, pressing his arm with a closer touch, 'that we are no longer living here?'
>
> I paused, then turned for some response; but my father had vanished, utterly melted away, leaving only his old green suit hanging over my arm.

She leaves the empty house, noting the garden vegetation is now tropical, a soil rampart around the garden is volcanic and fountains fertilise the earth. Outside, from the lane, she sees a mountainous region in the east 'touched by the first auroral glow.'

This return to the mainland is in the last chapter 'Projection' which, in Jungian terminology, is a casting off or releasing of emotional ties in the process of 'individuation' which involves a realisation of and integration with the depths of the unconscious. Something similar is implied earlier, when from one of the chambers containing her uncle's chaotic collections of objects resembling the Tarot suits of wands, swords, cups and discs, she selects a dartboard and rolls it towards her family. It doubles as the Wheel of Fortune. They must find release from the turbulences of their lives. From 'Multiplication':

> I set the disc bowling like a hoop . . . I watched it swiftly gaining momentum down a gentle incline, and knew it would reach its destination. After that my sisters and half-brother must read its message as I had done, and find in it their freedom.

There is a sense of spiritual completion - a voice heard earlier proclaiming softly 'The Silver Morn' from a heathery landscape showing a mere on a misty grey morning is now richer. It extols 'The Golden Eve' - the wheel of fate will either release her family to attain a higher level as destiny, or will return them to their world of form. In the rite scene in 'Exaltation', while she was in sleep state:

> I must have been borne away beyond the confines of the house, for when I next knew anything I was lying upon some eminence, a centre of grassy open space surrounded with trees, in a remote part of the grounds.

The light is pearly - aromatic odours pervade and droning music emanates from the bushes. A circle of people are crouched in the long grass. She glimpses her uncle, the anchorite, her sisters, monks, and females from the green-light district. Except for her jewels she is naked. She is made to drink a liquid, which is followed by erotic and sadistic experiences. Later she awakes fully clothed, still with her jewels, on a couch in the ante-room to her uncle's library. It is not clear if this is a dream experience or describes events actual to the story. It seems unfortunate that this sequence has been seized on by some rather luridly and, I think, to the detriment of a balanced perception of the character of the author.

The whole book is very rich with the essence of what Jean-Pierre Cauvin has termed *dépaysement*, the sense of the subject being out of her physical element, the unfamiliarity of first-time situation, and of exploration of highways and byways of a dream pattern. Some texts or themes published previous to the *Goose* have been incorporated, notably a metamorphic floor change in a room of her father's empty house, to a flower and water floor (9). References in the *Goose* to exploring chambers and passages, passing through archways, and the dartboard-cum-wheel seem to have a possible analogy to the kabbalistic Tree of Life, with its pathways to and from *sephiroth* which equate to states of consciousness, a system in which the return to the physical level for more experience as a destiny of the soul, a cyclic rebirth, is symbolised by a wheel. Or since Ithell refers to 'freedom' for her relations, it may improbably relate to a destiny which bypasses rebirth and allows the discarnate soul to proceed to higher states. The book remains as a formidable and skilful synthesis, if that is the right word, of hermetic doctrine within its more overt

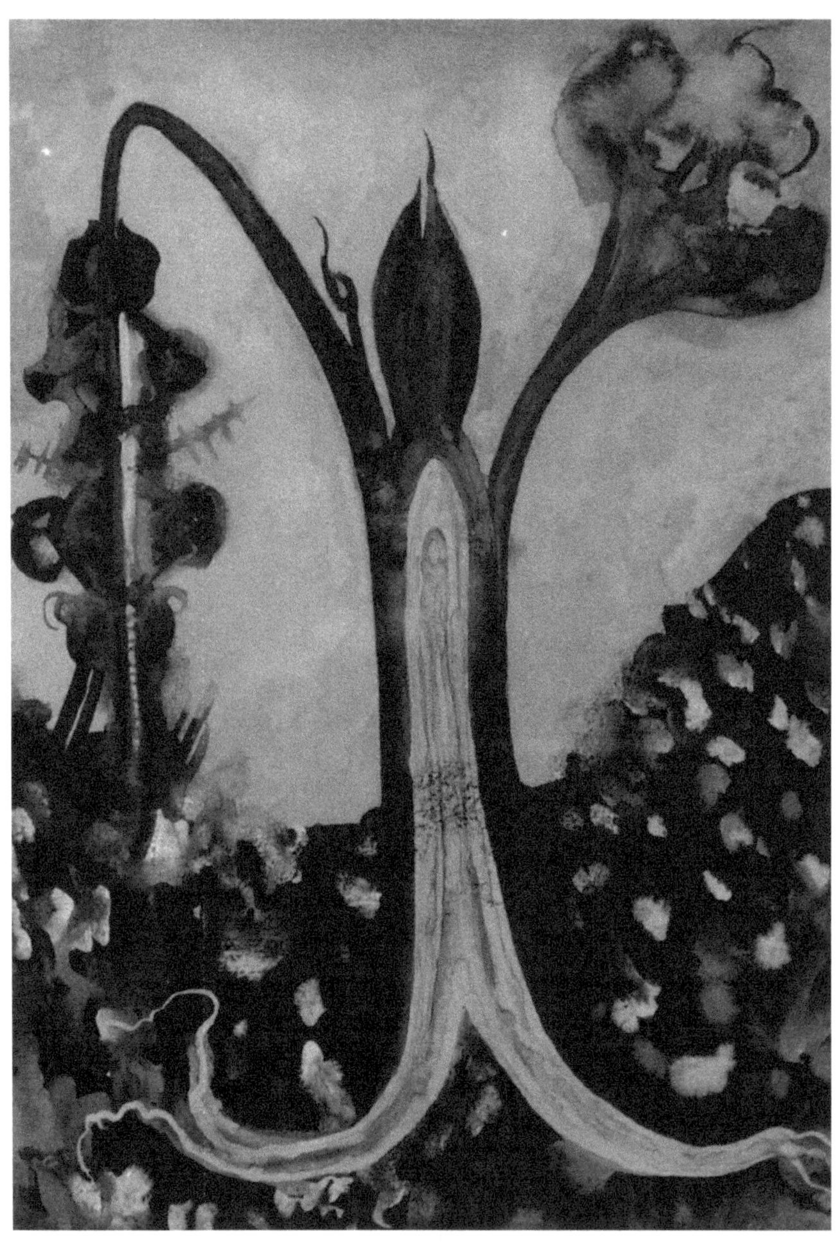

52. *The Trees* (1941, watercolour, 36.7 x 30.2 cm)

description as a surrealistic Gothic novel, and has since been reprinted by Peter Owen.

1959 saw Ithell engaged in correspondence with Tamara Bourkoun, a Manchurian-born Russian living in New York. The link leading to first exchange of letters cannot be traced. Tamara had received instructions from a medium to revive the Golden Dawn system (10). The outcome was the formation of The Order of the Pyramid and the Sphinx. Tamara left the States for England in 1963 and Ithell produced an artistic manifesto. The order was operative at least until 1975, when Ithell resigned, it seems, from ill health and a lapse from vegetarian regime on doctors' recommendations, which was contrary to OPS rules. Timothy d'Arch Smith, who was admitted to the Order in 1964, which operated from a room adapted for a temple in Hampstead, expands on the life and aims of Tamara, mentions other members, and gives some idea of the temple workings in a chapter of his recent book (11).

In 1961, Ithell, with Ross Nichols, both then associated with the London-based Druid Order A.D.U.B. (*An Druidh Uileach Braithreachas*), otherwise known as The British Circle of the Universal Bond, travelled in August to Brest in Brittany for the Breton *Gorsedd* as the start of an itinerary carefully recorded by Ithell in a handwritten diary (12). There they joined The Chief (Robert MacGregor-Reid), Pendragon (Dr. Thomas Maughan) and Companions of the Order to take part in the ceremony at the Place du Château. Ithell notes that no Cornish or Welsh druids attended. In journeys within Brittany they visited various holy sites, wells, churches, menhir monuments, dolmens &c; also Quimper cathedral. During the tour, Ross Nichols received conditional baptism into the Ancient Celtic Church, Ithell having received it the year before, probably after the 1960 Gorsedd. She describes features:

> Chrism imposed on the forehead, eyes, nose, mouth, ears, hands and feet. . . also the Oblature of St Kolumban – with

> cutting of a lock of hair – tonsure, and the donning of the capuchin.

Later that August, always vitally interested in her spiritual or secular position within the Celtic environment, she was ordained a deaconess of the church, the diaconal ceremony involving a floor ritual of prostration with arms crossed on chest. At the hermitage at St. Dolay, where all are robed, and the ceremonies took place, we catch a glimpse of Ithell applying meditative techniques in its chapel, using terminology well understood by those familiar with the Tree of Life and the consciousness expanding theories based on Sanskrit sources. Interpolation of Cymric mythology and French does not help the uninitiated but the statement does show her facility for association of different esoteric systems which is the mark of depth of approach. Before this she is careful to select her seating:

> It seems that the chapel is not sited due East and West, but more exactly North (altar) and South. I always place myself in the middle of the East wall.
>
> I attempted to make a meditation in the chapel: *oraison passive* - a sinking into *Annwon* (the *Muladhara*, *Malkuth* in one of its aspects?) the aim being to despoil oneself of all sense impression, emotion and thought, to reach the ground-base or 'chaos' of being, potentiality. When the human-being is thus denuded, its divine spark should fly upward automatically to *Ceugant* (*Sahasrara*; *Kether* or even *Ain Soph Aur*) though I doubt whether the last can be reached and a return still be made to conditional existence. Not much success – impressions distract – air from the open window to the west, the pallid gold of the sky behind birch-leaves, even the balsamic quiet of the chapel itself. The first effect is an immersion into the peace of the body – thoughts go first, then feelings and the body's warmth and silence alone remain.

On August 18th she left for Jersey, having been given 'a packet of sea-salt (blessed), and seeds and a sprouting lily bulb; also an omelette sandwich and fruit'. It had been a memorable fortnight. Her next participation in the Gorsedd on record is in 1964, at Paimpont (13).

Between her writing and painting activities, punctuated by travels in Cornwall, Ithell Colquhoun collected colloquialisms used by the inhabitants. Spoken Cornish was a thing of the past, although I believe that there was activity and still is, to revive it tutorially. From the memory of Cornishmen, Dolly Pentreath (1685-1777), fishwife and fortune teller, born in Mousehole, had been the last to speak Cornish (14). There is, though, a literary revival, and poetry in Cornish has been collected, with English translations (15).

Ithell, whose research included obtaining information from the elderly William Giles who looked after her garden, and her daily help Mabel Drew; and with some aid from Denys Val Baker of *The Cornish Review*, among others she talked to, had by 1970 made up her own glossary of words and phrases in the Cornish dialect, as current in Penwith. A lengthy dissertation by her was published in the *Review* the following year under the title 'Cornish Earth' (16). It casts some light on communication and beliefs in the period when countryside life in Cornwall was still truly rural, with no suburban encroachment. Ithell remarked:

> Before extreme mechanisation and the dismal concept of factory - farming had taken the zest out of it, life was, to quote Mr. Giles, 'heaven upon earth'; but this was an earthy paradise with nothing fey about it.
>
> Folk beliefs are dying out faster than dialect-words or phrases and people are shyer of admitting to them. Most of them concern weather, the calendar and herbal remedies - there used to be at least one woman in each street and even the smallest hamlet who could prescribe and supply herbs for use in sickness.

> These were still widely used until the advent of the Health Service and the expansion of the drug industry. In the same way, traditional knowledge of the weather in relation to the annual cycle played an important part in husbandry before meteorological forecasting by radio was generally available.

She pointed out that the phrases gave a tang to conversation, the words are often intriguing, that shreds of folk-wisdom are preserved within the beliefs; and that, although only a few words in the glossary are traceable to old Cornish, many words would then have not been understood by those from other parts of Britain. Her Glossary is reproduced as Appendix I. At this time, it seems that her 'Stone Cross Cottage' and garden provided the environment for renewed zest in creative writing, such as playlets of a supernatural nature, one of which, 'The Monument', apparently unpublished, has a gardener as a character relating the history of a stone cross which was broken up by those who saw ghosts around it, and how a boy had earlier identified the murderer of his mother (in whose memory the cross was later erected) during an identity parade. Her earthbound ghost appears looking for her old habitat in Monument Meadow as it became known. The versions of the tale of Monument Meadow, and the murder which occurred in 1793 will be found at the end of Appendix I, obviously providing the inspiration for Ithell's short play.

Her interest in The Order of the Holy Wisdom continued; it was about ten years since she had contacted Dr. Crow, reading the Order's literature and asking questions. Crow had by then moved to the Essex area from Leicester, and worked in London, and the two met in the mid-sixties. It is doubtful whether Ithell attended any of the Order teaching meetings, but she then expressed interest to be a Member, and on the basis of her activities and writings had conferred on her the status of Lady of Honour of the Order of the Keltic Cross, with a certificate dated June 12th, 1965.

Marian Green's *Quest* magazine, featuring occult philosophy, ritual

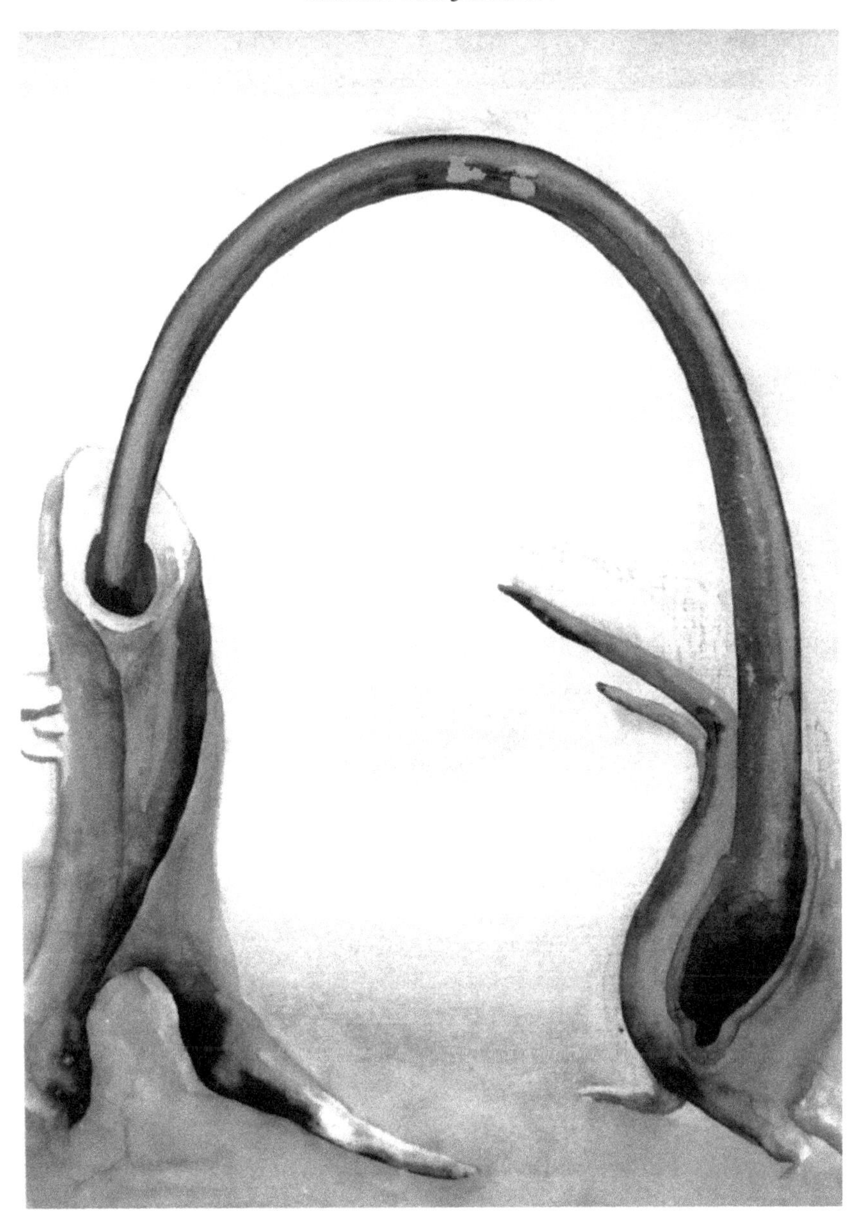

53. *The Bird or the Egg* (c.1940, watercolour, 25.8 x 16.3 cm)

magic and practical instruction commenced in 1970 and is still running today. The first number published an article by Ithell on Celtic interlace designs (17) – no mere patterns, and theorising that there were possible messages in the entwining sections. She drew parallels to designs in *The Book of Kells* and in the *Lindisfarne Gospels* with sacred languages in China and Peru which was conveyed by the twisting and knotting of cords, modified by the colours of the strands. She concluded:

> The 'Cord language' may have been brought over with other Druidic lore by the early Celtic church. In the same way, some of the traditions of ancient Egypt are preserved in the Coptic church even to-day, and the Interlace was first used in Christian art by the Copts.

No.4 of *Quest* published her 'The Openings of the Body' which queried the diagram in Blavatsky's *The Secret Doctrine* which showed existing relationships and correspondences between the openings or 'gates' of the body – what did Blavatsky mean by an 'opening'? Ithell concludes there are twelve in the male, which could be related to the zodiacal signs. On the other hand there were thirteen in the female body which may be adapted to receive that Mezla or influence which is said to stream downward from the thirteen strands of the Beard of Macroprosopus.

[Note. Macroprosopos is the Vast Countenance, a magical image of a bearded figure at the top of the Tree of Life in the Kether position representing the Creator, a unity from whom manifests the Lesser Countenance (supernal father, also with beard) and the Bride (supernal mother) - all an aid to visualisation of spiritual creation using these images. The strands of his beard are thirteen, the number being derived by numerology applied to the Hebrew alphabet. using the word 'Achad' which stands for unity. That is, Aleph (one) plus Cheh (eight) plus Daleth (four). The second `a' is surplus, being there to Anglicise the Hebrew. E.R.]

9 Cornwall (activities post-1971)

Ithell Colquhoun gave five one-person exhibitions between 1972 and 1977, viz: in 1972 at theCity of Exeter Art Gallery ('Paintings, Collages and Drawings'); in 1973 at the Orion Gallery, Penzance ('Flower and Plant Paintings'); in 1974 at the Leva Gallery, London ('Surrealist Paintings and Drawings from 1930-1950'); in 1976 at the Newlyn Orion Galleries, catalogued as Penzance but probably at Newlyn ('Paintings, Drawings, Collages 1936-76'; and in 1977 at the Parkin Gallery, London ('Paintings and Drawings 1930-1940'). The Exeter (65 works) and Newlyn Orion (90 works) exhibitions showed the broad range of her art, which included her later interests in convulsive landscape and collage. The latter divided the exhibits into categories of Pre-Surrealist (influence of the Slade), Surrealism or Magic Realism (influence of Dali), Surrealism - Psycho-Morphology (influence of Max Ernst, Matta, Automatism - from 1939), Collage (influence ofKurt Schwitters), Convulsive Landscape (from 1952), and the Condition of Music. These were roughly on the time-scale of her interests from work at the Slade up to late work at Paul. Condition of Music, so called, was a late phase and included her paintings *Delius's Irmelin* (1972), *Messiaen's L'Ascension* (1973 or 1974), and *Stockhausen's Poles* (1976).

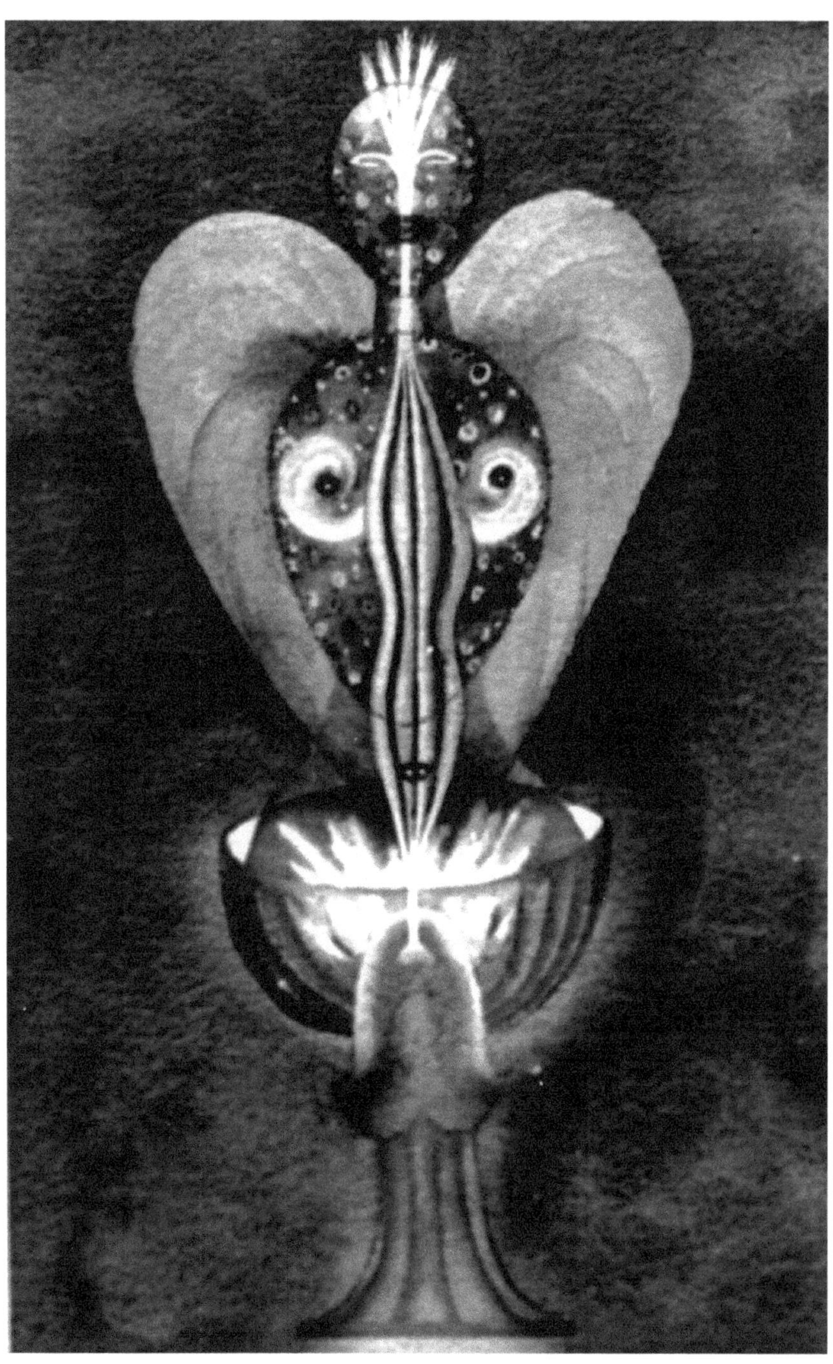

54. Linked Senses *(c.1946, watercolour and ink, 66 x 47.5 cm)*

Andrew McLaren Young said, in the Exeter catalogue, that her art 'belongs to the fantasy world of the dream and the imagination' and that there was magic in it – 'not magic in the ordinary every-day meaning in which the word is now used; but magic as understood in a past age . . .' The autumn 1973 exhibition at the Orion Gallery, although confined to 39 works, complemented after 37 years the selection of exotic flower decorations in her 1936 exhibition with the Fine Art Society. The remarks already quoted (Ch.3), still hold good - technical brilliance, mystical nature, uncompromising truth, magic realism - all could be re-echoed along the time corridor of decades past.

The exhibitions of past paintings and drawings went on, but there came a time in the seventies when Ithell's literary work overshadowed her then current painting. Illness had caused her to turn to collage when brushwork skills failed. Writing had not been curtailed. If the painting hand failed, the mind and pen were as active as ever. There is a correspondence record of Ithell consulting her friend Bobbie Gray at Cheltenham in the spring of 1973 (1), apparently over health and publishing difficulties, who provided a natal chart, with a back-up letter promised from her husband William. In this year, there is only a record of one painting of Ithell Colquhoun's - *L'Ascension* – inspired by Messiaen's early composition.

A major literary effort resulted in publication of her last book - *Sword of Wisdom* : *MacGregor Mathers and 'The Golden Dawn'* in 1975. We need to go back to December 18th, 1967 for the seed of the activity. Mrs Evan Weir of the old Alpha and Omega temple, whose acquaintance Ithell had made when in her early twenties, as a candidate for the Outer Order of the Golden Dawn, had since died. Without warning, just before the end of the year, Ithell received then a gift of a painting of MacGregor Mathers, from a relative (perhaps daughter) of Mrs Weir, who had been sorting out lumber, and had saved it from the bonfire. The circumstances in which it was known that Ithell should be chosen to receive it, have not been discovered.

Ithell was overcome with emotion; Mathers and the Golden Dawn Order were as close to her in the occult realm as were Breton's principles in the world of surrealism:

> Having only the haziest recollection from my student-days of the portrait I had seen in Mrs Weir's drawing-room, it was with some excitement that I now tore aside its wrappings! It seemed that I was rending a Veil, as in the Portal Ceremony. From the shadows 'the gaunt resolute face' of Yeats's Autobiographies looked out. 'The face of an angel', was my first impression : angel as messenger, perhaps, of Michael Archangel, leader of heaven's armies. In a surge of strange emotion, I kissed the portrait's lips; then crouching on the floor beside it, I burst into tears. I had fallen in love at first sight, not only with a picture but with the representation of someone literally out of this world. (*Sword of Wisdom*, p.40)

An additional interest was that the painting was executed by Mathers' wife, Moina, whom Ithell's cousin Edward had known, when she returned to England from Paris on her husband's death in 1918, and who had established the Alpha and Omega temple, in which Edward had held office and to which his mother had belonged, as mentioned in the chapter on Ithell's early interests in the occult. It may have been one of the paintings which Ithell had noticed in the Elm Park Road house. Blue-eyed and attractive, Edward remembered her as 'the sweetest woman'. Her attractiveness had been noted by Yeats, who dedicated *A Vision* in 1926 to 'Vestigia', part of Moina's magical motto *Vestigia Nulla Retrorsum* (I never retrace my steps). In her student days, Moina (then Mina Bergson, sister of Henry Bergson) also had studied at the Slade, from 1882. The title page of her husband's *The Book of the Sacred Magic of Abramelin the Mage* was drawn by her and she also wrote the preface to the 1926 edition of his *The Kabbalah Unveiled.* She died in poverty in 1928 after an unsuccessful period of portrait painting to earn a living.

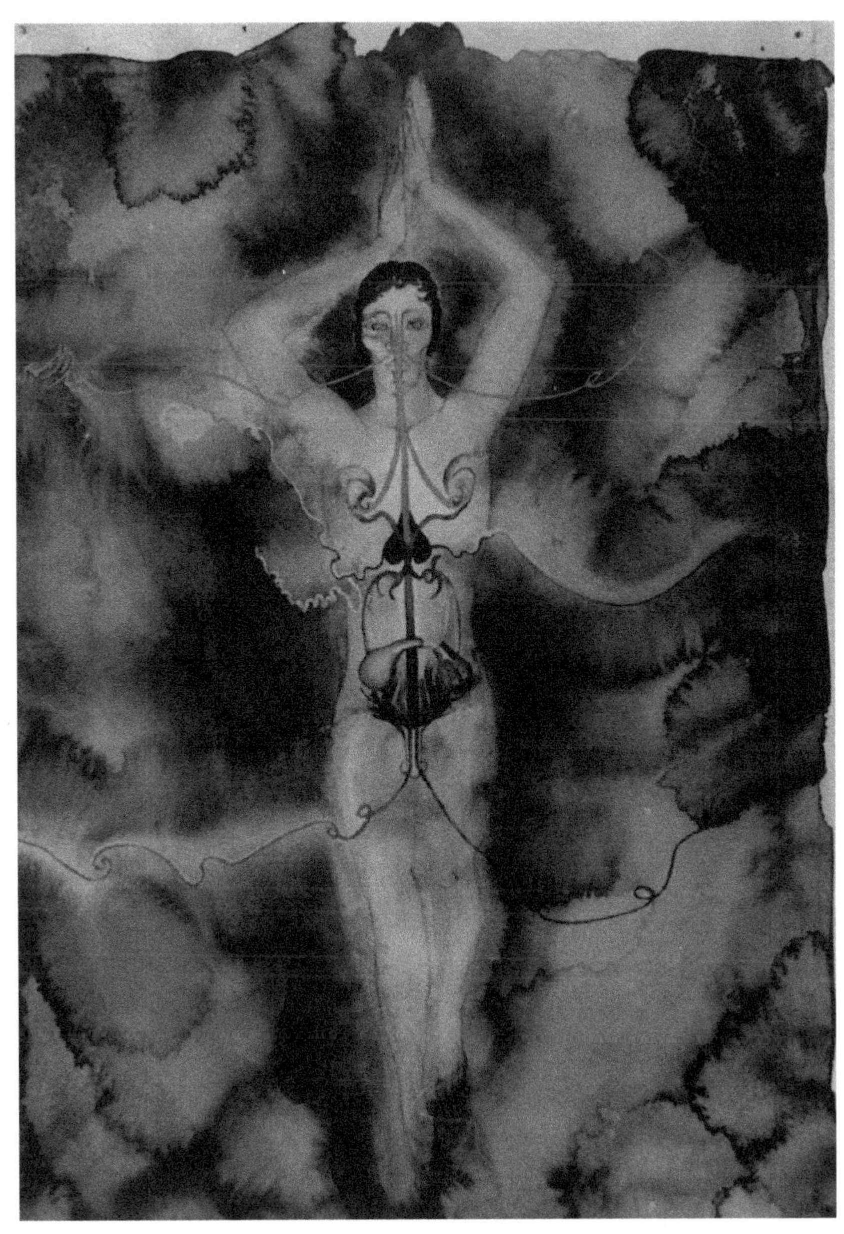

55. Second Adam *(undated, watercolour and pencil, 45.7 x 32.4 cm)*

The *Sword of Wisdom* is not a book for the uninitiated; it was written by a knowledgeable Ithell for the knowledgeable in occult and magical matters, and contains useful detail on Mathers, the Golden Dawn co-founder, and the Dawn temples and members, with a division for whom she called 'dissidents'. With the passing of years, and more and more information being available here and in America, some is 'history', but much is still valuable for its insights.

Briefly, for those not cognisant of events, the Order, founded in 1888, the history of which is well known, eventually had temples in London, Weston-super-Mare, Bradford, Edinburgh and Paris (the Ahathoor Temple from where Mathers and his wife ran the Order.) Details of the interaction and formation of Golden Dawn temples, and the relation of the Order to other organisations, such as those including druidry, freemasonry, theosophy, hermetic society branches and much else were provided in great complexity by Ithell. Personnel in the temples were listed, with summaries of the history of many (Edward Berridge, Aleister Crowley, Florence Farr, Annie Horniman, the Mathers, William Sharp, W.B. Yeats; and the co-founders William Westcott and William Woodman, were just a few). Names of popular interest crop up: - Sir Gerald Kelly, Arthur Machen, Sir William Crookes, Sir Edwin Arnold, William Morris, Charles Courtneidge (brother to Cicely Courtneidge who married Jack Hulbert).

Absorbing detail is provided of Mather's 'magical legacy' and in Ithell's themes of the usage and histories of the initiation vaults of temples. The book also defines the various assets of Mathers. Israel Regardie, in *Gnostica*, said at the time:

> . . . For the first time ever, insights are given into the history and character of MacGregor Mathers . . . the author has reproduced Mathers' natal horoscope, which is most useful. . . There is a great deal missing, though this is no reflection on Miss Colquhoun, who has done a yeoman's job . . . her writing displays profound dispassion and objectivity while expressing

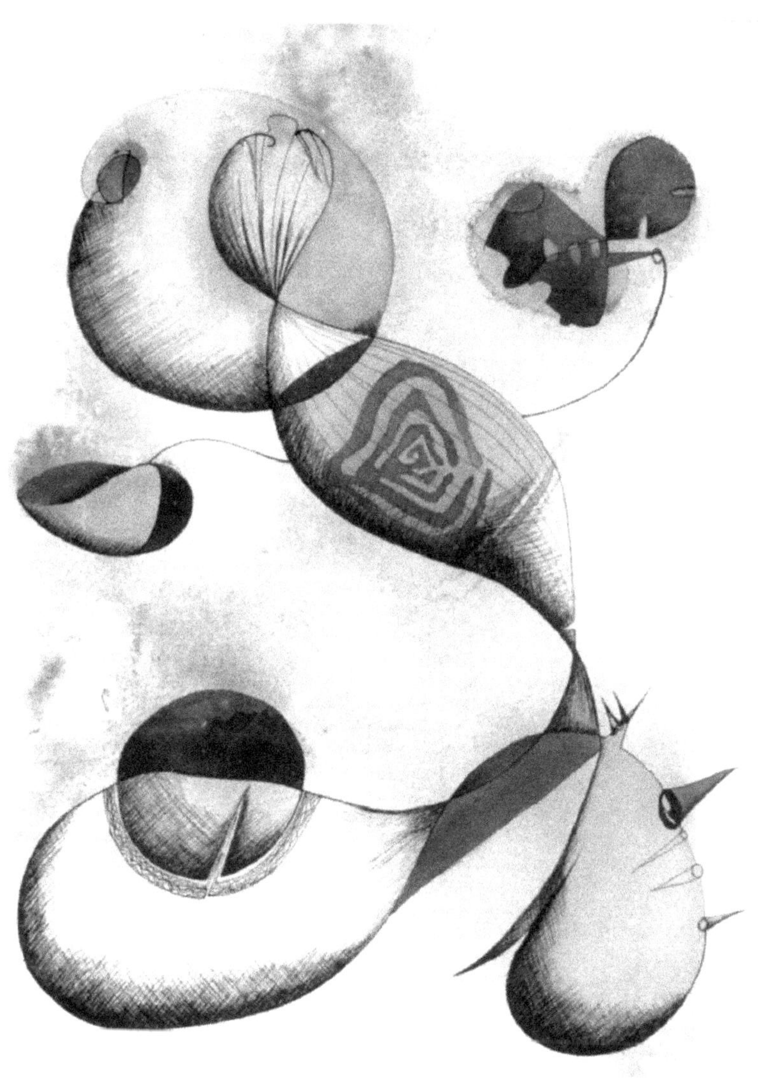

56. *Toy* (c.1947, watercolour and ink, 42 x 31.5 cm)

> her empathy for and even devotion to Mathers himself . . . she contributes some vital insights into the topics of magic, alchemy, Enochiana and, of all things, Tantra . . . In a word this is a book of the utmost significance to anyone interested in practical occultism or magic.

Regardie, London-born, had emigrated to America, and rekindled interest in the Order there, breaking secrecy for the good of the many, resulting in revival of interest as the remaining British temples gradually failed to prosper in the thirties. Practical Tantric methods of advancement are now not uncommon, unfortunately often seized on by media programmes without sufficient technical and historic explanation of the spiritual aspirations of the sexes involved. In earlier days, however, the Arts Council exhibited some Tantric art.

That *Sword of Wisdom* (1975) was already in Ithell's mind after that December day in 1967 is probably evidenced by her articles in *Man, Myth and Magic* (2) and *Prediction* (3), which provide useful summaries of the lives of Mathers and his wife, with some details of the Golden Dawn Order. She was 'Bergie' and he 'Zan'. The latter pet-name because he reminded her of Zanoni, hero of Edward Bulwer-Lytton's occult book of that name (4). The articles and Ithell's book are illustrated with a photograph of the painting which shows Mathers in ceremonial regalia, seated, arms folded over the hilt of a ritual sword. In addition there is a head-and-shoulders illustration of Moina in the *Prediction* article. Ithell's cousin Edward had the original on his bureau, which showed her, attractive, in an art nouveau dress. The other article does not show Moina but four drawings by her of Egyptian deities (Osiris, Horus the Child, Horus the falcon-headed, and Nephthys, sister of Isis). These, once in the hall of the Mathers' Paris house at 87 Rue Mozart (which was decorated like an Egyptian temple), re-surfaced as possessions of Ithell which are now held by the National Library of Ireland following her death. Sadly the painting of Mathers was bequeathed to the National Portrait Gallery of Scotland, but was refused and sent for auction, and so lost sight of.

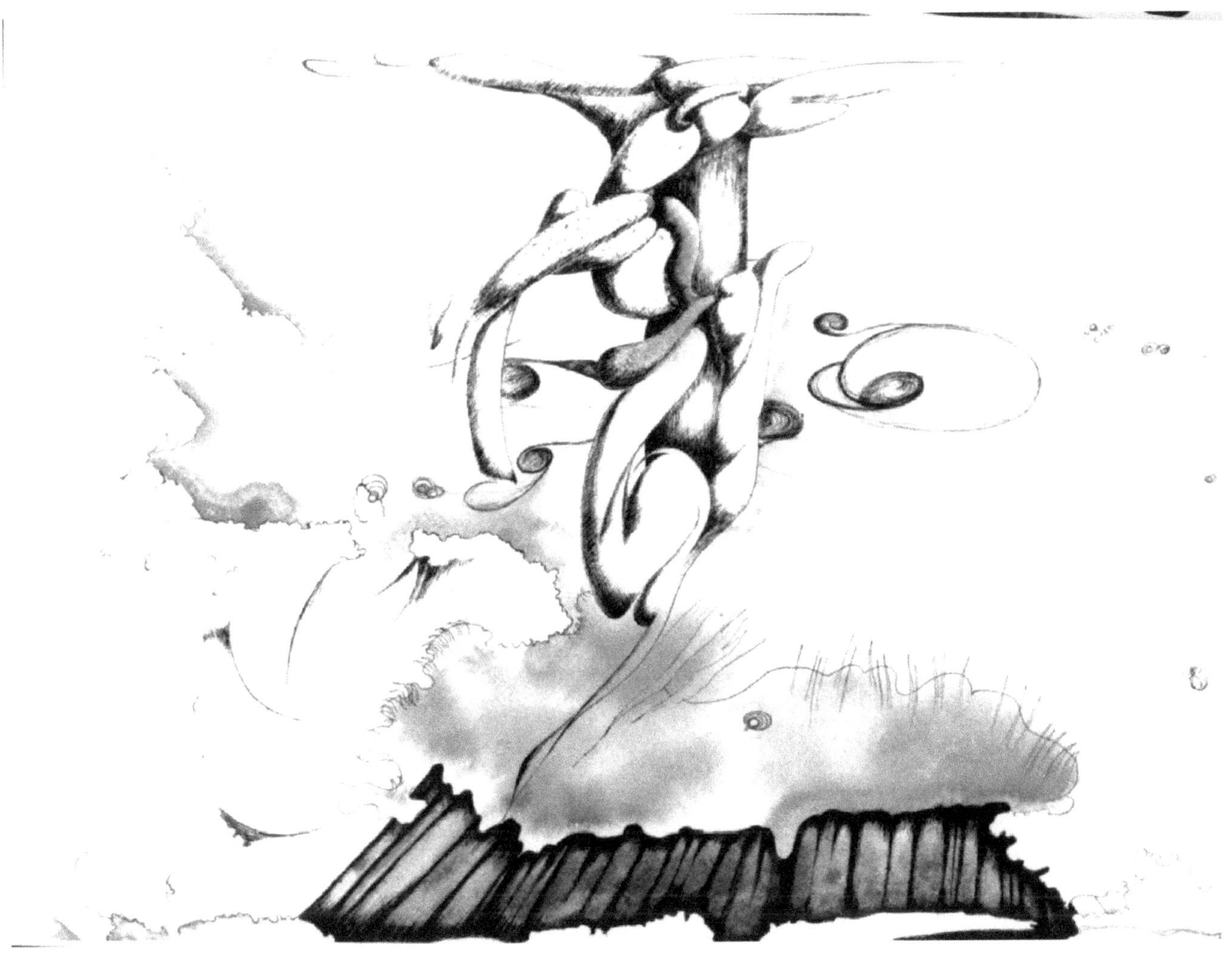

57. *Eruption* (undated, watercolour and ink, 32.5 x 45.8 cm)

The title for *Sword of Wisdom* was suggested to her from words in a poem by George Bataille and André Masson: '. . . his two hands resting/On the sword of wisdom' – lines actually referring to Paracelsus. Here is Ithell's praise of Mathers:

> There remains his considerable achievement in Ceremonial Magic, in the Hermetic Qabalah, in Skrying and the allied Projection of the subtle body and in various techniques of Divination. These latter include initiated Taro and Astrology, Geomancy, Enochian chess . . . Mathers was above all (and above any of his contemporaries) a creative occultist, working upon remnants of esoteric tradition to weld them into a unified and revitalised *corpus* without distorting their essentials.
>
> (*Sword of Wisdom*, p.243)

Other data include discussion of the GD tarot card designs, a dissertation on alchemy, and many pages on Enochian magic. At the time, useful to her if obtained would be the unpublished Glossary of the Enochian language by her cousin Edward Langford Garstin, who died in 1955; and Regardie's *Golden Dawn*, Vol.4 dealt with the system. Since then, subsequent writings have superseded the early interest. A quote from Ithell shows the sensitivity of her particular intuitive perception of an abstraction which would have demanded a raised level of consciousness when she suggests that the manipulation of sound in the Calls can 'give access to an early world of Atlantean pellucidity: based on an employment of occult mathematics, it raises a superstructure unimaginably attenuated and jewel-clear, what the *Egyptian Book of the Dead* symbolises as "the lily of green felspar".' (*Sword of Wisdom*, pp.256-7)

Ithell, in a summer 1977 exhibition at Newlyn, exhibited a set of paintings of tarot cards with particular reference to colour modes, rendering 'the essence of each card by the non-figurative means of pure colour, applied automatically in the manner of the Psycho-morphological movement in Surrealism'. She used a traditional

Golden Dawn pack. She is talking about the cards as meditation glyphs:

> Basic to all [cards] is the concept of the Four Elements: Air (Swords, pale yellow), Water (Cups, deep blue), Fire (Wands, scarlet) and Earth (Disks, indigo). Four family groups appear, each dependent from one of the Aces or Roots of Power. Each Ace attracts to itself one card from among the Major Arcana as its *Shakti* or formative energy to co-operate with it in manifestation.

She gives examples of the 'capturing' or 'attraction' relative to each Ace:

> Ace of Swords (central colour pale yellow) is entitled the Root of the Powers of Air and captures the Fool, entitled the Spirit of Aether, the Air-card . . . Together they produce the Court Cards : the Prince of Swords (central colour pale yellow), the Queen (deep blue), the King (scarlet) and the Princess (indigo). These represent respectively Air-of-Air, Water-of-Air, Fire-of-Air, and Water-of Air. . . Regarding the other Aces - Cups captures The Hanged Man, Wands captures The Angel, and the Ace of Disks The World. The article in full should still be of interest to professional Tarot experts.

By this time she had resigned from the Order of the Pyramid and the Sphinx, as previously related, and we find her in correspondence with Dr.Robert Wang (5) in the mid-seventies. the designing artist of a new deck of Golden Dawn tarot cards, in association with Israel Regardie. Wang kept her up to date with progress, during which he sought and took Ithell's advice on a design detail for the Ace of Wands.

Some expansion of her articles on automatic processes originally published in 1949 and 1952 was made by Ithell in *Melmoth*, probably in its second and final (?) issue of 1981 (6), sparked by an earlier

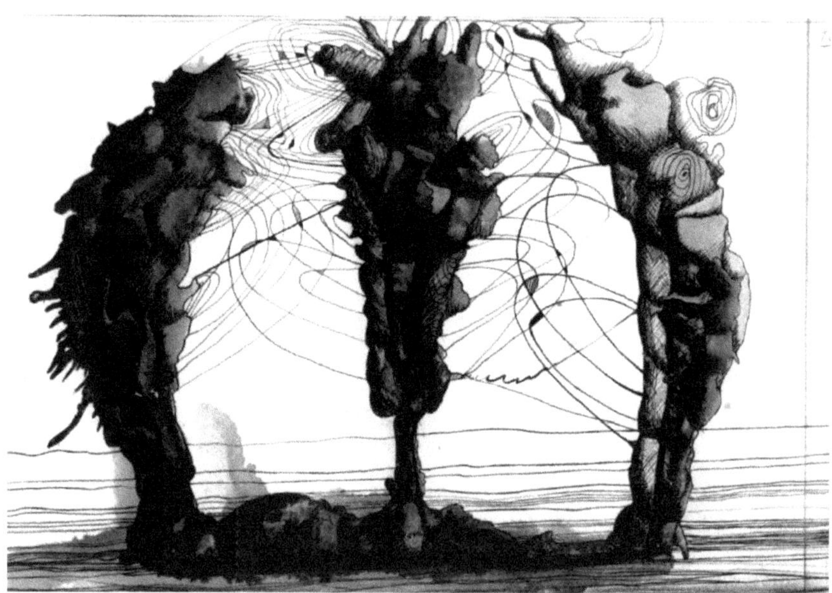

58. *'Composition : Three Growing Forms'* (given title, 1941, watercolour and ink, 32.4 x 43.5 cm)

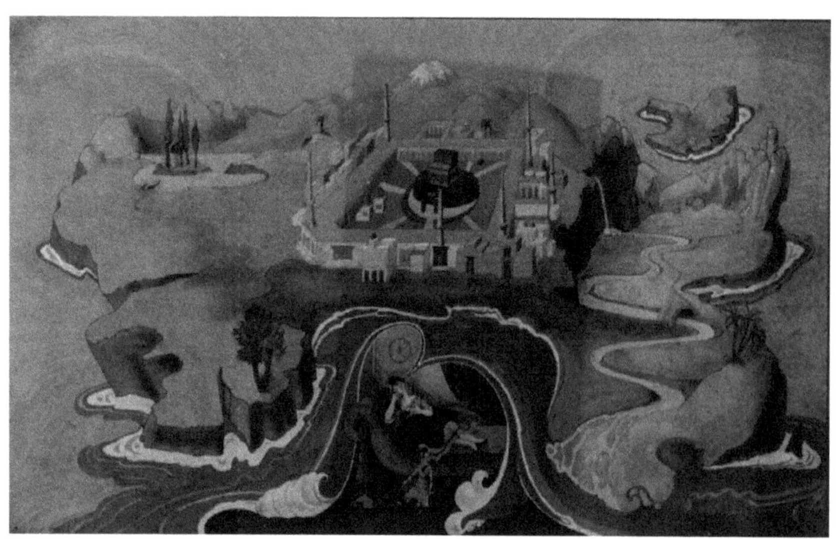

59. *Decoration for a Children's Waiting-Room in a Hospital* (undated, gouache and pencil, 35.7 x 68.5 cm)

essay by Michael Richardson, 'Automatism and Surrealist Poetic Practice'. Now very much the experienced 'operator', she reminded the readers that she was the author of the first accounts in English ('The Mantic Stain', 'Children of the Mantic Stain'). She went on to distinguish between two types of automatism. Breton had no time for a mediumistic source of automatic writing or painting, and was scornful, considering only the plumbing of hidden psychological depths. Examining the implications of suspension of both will and intellect, from the dictionary definition of automatism, in her 'Notes on Automatism', Ithell continues:

> It seems therefore that some degree of dissociation must take place in the Operator, though this seldom reaches the stage of trance. One also finds psychic force defined as 'non-physical force assumed to explain spiritualistic phenomena', which brings one to the point of distinguishing two usages of the word 'automatism', namely surrealist automatism and spiritualistic automatism. For the general public the latter is what springs to mind as 'automatic writing' but Breton's poem 'Tournesol' is an example of the former, which marks the difference between exploration and regurgitation. His writing could not be confused with the cosy platitudes delivered by the average spiritualistic circle.

She noted an exception to 'poor spiritualistic results'; namely, that of Bligh Bond who made archeological discoveries via automatic writing, with John Alleyne. She quotes Bond's definition of automatism in *The Gate of Remembrance* (7) – '. . .a willingness to hold back all mental preferences and preoccupations, and to restrain also the surface activities of the brain, so that the channel of pure 'idea' which resides in the subconscious mind may be maintained. . .' which was reminiscent of Breton's 1924 Manifesto's definition of surrealism in respect of psychic automatism. She considered that Bond's advocation of restraint of brain surface activity must be equivalent to Breton's assumption that this kind of control is attained by assuming a passive state of mind. She had found endless variety in the flux of imagery below conscious level, which could be tapped via the various automatic processes. Ithell Colquhoun thought that there was much more potential in these processes and that the 1978 exhibition at the Hayward Gallery(8) had 'underexposed' automatism.

The work of Bond, a member of the Society for Psychical Research, involved the receipt of automatic script from 1907 to 1912 via the pencil-hand of a friend covered by the right hand of Bond. Now, Bond (incidentally descended from the infamous Captain Bligh) had been appointed as Director of Excavations in the grounds of Glastonbury Abbey and, in brief, published his findings in *The Gate of Remembrance*, which involved monkish and other scripts and included drawings, obtained by automatic writing. These led to the claimed discovery of a lost chapel and other previously hidden archeological features which added to the knowledge of the Abbey. However, custody of the Abbey was with trustees acting on behalf of the established Church, and Bond eventually was dismissed in 1922 after his methods became known. Religious prejudice was uppermost and he was not given the benefit of the doubt. The Abbey trustees directed the removal of all his books from the Abbey book store.

In view of the multiplicity of data, sometimes in Latin and Middle English, it is not unwise to cogitate whether any such mental literary panorama attributable to the subconscious belongs naturally below the surface of the conscious mind, or is foreign and placed there by activity of unknown origin. This could lead to a doubt that some automation could be claimed as original work by the whole mind of the writer or painter. Can we without qualm unload everything not attributable to conscious reasoning to a place in the subconscious mind? It is worth quoting the remarks of Sir William Barrett, F.R.S.

> As is so often the case in automatic writing a dramatic form is taken, and messages purport to come from different deceased

people. The subconscious or subliminal self of the automatist doubtless is the source of much contained in the scripts, and may possibly be responsible for all the insight shown. But in that case we must confer upon the subconsciousness of the automatist faculties unrecognised by official science.

(*Gate of Remembrance*, pp. ix-x)

10 Poetry

The poetry of Ithell Colquhoun has been left to this penultimate chapter. Her creative application in numerical terms of titles rivals that of her paintings and drawings and it is impossible to provide a full selection. Failing a separate volume, this chapter provides a minor cross-section. Except for known published collections, many poems cannot be dated, or now linked to publications without exhaustive search. Some of her translations were included in the programme of joint readings with Toni at the International Arts Centre between 1940 and 1942. Two small collections of work in her own right were *Grimoire of the Entangled Thicket* in 1973 (1) and *Osmazone* in 1983 (2), referred to in the Introduction. Some uncollected poems were published in *The Sword of Wisdom* and various issues of *Ore*; prose poems appeared in *Fantasmagie*, *The Fortune Anthology*, *The Glass*, *The Scillonian*, and *Springtime*. One long personalised sequence of love poetry, 'Diagrams of Love' (3), is very fine indeed. Order of the typescript pages was difficult to establish. It is presented as an order-edited undivided sequence, retaining all line-wording.

Transformaction, in 1971 and 1973 (4), respectively published six of her poems and an article on the chain poem. Examples of chain poems as a surrealist activity can be found in *Surrealist Poetry in English*

(Penguin, 1978). However, the editor says, regarding these group poems, that in most cases, a participating poet contributes one line after reading what has preceded. In this case the conscious mind of the next person has influencing freedom. I do not think that this is the kind of Breton-aligned surrealist exercise, which strictly involves only subconscious levels, as described by Ithell Colquhoun. Quite rightly, she treats the process seriously although on the surface it is a fun exercise. Her views on the chain poem are at the end of this chapter.

DIAGRAMS OF LOVE

The world makes me wear
Disguise and concealment
An outer dress

You put on me
An inner clothing
A glorious robe

None but the words of love
Can I give you - or silence only

Commonest phrases from you
To me became a message

Already so many times
Have my hands travelled over
The sacred bone
And the space like a root
All that you most detest
All that you most revere

Do not be afraid
Do not be ashamed
My hands knowing all
Can only caress
Only convey love

It is as though
We were both dead
Not lifeless, free
From conditions

Our coats of skin
Cast aside
We meet in a mother-naked
Flame

  Be the messenger
  Be the messenger even
  No more

  Yourself
  Seminal essence
  Be all

He said in the shade
Yours is the breast of a dove

I knew that our love was deeper
Than all the qualities
And had existed
Before circumstance was

O plasmic content, ever to be renewed
Nothing can annul you

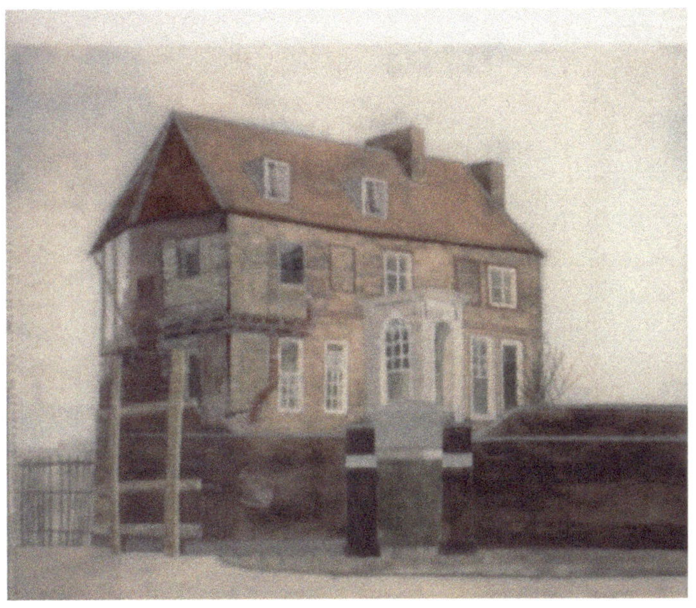

60. '*Hogarth's House at Chiswick*' (given title, 1941, watercolour and pencil, 35 x 45 cm)

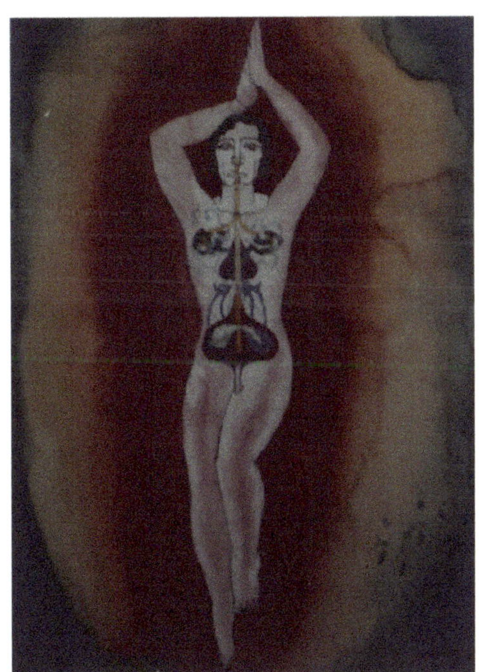

61. '*Mystic Figure*' (given title, undated, ink and gouache, 35.5 x 25.4 cm)

Nothing destroy

Far from idyllic gleams or
The sun-warmed torso
I choke in the dark
And smother with regret for
That draught of well-being
Swallowed and still tasted
A constant air

She saw his image in the clouds
In the sunset sky he saw her breasts

Snow makes us aware
Of presences
The thaw may sometime remain
Like snow in your garden
To take my footsteps' imprint

I knew that our love was deeper
Than all the qualities
And had existed
Before circumstance was

A leap a spark
Victorious metal's
Clang of triumph
Here acclaims his
Wished-for child

At your finger's touch
The harp of my accord
Sounds its most vibrant string

The wise say, Wipe out
Desire and ensue
The void of bliss

But what is content
If empty of you?

Tears, a spray
Of the ocean
That which divides
Is all our link
If he should pray O three angel-weavers
Receive his words and make them garlands
Make flowery crowns as you are said to do

I cannot enter by the door
That is unlocked at morning
I slip in at a side-door
The chink that's wide at dusk
The narrow door between the ribs
That gives on the heart

How steps drag
Moving away from you
Hours lag
When you are not near

The springing step
That goes to meet you!
Moments that leap
Like an early breeze

The two moons coincide
What if my head pains me?

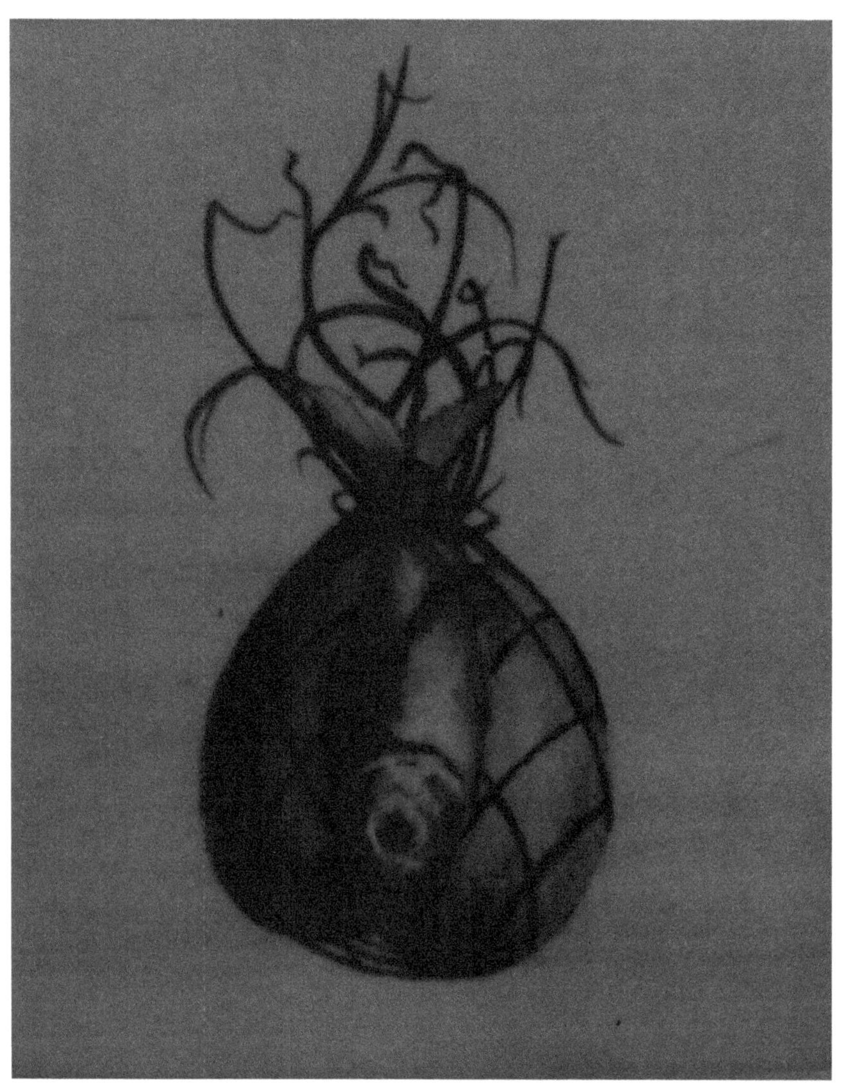

62. *Sardine and Eggs* (undated, watercolour, 22.3 x 17.3 cm)

You in my heart
Make full-moon always

Do not beg me
Never to leave you
When your love ceases
That day I go

Already he is living
Where? On the earth's ground.
Even now does
The first shiver touch him
The first tremor seize
At night, crossing a river?
I write letters
I write nonsense
He will not receive
The one letter I would send

In phantasmagoric dark
Before sleep instead of folding
Into myself as I was taught to do
I plunge into another being
And touched by tendrils of forest
Or foam of ocean's tongue
At one with you then
I sink into the abyss.

The skin is smooth
Between my breasts
The flesh whole
The bone unbroken

But the sternum's bland furrow

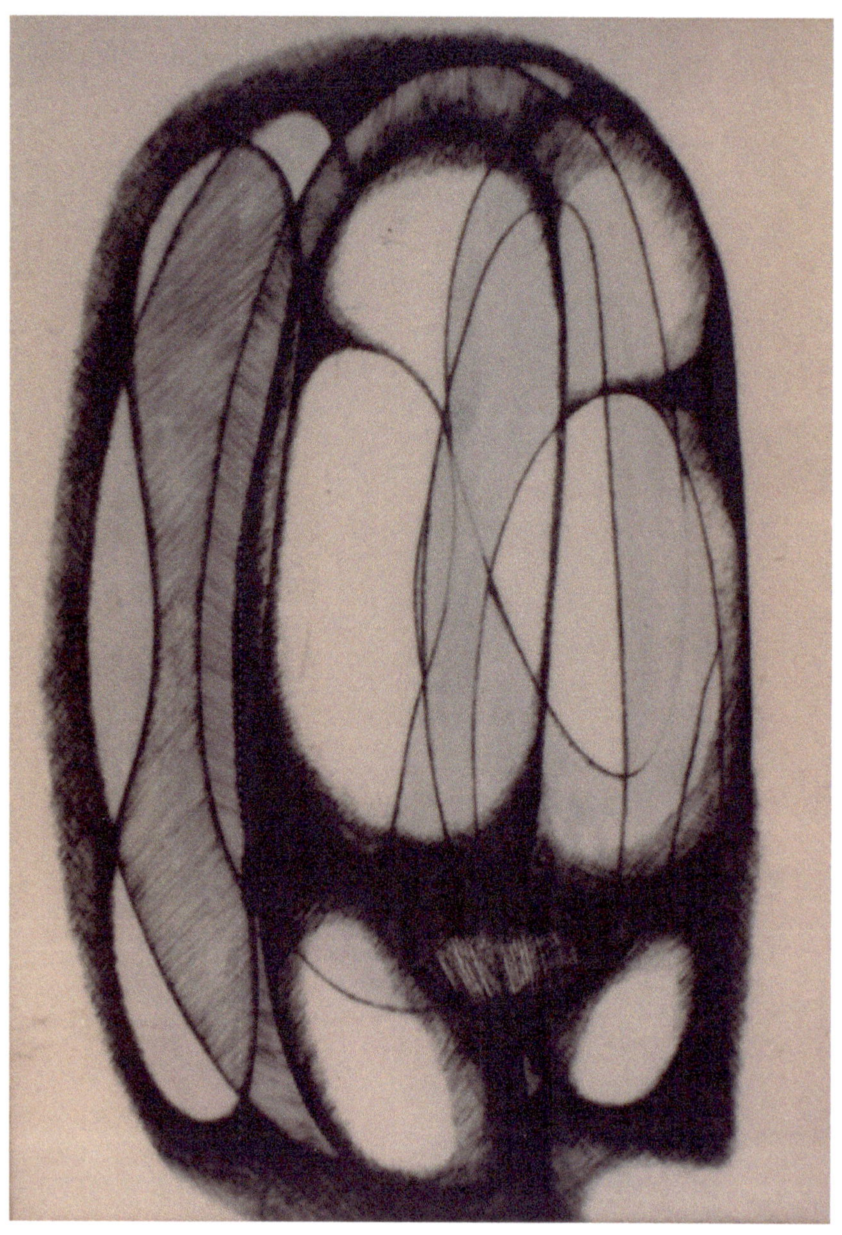

63. *Depression* (c.1947, ink and wash, 44.2 x 31 cm)

Hides a gash filled with flames

Are you covered?
Yes with linen
Satin fleece down
Still I shiver
You also, or why do you ask?
You also are bare.

SENT AWAY

Sent away
By light of day
I return
When candles burn

A mischievous but attractive poem is 'Love Charm I' (5).

LOVE CHARM I

Messengers, listen to me!
Take him the symbols he understands
Here is a dove, a swan
A lynx leading the tribe of cats
A garden with clover
Honey, a grove of myrtle
An apple-tree, the opening flower of a rose
Bensoin, red sandal-wood, the soft odours
I give him the drug damiana, drink!
The image of a doorway
And all enclosed in a girdle

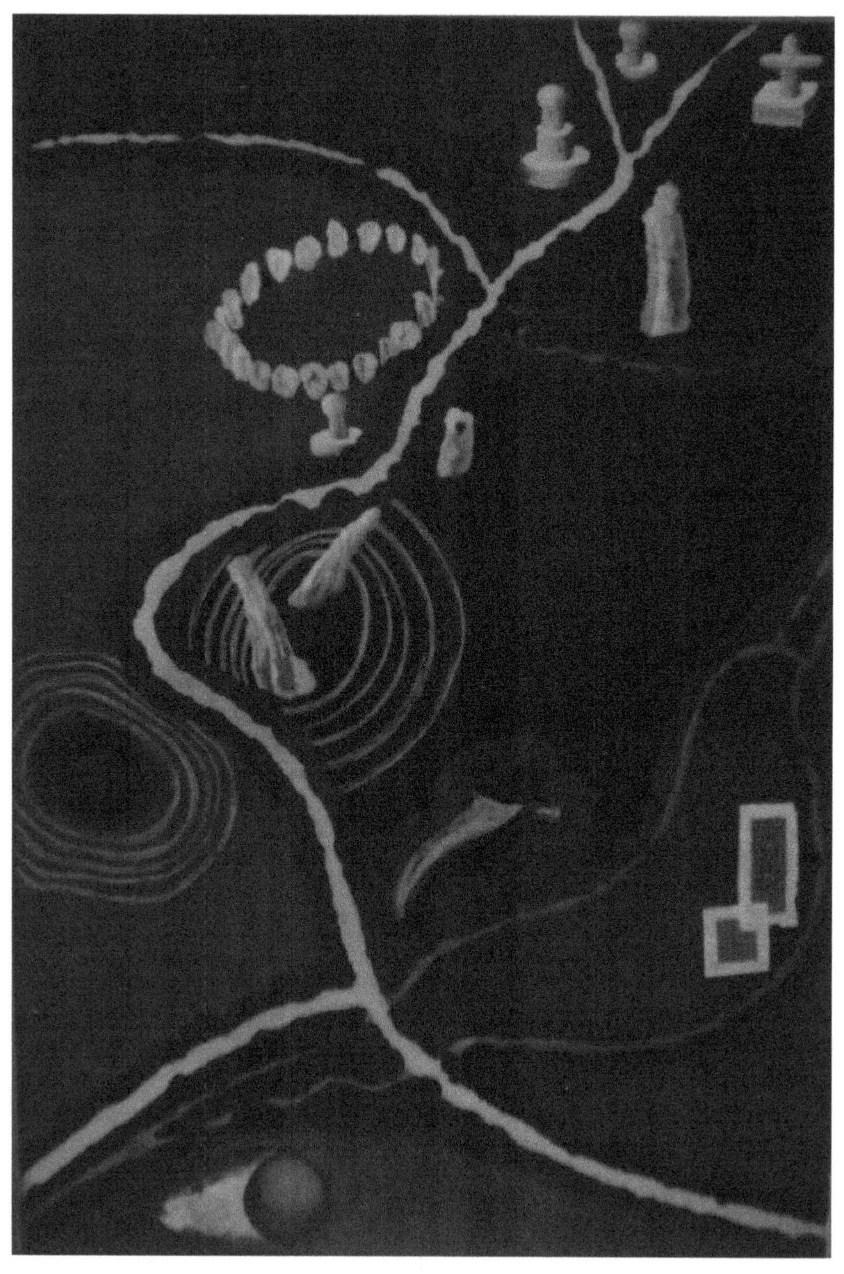

64. *Landscape with Antiquities*, Lamorna (1955, oil on canvas, 92 x 61 cm) Royal Cornwall Museum, Truro

A few poems prior to or the same as those in the *Grimoire of the Entangled Thicket* appeared in *Ore* - those not repeated in the collection included 'Moyslaght' and 'Swannenbrunn' in 1968 and 'Here' in 1971 (6). 'Here', i.e. Cornwall, traces in geographic/bodily terms the 'magnetic force line' she and others believed ran from the East Anglian coast to Cornwall and out to the Scillies, then out in the Atlantic to the American coast. These ley lines connected 'power vortices'. There is an analogy between the 'skin' of the Earth and its power points and ley lines, and the human skin, in mapping the pressure points along the meridians in acupuncture.

HERE

From the left iliac crest
To the smallest toe of the right foot
A magnetic line drawn by the Brothers
Tingling through England retains its power.

The current drew you, is still drawn through you.
From north of your home
You followed it, crossing the navel
And reaching the furthest point
Marked by the phallic tower, the peninsular breast
Before the line plunges into the sea
To emerge again as an island
Twenty-seven miles out.

Something of you remains here. Your own force
Mingling with that of the ancients, both are intensified
And your tweed after three years
Breathes from the downland flowers, the weathered lichens
Undissipated by Atlantic storm.

The poem 'Moyslaght' (alt. 'Moy Slaght' or 'Magh Sleacht' - the Plain of Adoration, then a wide limestone ridge) takes us probably to

Ballymagauran in ancient Ireland. There was a high central stone, surrounded by twelve smaller ones, known as Crom Cruach (a kind of Gaelic Moloch). In the legend, St. Patrick approached with his crozier (7) to strike it but obviously Ithell yields to its pagan persuasion.

MOYSLAGHT

Prostrate on the plain of
Adoration's expanse
I look to a hill

Stretching my limbs before
Inaccessible height

What are you, idol?
I cannot see
Is it the snake's form you wear?

Immolated I yield
To a smothering caress

In *Sword of Wisdom*, Ithell added a 9-verse, 36-line end poem, 'Elegy on the Hermetic Order of the Golden Dawn', lamenting the passing of the original impetus of the main Order, the unfulfilled promise:

The gods that Mina made to deck
The inner vault of mystery
Are now sewn up inside a sack
Stored in a dark repository

But it is to the introductory poem, also used in *Ore* two years before the *Sword* was published, that we turn our attention. It refers to the painting of MacGregor Mathers by Moina which Ithell received at the end of 1967. The magazine printed it under the given title 'On the Portrait of S'Rioghail Mo Dhream'; the book poem was titled 'On the Portrait of Deo Duce Comite Ferro'. Of the two mottoes of Mathers involved, 'S'Rioghail Mo Dhream' ('Royal is my race') refers to the MacGregors, whose arms include a sword supporting on its point an antique crown bearing this Gaelic motto. The other motto ('God my guide, my companion a sword') was found by Mathers when he consulted a manuscript which included an illustration of a talisman of Mars showing a snake twisted around a sword - on its coils was inscribed Deo Duce Comite Ferro. It was this magical motto that Mathers used within the Order.

ON THE PORTRAIT OF DEO DUCE COMITE FERRO

You come to me at the Solstice of winter you come
As a boat that reaches the nadir of night and turns
Helm to the east from south. For fifty years
You have lain in a coffin, a lumbered vault

I lift the lid, unwrap a silk swathing
And find no human skeleton but a sword.
A transmuted corpse bequeaths to me this token
With garnet gleaming darkly at the cross

Mists of nacre film the Egyptian sky
And soon a dusky beetle will fly upward
Hawk-like, the hidden sun gilding his wings
And, lord of the two horizons, regain mid-day.

(*Sword of Wisdom*, p.12)

Regarding corpse transmutation in line 7 above, see note 8).

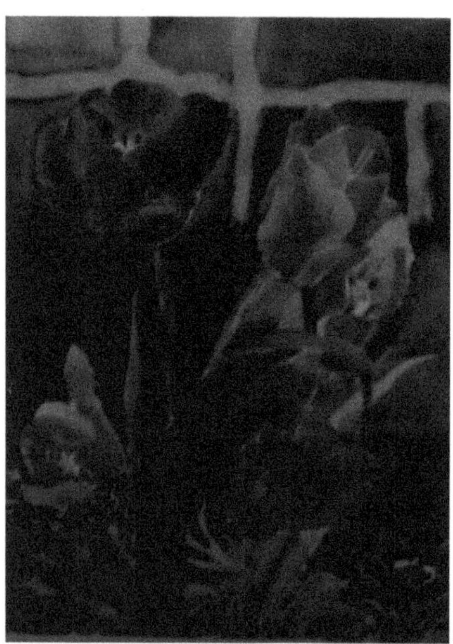

65. *Flowers* (c.1921, watercolour, 21.8 x 16.8 cm) Painted when 15

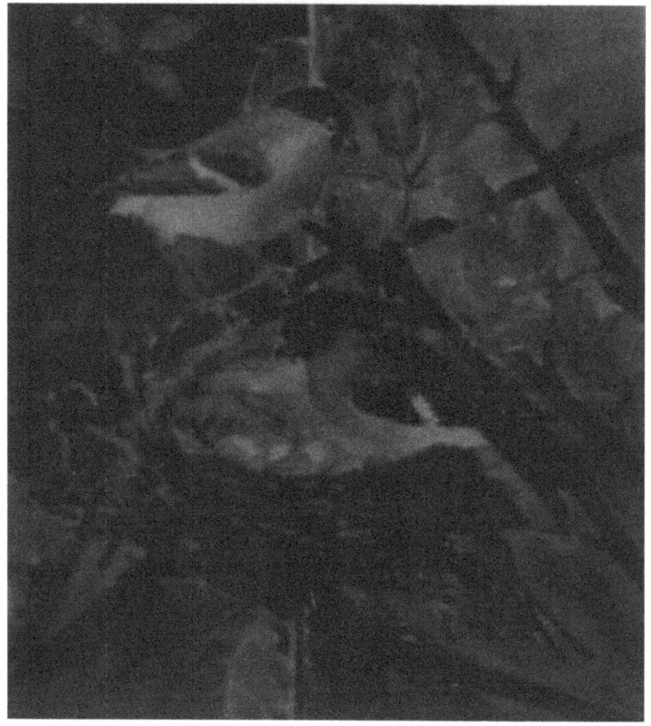

66. *Nature* (c.1921, watercolour, 17.4 x 15.8 cm) Painted when 15

The scheme of the poems in the thematic, illustrated *Grimoire of the Entangled Thicket* is that of part of a sequence intended to create one poem under its appropriate title of tree or vegetation, for each period of a thirteen-month calendar which the Celts associated with the annual cycle. These have also letter equivalents which were used in ancient tree-alphabets in ogham. In addition, Ithell intended to create a poem for each of the Celtic festivals. There are just eight poems in the book, so the theme is incomplete. There was a link between the poems and drawings. She wrote in the collection:

> 1972 was an important year to devotees of the Silver Crescent, for the thirteen months of the Calendar coincided exactly with their New Moons; this occurs only once in twenty-one years. It may be significant that in 1971 I made a number of drawings based on the automatic process known as décalcomania, which evoke the spirit of various trees - Beech, Rowan, Ash, Willow, Oak, Vine, and Silver Fir. Some of these, and the poetic sequence, I offer to the White Goddess at a time when wasteful technology is threatening the plant-life (and with it all organic life) of earth and the waters.
>
> (*Grimoire of the Entangled Thicket*, p.3)

Since there were twenty main letters in the Celtic alphabet concerned (the Beth-Luis-Nion) and a few subsidiary ones, and each was linked to a tree and/or other vegetation, there were differing interpretations as to which (perhaps one or more) vegetation fitted into the thirteen lunar-month slots. Ithell seems to have followed Robert Graves' interpretations (9). One poem on a festival day and one illustrative of a tree-month are given:

IMBOLC (Feb.2nd)

The celandines' array of chrysolite*

Calls out with vibrant tongue St. Brigid's praise
And oyster-catchers, where her grown lambs graze
Along the strand, proclaim her earliest light
With covens of sharp cries. Bride-shepherdess
Revealed in them and in the celandines
Their zig-zag wing your territory defines
Who wear the yellow flowers like a dress.

* Changed from 'chryolite'. The pale-yellow gemstone is meant, equating to the yellow and star-shaped flowers of the celandine.

February 2nd is the Christian Candlemas, dating from the sixth century, when Mary the Virgin's purification overlays a Brigid of history who also died in that century. But the pagan Bridget was a triple goddess invoked much earlier, traditionally golden-haired in her prime, and also conceived as a shepherdess in a period of lambing at the Imbolc or Imbolg festival on February 1st. Toulson (10) gives the snowdrop as her flower, Ithell mentions the celandine.

MUIN (Sept.2nd-30th)

I am the month of Muin, month of the vine
Exhilaration is mine through the garland of fruit
Draped from the right shoulder across the swell
Of a belly like Primavera's; yet mine of early
Fall is the realm. On the head too are grapes
And vine-leaves wreathing my autumn-coloured hair
My robe the bluish mist of a sky pregnant
With the first heavy dews

How calm I am! Yet is there perhaps hidden
An anger that gives authority to my poise?
I drank from the horn-cup and swam into a trance

So deep that only attraction amethystine*

Recalls me, after a voyage through gates of horn
I come now to bless and renew dreams that are true.

* The amethyst or 'wine stone' is said to protect against drunkenness.

The *Grimoire* included drawings – 'Ogham-Stone', 'Tree Trunk', 'Rock-Pool, Lamorna', 'Interlaced Boughs, Lamorna', 'Beth-Luis-Nion on Hand', 'Beth-Luis-Nion on Trilithon', 'Leaves of Muin, Ruis, Nion, Straif', and 'Sea-Anemone' which was repeated on the cover. In later years, Ithell Colquhoun added three other tree-month poems, which were used in *Ore*. These related to Saille (willow: April 15th-May 13th, *Ore* 20), and Fearn (alder: March 18th-April 15th) and Uath (hawthorn: May 13th-June 10th), both in *Ore* 27.

The early 1980s saw an 18-poem collection of mixed theme published for Ithell by Tony Pusey (11) under the title *Osmazone*. Whitney Chadwick has commented on the mystical partridge in 'Translated from the Galvanese':

> One evening I was standing by a lake when just below the surface of the water a large bird like a pheasant darted very swiftly by. It was golden-brown in colour and luminous, with markings like pale crescents on the tail-feathers; my companion said 'the sun and moon are the light of air, this is the light of water.'

Chadwick (p.210) points out, while also considering egg and partridge images in the work of Leonora Carrington, that in ancient times the partridge was 'variously identified with the sun or the moon, and was often sacred to the love goddess.'

The collection also seems to have given Ithell the opportunity to let her hair down and to delight in puckishness and whimsicalities as an antidote to the seriousness of her interests in alchemy and hermetic matters generally. One such poem was 'Living Boy':

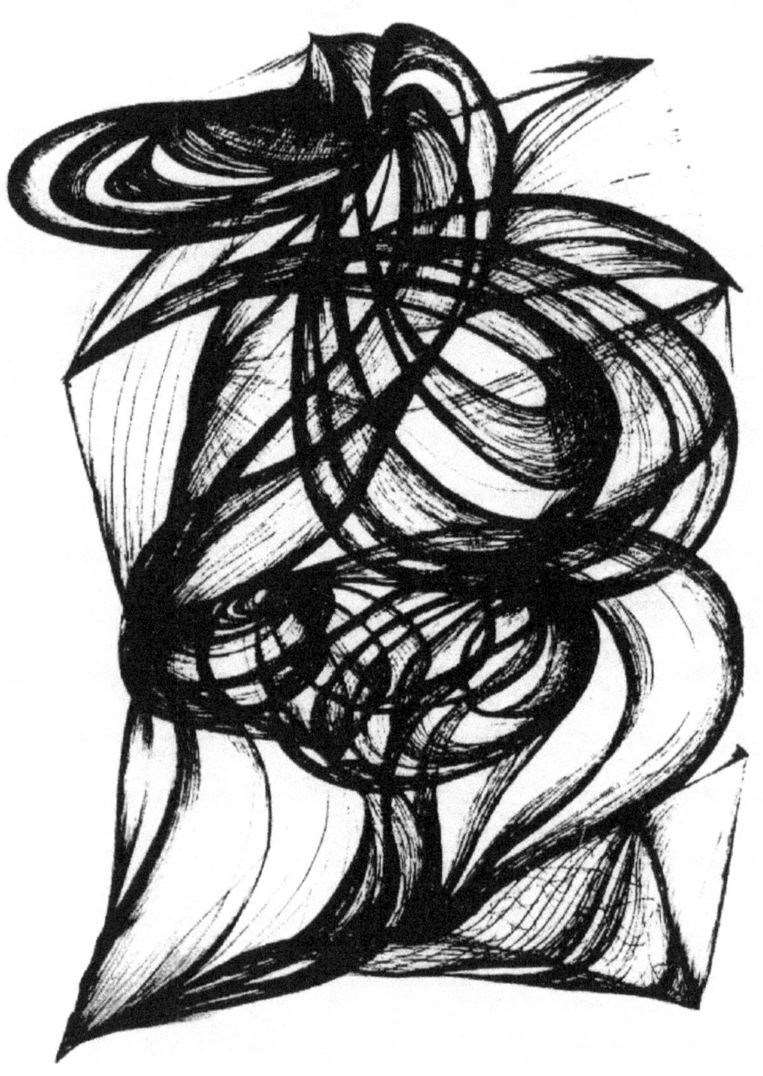

67 *Leave Uncombed Your Darling Hair* (ink drawing, 44.4 x 31.2 cm)

LIVING BOY (to P.G.)

The boy who is most alive
doesn't exist on paper
The boy with the toughest muscle
wears his hair like a girl's

Padrig Padrig don't cut your hair
Let people wonder let them stare

His mother didn't register
The birth of her twelve children
because she wanted to be free
of the State and call them by ancient names
Rebel-mother rebel-son
Token to all who would be one

Garlone Padrig Kathy
Gwen Morgane Yann
Adraboran Maiwenn Gendal
Sklérijenn Diwhezha Bran

Rebel-mother rebel-son
Token to all who would be one

Among his sisters are Last One and Light
his brothers are a warrior and saints
he works their land like his forebears
and like them lets his hair grow long
Padrig, Padrig don't cut your hair
Down to your shoulders let it flare

The family resisted the planting of a pole
in their courtyard and lines of wire
that would destroy their trees

68. *Horus*
(undated, ink and wash, 25 x 26 cm)

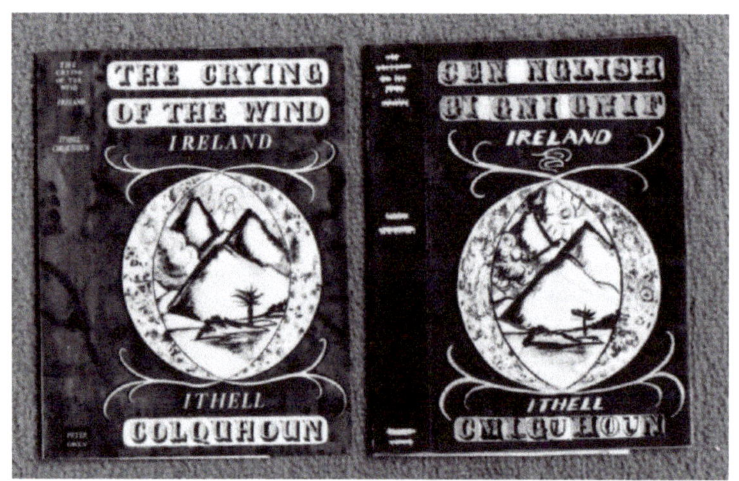

69. *Designs for book-jacket for The Crying of the Wind* : Ireland

for needless messages

Rebel-mother rebel-son
Token to all who would be one

Police in twenty truck-loads
drove up to the farm-place
with steel helmets revolvers
truncheons tommy-guns the lot

Rebel-mother rebel-son
Token to all who would be one
Breaking their own laws
they took his mother to prison
with two of her children
the eldest but sixteen

Rebel-mother rebel-son
Token to all who would be one

The boy who is most alive
in the centre of tumult makes no noise
keeps to himself in spite of those
who make newspaper and radio

Padrig, Padrig don't cut your hair
Down to your haunches let it flare

The living boy is strong
as horse and bull he wrestles
for sport and always wins
to prove himself he crossed the sea

Padrig Padrig don't cut your mane

Down to your thighs let it now rain

He comes from an early world
enfolded in pagan stillness
no telegraph or barber's shop
machine or science Church or state

Padrig Padrig don't cut your locks
Let them ripple down to your hocks

His smile opens
the earth's morning
Nature bred him
to be himself alone

Padrig Padrig don't cut your hair
Let it touch earth let it breathe air
Never mind mockery threats or please
Let it grow long like lichen on trees
Long Long Long

The mood behind the verses shows Ithell Colquhoun's mental range was broad. Apart from her ability to analyse and project her ideas on the profound, she was accommodative of simple truths and peasant humour. Some may find amusement in the following concrete poem, also from *Osmazone*:

DANCE OF THE FIGURE COUSINS

<table>
<tr><td></td><td>1</td><td></td></tr>
<tr><td></td><td>2</td><td></td></tr>
<tr><td></td><td>3</td><td></td></tr>
<tr><td>1 - 4</td><td>4</td><td>4 - 7</td></tr>
<tr><td>2 - 5</td><td>5</td><td>5 - 8</td></tr>
<tr><td>3 - 6</td><td>6</td><td>6 - 9</td></tr>
<tr><td></td><td>7</td><td></td></tr>
<tr><td></td><td>8</td><td></td></tr>
<tr><td></td><td>9</td><td></td></tr>
</table>

Finally, Ithell's delight in the expansion and telling of the old stories of the areas to which she had a magnetic empathy (in this case, St. Agnes in the Scillies and its patron saint St. Warna) (12).

THE MYTH OF SANTA WARNA

Arrival

Not a ripple, a pure day, gay and free. Only to breathe is a joy. The warm air shines, the island respires. Thyme and white camomile give out their scents by the shore. Santa Warna approaches, a figure wrapped by transforming sleep, lying furled in a coracle. From Ireland she comes, on a weather-surface level as a glass for her journey. The skin-stretched basket is drawn to an inlet, moors itself in the yielding sand: cries of the toweelies * awaken its passenger.

Landing

She rises, pauses between water and earth; robed with the swaying air, she steps ashore, her tresses still fathoming the shallows. The process of her subsuming begins; her presence is from henceforth unseen, though acknowledged in every blade and pebble. Now for

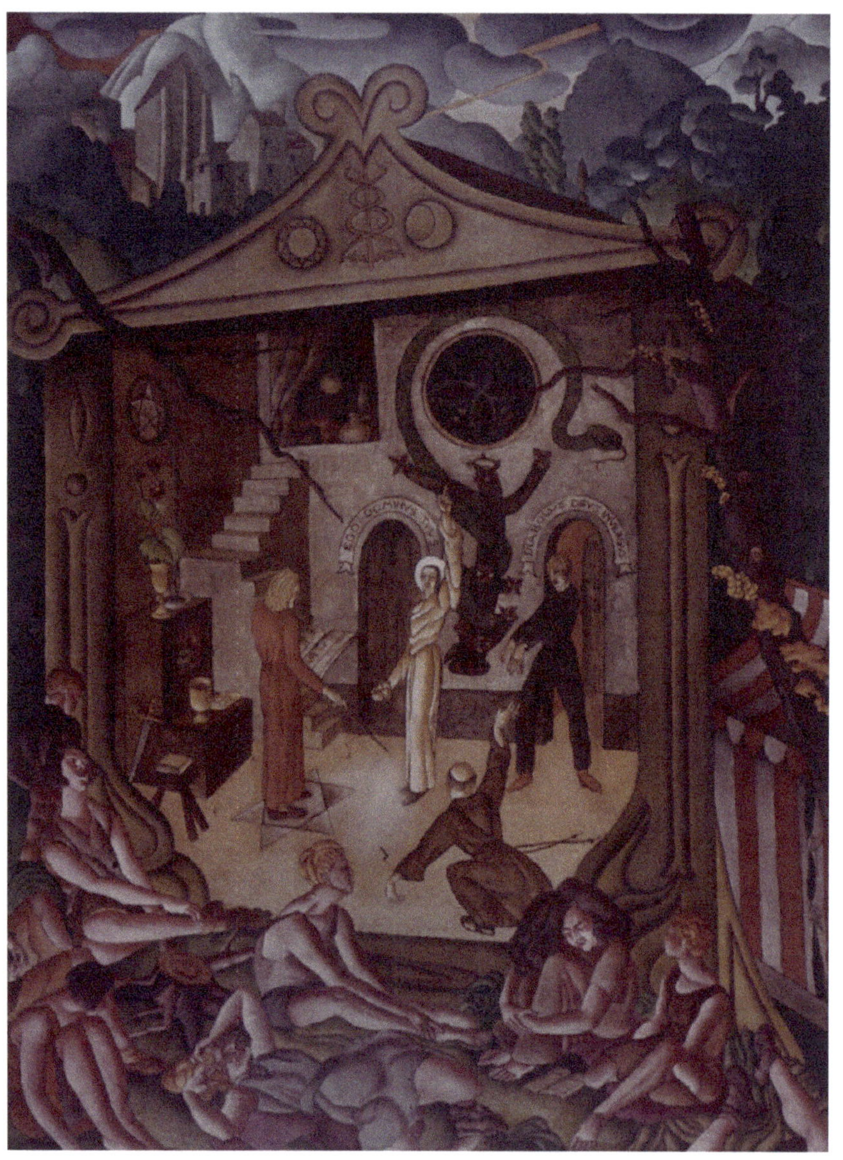

70. *Scene from Marlowe's 'Doctor Faustus'* (1931, oil on canvas, 48 x 36 in., 121 x 90 cm) Government Art Collection

ever this western island under its gull-breasted skies is an outpost of her home.

The Old Man

Only a channel divides the west and east, the near and far; a bar bared at low tide connects them for half the day. When the sea is flowing, the way over is dangerous - a few feet of water and one is swept away by the undertow to drown.

Santa Warna takes root in the west, recognising on the eastward semi-isle a presence older than her own. There on a ferny incline stands the Old Man of Gugh, his roots ringed by bell-heather.

Voice of the clashing sea! Spray and whirlpools, currents and rocks, jaws, teeth and tendrils, a sucking tongue. Ramparts of hurtling water, bastions of wave! She is defended but imprisoned.

He is of stone. Sometimes she turns to gaze at him; but his petrifaction leans another way, in the direction whence boats of the dead once came. Laden with chieftains fallen, they landed their ghostly tribute at his feet. Has the last boat called?

Wishing Well

The coastline of the south is her sanctuary, the southern bay where she beached her coracle is ever calm. Did some of her beads slip into its deeper pools, that they are still to be found at low-water, jewels of glass? Here on the sloping shore the coping and steps of her well are established, a fountain that brings all desires to fruit. Form-taking water, denuded of deathly salt! Water fresh with suspension of unseen qualities, agents of wonder-work. Life of crystal, life of sap and xylem, bast, bone, sinew and blood! Quick of the island, a sweet spray.

Patroness of Wreckers

Night advances in a strategy of clouds, a coppery light from the west turns purplish on the horizon, copper-green inshore. Anadyomene! Saliva whitens the rocks' fangs.

Through soil strangely fruitful springs a giant growth, topping veronica scrub and curtains of fig-marigold, the shrine's triumphant core. Break the ships, Santa Warna, show them a false light! Raise a baffling wind, tear them apart on the pinnacles, split their ribs to shed a rich cargo! Silk and gold of the suntise, dark wine from a distance, knives and ivory, treasure on our beaches in the dawn.

Latent

Peace, a cloudless heaven, a sea clear to the depths. The moment is lasting; is it sunrise or dark? Santa Warna shows her power no more, but hides it, permeating the island serenely afloat. Where does the turf end and Santa Warna begin? Rocks breathe, springs circulate; now is the change complete. She is absorbed in the body of the island, visible to the seer's eye alone.

* A toweely is defined in 'Cornish Earth' in Appendix I as a name for several small wading birds, often the ringed plover, a name which is onamatopoeic from the cries of the bird.

THE CHAIN POEM

(Reproduced from *Transformaction* No.5, 1973)

Is just one more Surrealist method for exploring and exercising the unconscious. Like the *cadavre exquis*, once called 'Ghosts' but much developed in the gouaches of my latest exhibition (Newlyn, 1971), and the 'Heads, Bodies and Legs' used by Surrealist operators to create monsters, it began with the flippancy of a party-game.

The chain-poem may evolve from any number of participants and is thus a step towards the ideal of 'Poetry made by all, not by one'. For practical purposes perhaps four or six 'players' work best together.

The first player writes a line, covers it and passes on the paper to the second player who writes a line, covers it and passes it on to the third and so on. The essence is that no player should be aware, at a conscious level, of what any other player writes. That there is often a striking interchange at unconscious levels (transference of thought, emotion and imagery) will be evident when the script is read aloud at the end of the session.

Each line should be set down with as nearly-complete spontaneity as possible, without deliberation or censorship: compare André Breton's definition of Surrealism as 'Pure psychic automatism — without any preoccupation, aesthetic or moral'.

However, the players may decide before the beginning to erect a scaffolding: the first player's line to take the form of a question; the second's, of an answer and a further question; the third's likewise, and so on. In answering, the players are of course unaware of what the others, as querents, are asking.

Or, with a deeper intention than the old-fashioned 'Consequences', the outline theme may be 'If and Then'. The first player writes a line beginning with the word 'If' while the second player answers it with one beginning with 'Then', in his turn contributing one beginning with 'If', to be answered by the following player's 'Then'. Any number of couples may thus answer each other in turn. Or again, the first player's line opens with 'Do you believe. . .' and the second replies either 'No' or 'Yes', in either case following it with a reason, and then his own 'Do you believe . . .' question.

If the number of players is composed equally of men and women, a sexual tension often produces a heightening of E.S.P. faculties. Threesomes and foursomes can make their characteristic contribution;

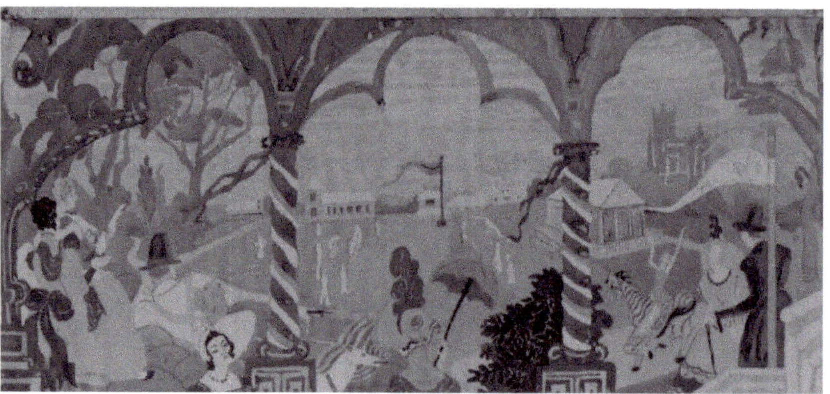

71. *Design for a mural painting for the café at Lord's cricket ground* (c.1930, watercolour and gouache)

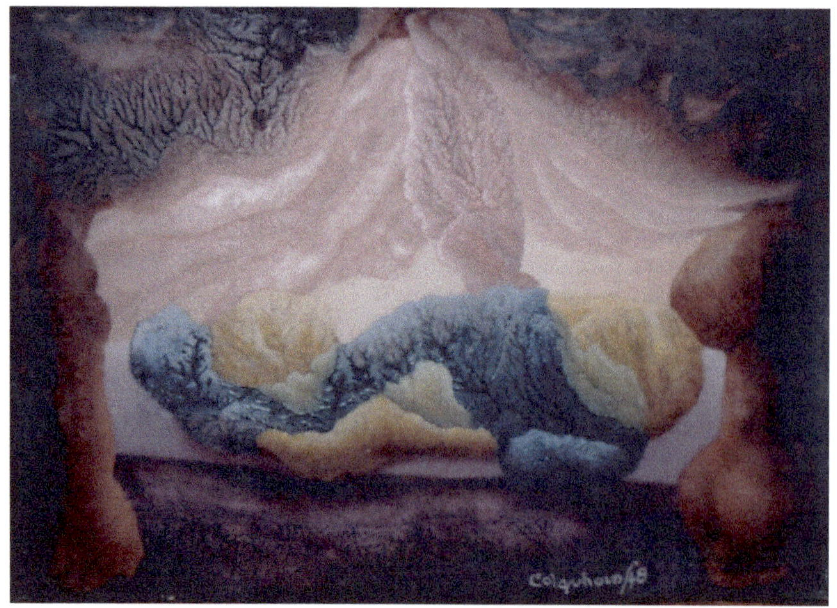

72. *Alcove* (II)
(1948, oil on board, 9 x 13½ in.)

but games conducted by post, though possible, can scarcely provide the same immediacy of impact.

What Ithell Colquhoun is describing, having participated in, is just one of the methods of evading the rationalising behaviour of the conscious mind and giving the unconscious free rein; in fact there had been also a pictorial version where a drawing was attached to one hidden by the paper fold. Some may remember this as a children's game – the 'heads, bodies and tails' which she mentions. The blanket name for such a game was the *cadavre exquis*, the exquisite corpse, from an actual result: 'the exquisite corpse will drink the new wine'.

For future research, a list of titles of all known poems by Ithell Colquhoun is given alphabetically in the Notes (13).

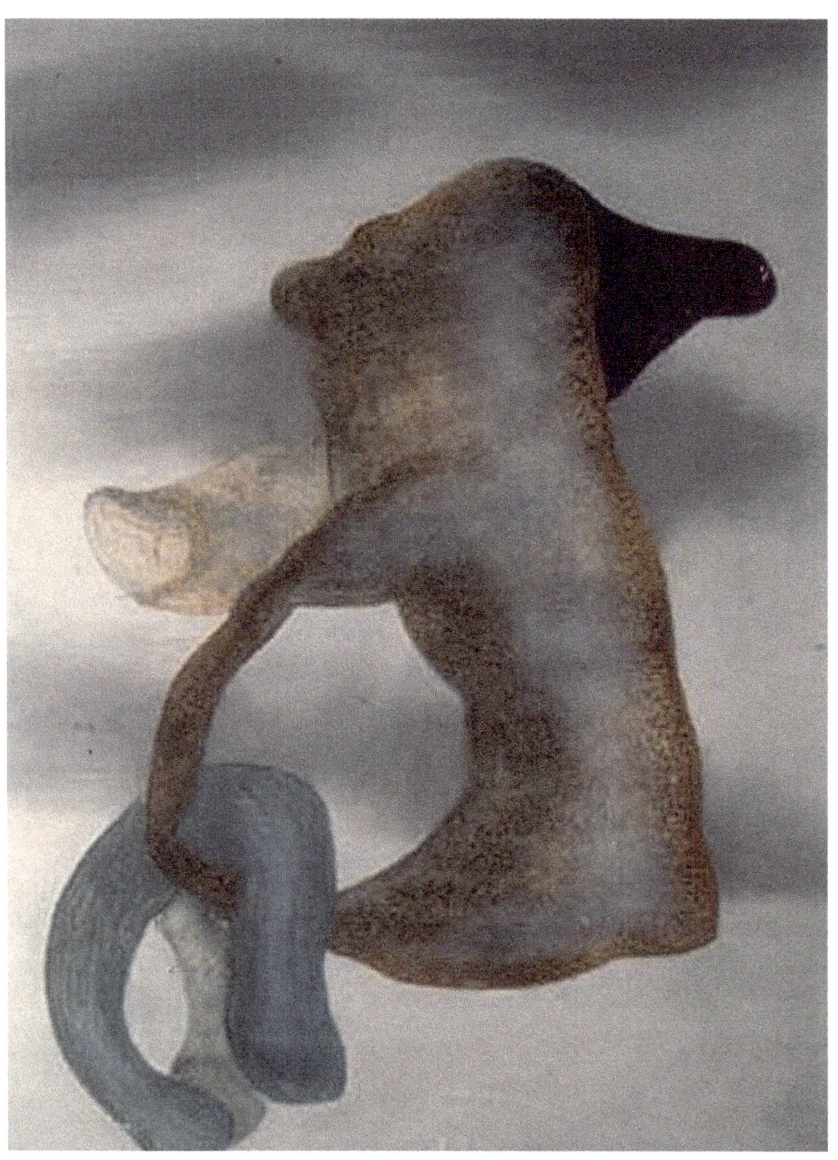

73. *Desert Growth* (c.1938, oil on board, 13 x 9 in., 33 x 22.8 cm)

11 Epilogue

The sixties and the beginning of the seventies saw Ithell Colquhoun creating collages in her compositions, with less and less brushwork as the years advanced and her eyes and hands failed to assist in completing paintings to the high standards she formerly attained. Consequently, the last wide-ranging retrospective viewing of her work, the 1976 exhibition at the Newlyn Orion Gallery, as well as showing earlier work, and many items created by automatic processes (décalcomania, stillomancy, parsemage, fumage, frottage &c), had a large proportion of works produced in collage form, or using the Merz collage system of chance contact with 'rubbish' influenced by Schwitters. Interestingly, there are musical themes in the titles of her late works - *Stockhausen's Poles* and *Messiaen's L'Ascension.*

It must be probable, with hindsight, to judge that both recognition and rating of Ithell eventually suffered from the wartime break with surrealists who followed the well-intentioned guidelines of Mesens, perhaps more than expected through alliance with her temporary partner, Toni del Renzio. Her 30-odd years in Cornwall were extremely

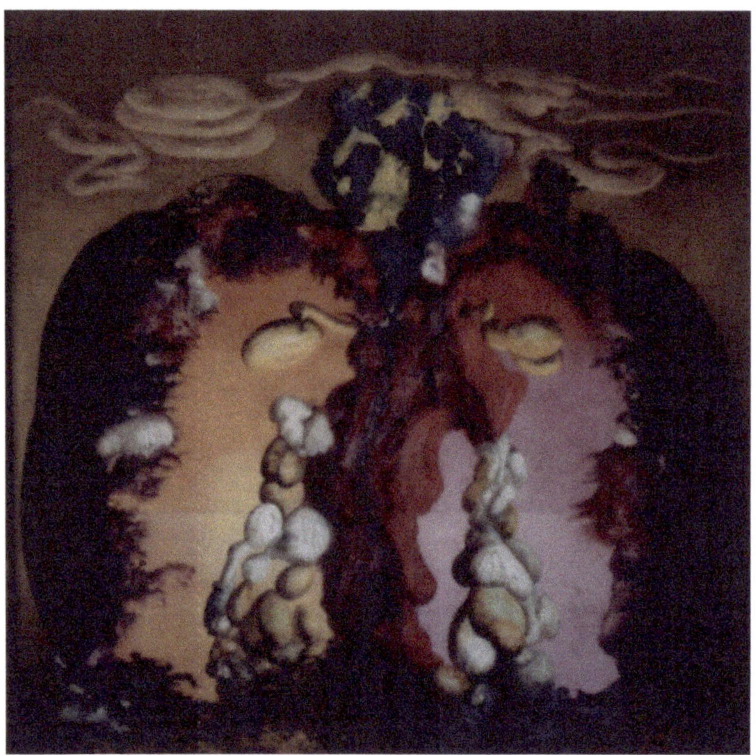

74. *Gorgon*
(1946, oil on board, 22 x 22 in.)

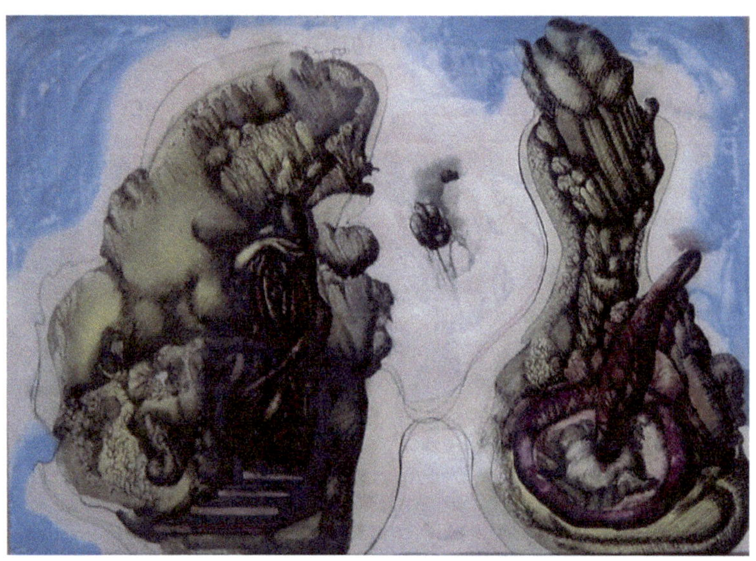

75. *Linked Islands* (II) (c.1950, ink and gouache, 12¼ x 17½ in.)

productive in many directions and should not have affected memory of her as a pioneer of the thirties. A review of her exhibition of flower and plant paintings in 1973 in Penzance pointed out that two years previously she had been included in the London Hamet Gallery's exhibition of British contributions to the surrealism of the thirties and forties. Also that

> She has always ignored prevailing fashions in art and remained true to her beliefs and highly personal style and approach with an integrity that is to be admired. Unfortunately, as a result she has often been under-rated . . .

Many of Ithell Colquhoun's late activities in writing have been described, and can be seen in summary in the appendix bibliography. These include a not untimely reply (1) to the article by Dawn Ades in a 1980 issue of the *Oxford Art Journal* (2), in which reply Ithell needed to remind her of some aspects of her long art career, including her books. The article understated Ithell, dealing with Eileen Agar more fully as 'the only professional woman painter to exhibit at the International Surrealist Exhibition in 1936'. Ithell Colquhoun did not exactly profit from, as an artist already represented in some 80 exhibitions at least by the eighties, the quote by Ades from the 1939 'Living Art' catalogue that she learned to draw at the Slade and 'I have not yet learnt to paint. I am teaching myself how to carve and write . . . My life is uneventful but I sometimes have an interesting dream', while missing out later accomplishments.

Seven years the senior of Ithell, Agar had left the Slade the year before the former had first attended, and her work had matured in time for the 1936 International Exhibition. Also she had been re-admitted by Mesens to the official group in 1939 after an apology, whereas Ithell had remained independent and did not intend to apologise for her principles. Chronology and circumstances are seen to have played a part rather unfortunately for Ithell, irrespective of any comparison of artistic merit between the two artists. It is true that Agar virtually became a surrealist overnight. Roland Penrose and Herbert Read, who selected the artists after visiting Agar's studio in spring 1936 were very impressed with her work. She well deserved early recognition; Ithell missed this important surrealist milestone.

The 1985 exhibition 'British Women Surrealists' confirms this perspective. Showing work by Agar, Bridgewater, Colquhoun, Pailthorpe and Rimmington, the point is made in the catalogue by Jonathan Blond (3):

> That the women artists made such an outstanding contribution to the movement is a tribute not only to their talent as artists but also their spirit and tenacity in pursuing their ideals. Eileen Agar alone among the British women artists has received any degree of recognition. The remaining four artists in this exhibition, despite the power and originality of their images, have been completely neglected.

Against this background it is still disturbing to find, 20 years later, at the start of this millennium, in the book-size catalogue to the Tate Modern exhibition *Surrealism: Desire Unbound* (4), no references to British women surrealists save the photograph with Eileen Agar of the surrealist group in London in 1936; a photograph taken by her at Juan-les-Pins in 1937 of Roland Penrose and Lee Miller on the beach; and an often-repeated version in exhibitions and illustrations of Agar's effective head-wreathed object, *Angel of Anarchy*. It seems that an invisible array of stacked social influence over a long period is stronger than exhibited skills over long periods. Is this imagination or does the statement of Jonathan Blond ring true? This massive luxury catalogue was to be made available in America on the exhibition tour to the Metropolitan Museum of Art in New York in early 2002. Some have visited Cornwall for holiday parties. Ithell went there as a kind of 'nature fundamentalist', taking from and giving back to the land. She was a part of it and it almost a part of her. By then the surrealist *milieu* had lost importance as an aid to recognition, although such would have been influentially welcome.

The exhibition lists 1985-99 in Appendix IIB, around her terminal years, made a late but welcome offering to the public. I think that her long dedication to painting combined with a multiplicity of writing skills and fantastic occult knowledge have been inadequately presented by historians, unaware of this totality within her character.

Many undated poems and prose articles offer difficulty in determining when Ithell ceased creative writing. *Osmazone* (1983) was her last published poetry collection; just previously there had been three poems in the second issue of *Melmoth*. Articles on magic and the occult generally continued up to 1979, with several items in the *Hermetic Journal* (5); and she wrote a Foreword to an edition of *The Rosie Crucian Secrets of John Dee* which her late cousin had originally edited (6).

Her topographical writing was of a high order since she was always a part of the land itself and her sensitive feelings for the 'spirit of place' often inspired her art:

> It is difficult to describe the subdued weirdness that surrounds Braine. The day on which I first came here was grey and chilly; a faint mist which stood over the whale-back of Bartinney Down, just ahead, threatened to descend and cover all; but somehow it held off. One felt that this faintly marked pathway, winding into the west, must soon vanish altogether . . . Here was St. Uny in neglect . . . her strange powers, unused, seemed to hover about the grey hill, the unchannelled water, the rank leaf. A presence that had once been drawn back into soil, weather and plant, to become one of the 'self-born mockers of man's enterprise.' I expressed in an ink drawing called *Interior Landscape* something of this semi-human entity who still pervades the place. (*The Living Stones*, p.58)

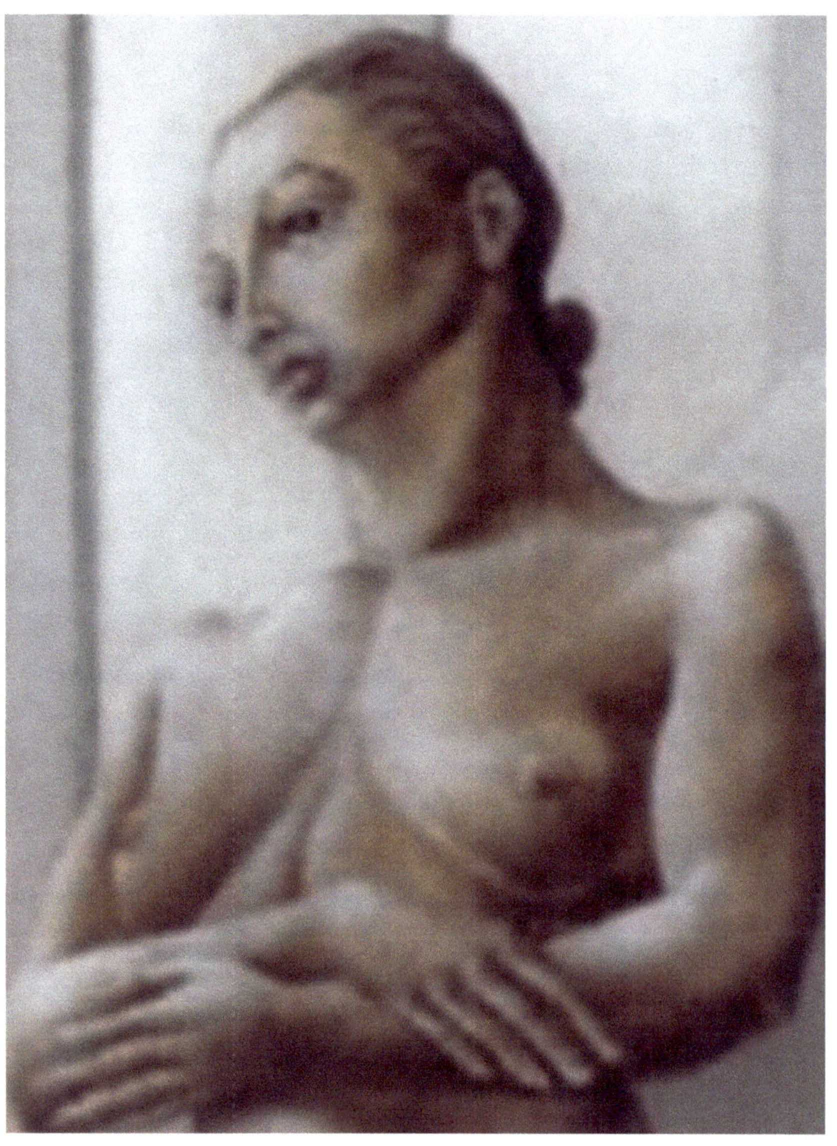

76. *Head* (1931, oil on canvas, 8 x 6 in., 19.5 x 14.7 cm)

The degree of her empathy with the vegetation of the Lamorna valley, as well as with external ancient features, is very noticeable:

> Stirrings of life, expanding spores, limbo of germination, for all you give me, I offer thanks . . . I bathe in you; genius of the fern-loved gully, do not molest me; and may you remain for ever unmolested.

It is important to realise that, although she has transmuted the state of her feelings as readable text, available to the public, Ithell is not romanticising for effect – she did, actually, on a non-physical level of consciousness experience the power behind soil and vegetation, sensing a personalised force, some primitive pre-Christian phenomenon emanating from 'mother-earth'.

So far as she participated as member or guest or was otherwise vitally interested in the outdoor ceremonials of the Cornish and Breton Gorsedds, and those elsewhere, this force aspect and the use of ritual involving the elements of earth, air, fire and water were the attractions. Philosophies involving these elements go back to at least 500 B.C. in many traditions. Yeats had a chessboard representing the four gates to the 'cities' of the elements; and it seems that the squares themselves were connected with standing stones.

Late in life, she was ceremonially ordained as a Priestess of Isis on Sept. 10th, 1977 by the Fellowship of Isis based in Eire, then a 'pioneer' in an organisation which now includes over 22,000 members in 96 countries. Of her Masonic activities, we know little, but in 1976-7 she was still paying annual dues to a Lodge in Maida Vale, no doubt dating from the time she lived in the Hampstead area.

One would like to feel that, if an initial influence in occult interests was her cousin Captain (later Major) E.J.L. Garstin, that later she was closely watched by the shade of another captain, her 18th-century relative Captain John Manley, who once guarded the Cornish coastline in the sea-fencible system. If he could have known his great-great-

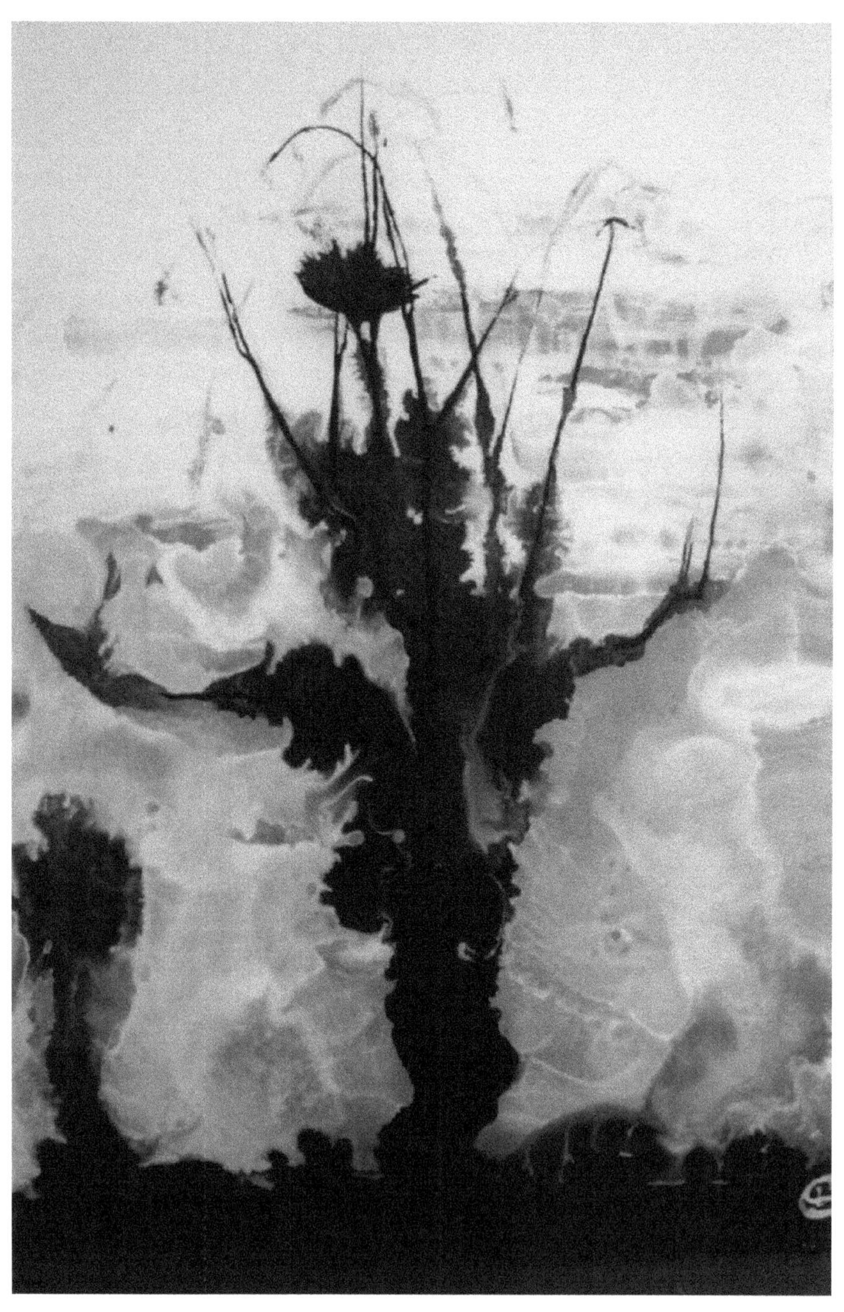

77. *Winter Tree* (1977, enamel on board, 30.3 x 25.3 cm)

grand-daughter, he surely would have approved her ultimate choice of residence in Cornwall. Inherited behaviour from her maternal military grandfather, an Irish V.C., appears irrelevant until it is remembered that this Manley earned this award in the saving of life, not in killing, at great danger to himself; and that his daily task was that of a surgeon's. So each of these distant relatives had protective roles. Then we remember that the Cheltenham College records pointed to her ability in humane subjects; and that in *The Living Stones* she stated, when at Vow Cave 'I am identified with every leaf and pebble, and any threatened hurt to the wilderness of the valley seems to me a rape.'

There was a tribute to Ithell in 1988 by Jo O'Cleirigh in *Meyn Mamvro*, the journal of Celtic Cornwall (7), telling of Ithell's animistic feel for the natural world, especially for stones, wells, trees, wild plants and the sea – her interest in Celtic traditions. Reading *The Living Stones* had led Jo to live in the Lamorna valley. Here she also learned of Ithell's interests in things Egyptian and of her Nile cruise when they chatted. Jo records:

> Two weeks before she died, we visited Ithell for the last time and talked long about the return of the Old Ways in Cornwall . . . That day she tried hard to keep us beyond our time . . .

Sheila Hicks, a close friend of Ithell, companion on many long walks, said that in later years she became frail and lonely, and spent a lot of time in bed with her adored cat Ginger for company. (In the 1990 listing of items then in National Trust possession, reference D/119 is of *Ginger Cat*, a painting in watercolour and enamel.) Towards the end of her life, having bequeathed her Paul 'Stone Cross' cottage and its contents of many paintings, collages and drawings to the Trust, she had moved into the Menwinnion Country House Hotel, then possibly a residential home for the elderly (a now relinquished role) in the Lamorna Valley.

Following admission to the West Cornwall Hospital in spring 1987 and later in the autumn of that year to the City Hospital, she died from heart failure at the Menwinnion on April 11th, 1988. Her friend Sheila Cavell-Hicks was with her at the time. I think that her cottage was sold privately and not via the National Trust by the terms of her will, although the contents were stored, passing to the Trust. Information about this is unimportant now, but it was extraordinarily difficult to discover what happened. It may have passed to her brother who sold it on without contents. Speculation as to whether all the contents eventually reached safe storage near Llanhydrock under National Trust ownership may be made, but the works were all carefully itemized in the listing referred to earlier.

Her will included bequests to other relatives who could not be contacted. The Tate Gallery archives received some art items, after legal interpretation of her will, and they also hold many of her literary effects and collection of books, which were transferred there after her death, during the illness of her literary executor, Derek Stanford.

It seems that, for those sensitive enough, part of Ithell was always present in the landscape she loved. One of her friends, Clare, who visited her when she was in hospital and later at the Menwinnion, wrote how in her younger days she roamed across fields and through lanes and woods, saying how deeply she loved the ancient earth and the ancient places, where her feet retraced footprints of older days. Literally, although sometimes suspicious of the motives of the more worldly human being, Ithell often found herself in a state of loving energy within the Cornish landscape itself. Clare wrote a poem 'To Ithell' - part of it reads

> So, you have gone: you rose and left
> quite suddenly, so now, bereft,
> we offer thanks - for all you were
> and all you wrote that helped to stir
> so many hearts and opened eyes

79. *Exposed on the Mountains of the Heart* (undated, oil on card, 25.8 x 38.3 cm)

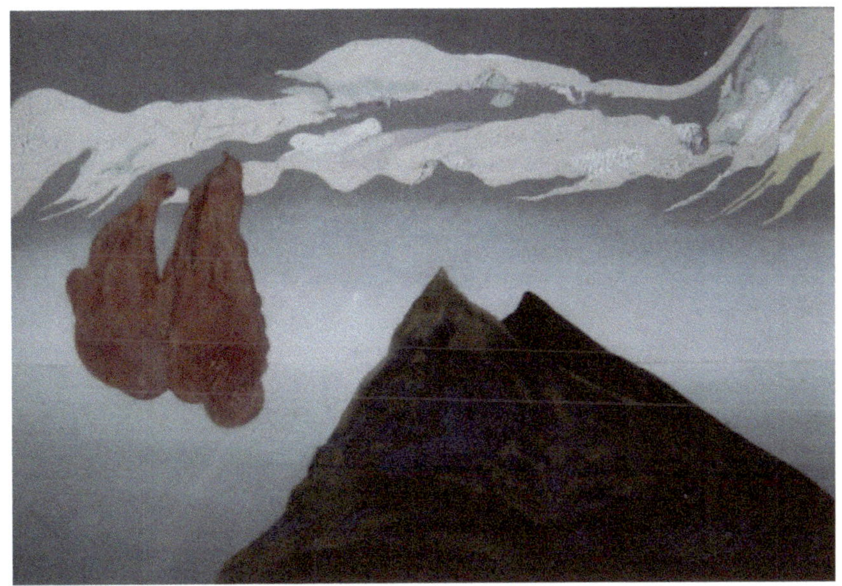

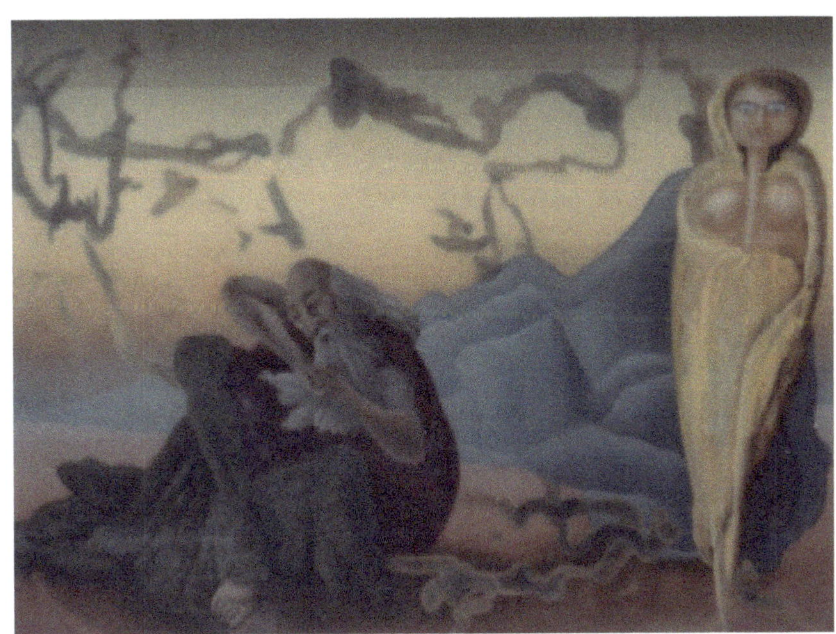

80. *Temptation of St. Anthony* (1962, oil on board, 57.0 x 89.5 cm)

that never saw before. . . stars, skies,
woods streams and marsh, moors - open space -
where nature rules; a brooding place
of standing stones and circles, where
you lived and loved and tasted rare
Lamorna peace . . .

You could ask about Ithell today of those who still remember her, and many will tell you much the same. It is as true as the tail-feathers of a bird of passage. And, as I have omitted to mention it, one of her bequests was a donation to the Noise Abatement Society!

Appendix I Cornish Earth

From a copy MS in handwritten-amended typescript for the September 1971 article in *The Cornish Review*.

'CORNISH EARTH'. A GLOSSARY OF PHRASES, WORDS AND BELIEFS BY ITHELL COLQUHOUN

Phrases

A brown voice or heavy voice: A deep or masculine voice; a voice of feminine timbre is said to be 'blue'.

As bad as John Stone: Anyone who indulges in zany humour. John Stone was a little man who lived by a stream. John Stone's 'shote' was his water-chute. He lived in Newlyn about the mid-19th century. His house, opposite Primrose Place, has since been demolished. He seems the Penwith equivalent of Nastradin Hodga (the Mullah Nasr'udin). There are many stories of him. When a doctor directed him to take some medicine in water, he drank it neat, standing in a full bath-tub. When queuing at a station ticket-office, he heard a girl ahead say 'Nancegollan, single'. When his turn came he shouted out 'John Stone, married !' When once carrying a sack of potatoes he was overtaken by a carter who offered him a lift, so he climbed in. 'Why don't you put down your sack, John?' asked the carter. 'You offered a lift to me, not to my sack,' was the reply, and John continued to carry the sack over his shoulder. (A variant records that he kept the load on his lap, saying this was 'to spare the horse'.) Another time he was helping a builder who was on the roof and warned him 'don't come down the ladder as I've taken it away!' A corresponding character from the Camborne area was Agie (Agar) Russell.

Down on his (or her) nerves: In a nervous or neurotic state.

Fat as a truff: Very fat. People say they don't know what a 'truff' is, though they use the expression.

Going to coming, like the old woman's butter: Said of anything that takes a long time - an old woman not having the strength to churn butter quickly.

Head'n chief: 'He (or she) wants to be 'head'n chief' describes an ambitious bossy person.

If you will: If you like.

I wouldn't do it for a gold watch: I wouldn't do it for anything.

Kiss my arse! (pronounced 'me ass') : 'Tell me another!'. Disbelief or rejection.

Like Billy Tink: Swiftly, violently; euphemism for 'like stink'.

Like rats pissing on hot iron: Sound of the violin-playing of a certain lady as described by a Newlyn fisherman.

Like Tom Rowe's mouth (pronounced 'Rosmuth'): Exactly right, fitting exactly. Tom Rowe, finding the meat at a feast rather tough, cut it into pieces which would just fit his mouth.

Like a turf-rick toad: A woman with a wide, flat figure. Before coal was generally available, turf for fuel was cut with a special tool from the then-extensive moors of Cornwall - as it still is today in tthe Gaeltacht of Ireland - and stacked in a rick beside the house. Toads sheltering in the crevices between the turves would become flattened out. See *Tubble.*

Lousy as a keet: Filthy, dirty, smelly, verminous. See *Keet.*

Nicknames: Many villagers were known by nicknames, such as 'Double Dick' for Richard Richards. There was 'Cake' for a fisherman who ate a slice of cake before a meal incase he should miss the meal; 'Parrot Nose'; and 'Bull-Back' for a man with hunched shoulders.

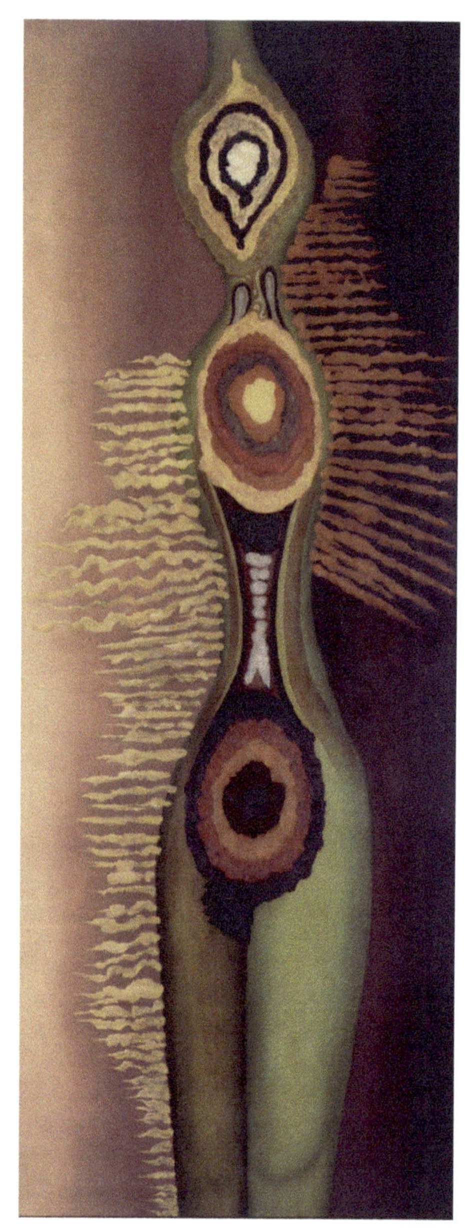

80. *Autumnal Equinox* (1949, oil on canvas, 81 x 32 in., 206 x 81 cm)

'Rattle-Pence' was a man employed in the building of the Wolf lighthouse who would rattle the coins in his pocket to pretend that he was rich. A man named James was known as 'Jimmy Donkey' (pronounced 'Dunkey') because of the rough, practical jokes he used to play, such as blocking up a neighbour's chimney, or nailing up a woman's door when she was thought to be entertaining her 'fancy-man'. Fifty years ago there was more disorder and less police activity than to-day, villagers tending to settle scores amongst themselves without resort to litigation. The use of nicknames suggests a fellow-feeling between neighbours which has almost vanished - everyone now likes to be called 'Mr'.

Not behind the door (or gate): Forward, cheeky, usually with a sexual implication.

Not quite exactly or Not striking twelve: Half-witted, 'simple'.

Nothing but muck and stink: Anything considered worthless or unnecessary.

M'Nabs: A name for the hare; MacNab pronounced in the Irish way with 's' added. Also may refer to the magpie (*Pica rustica*) or any kind of animal or bird thought to be wily.

Sour as a wig: Looking cross or resentful.

Take the paint off her and she i'n't no more 'ansome than a frying-pan of arseholes: A lady whose looks you don't admire.

Terms of abuse: *The heller! The old stink! The dirty hound!*

Terms of endearment: *Dear beauty, my beauty, my bird (or burd ?), my cock, my flower, my handsome, my lovely, my lover, my robin.*

The body of a cow on the legs of a sparrow: A plump woman with spindly legs.

The Devil shits luck for some but when he comes to me, he's hardbound: Said

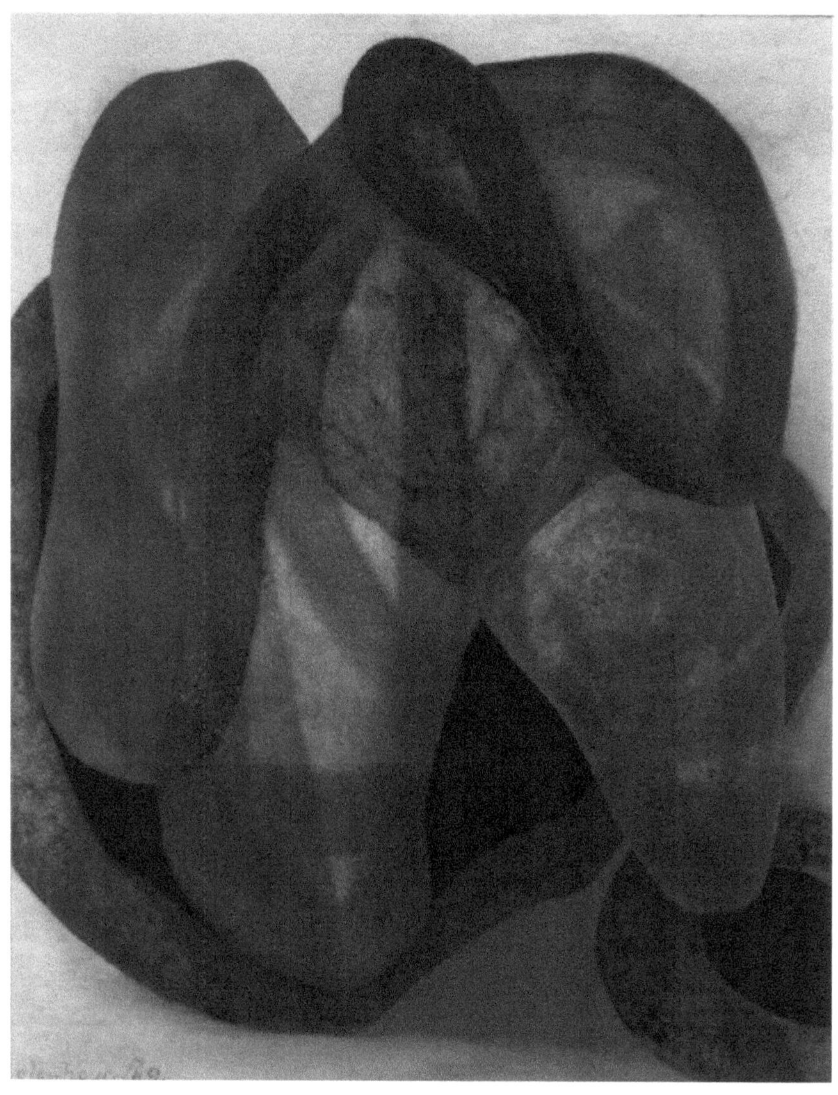

81. *Desert Growth* (I) (1949, oil on board, 12½ x 10 1/8 in., 31.8 x 25.5 cm)

in envy of someone who has inherited money - compare the Freudian equivalence of money and excrement.

There's that upon it: There's that about it.

The sun is cracking the hedges: Very hot weather.

To break one's English: To swear, to use bad language.

To be about it :To be doing it.

To die like starlings: To die like flies.

To have the fault: To be to blame.

To turn around like the cat in the pan: To change one's opinion or actions, usually for the worse; to upset arrangements; to quarrel. The origin of this saying does not bear speculation.

Words

APPLE-BEE: n., wasp; it appears when the first apples are ripening.

ARRISH: n., stubble, stubble-field; often used collectively.

BELKING: verbal adj., belching, hiccuping.

BELONG TO: vb., ought to, reckon to.

BELVING: verbal adj., bellowing (of a bull).

BLEATING: verbal adj., lowing (of a cow, especially when separated from a calf).

BLOND UP: vb., 'chum up', become friendly with.

BREAK AWAY: vb., clear up; referring to cloudy weather.

BROWSSE: n., dry undergrowth; vowel sound as in 'cow'; cognate with Fr. *Broussaile*.

BUCCA: n., scare-crow; cognate with Ir. *Pouka* ?

BULLAUN: n., sloe; seems to be the Ir. *Bullán*, a small rock-basin, but why applied to the sloe? See SLONE.

BURN: vb., wither by a sea-wind; vegetation is said to be 'burnt' when it shows brown after a sea-gale.

BUSH-SPARROW: n., hedge-sparrow (*Accentor modularis*). See HEDGE.

CAG : n., stomach.

CAGGLE: n., filthy mess. Also as vb., 'to be caggled with shit'.

CAUDLE: n., mess, muddle. See KILTER and RUBBYDULLYAN.

CAUNTZ: n., granite paving-stone.

CHUCK: vb., choke. 'You're either chucked or starved' means you have either too much or too little.

CLIBBY: adj., tacky, clinging; cognate with 'clip', also perhaps with 'clobber' (as n.).

CLOAM: n., earthenware, crockery.

CLUNK: vb., swallow.

COMB: n., ridge or crest in lines of ploughing. See VOR.

COMMEND: vb., agree with; I commend you, I agree with you; you're in the right.

CROWST: n., snack; vowel-sound as in 'cow'; originally splits and unsweetened tea taken about 10 a.m. and 3 p.m.

DAWNY: adj., damp; like dew at dawn (?)

DOOLALLEY-TAPS: adj. phrase, dotty, 'touched'. 'To be doolalley-taps', to be a bit crazy. See KYTIE and *Not quite exactly*. [This was around in the army environment in India, probably referring to the state of personnel entering a sanatorium in Deolali. Maybe adapted to the Cornish via this route. The meaning was the same. E.R.]

FARM-PLACE or TOWN-PLACE: n., small hamlet, farm with outbuildings and labourers' cottages; equivalent to the Irish 'town-land', *Baillé*.

FENCE: n., hedge - in the English sense, a Cornish hedge being always constructed with stones. See HEDGE.

FITCHER: n., terrier - the breed once used for rabbitting with a ferret or 'fitch'.

FITTY: adj., convenient, proper.

FLAG-STONE: n., large flat stone set in front of the SLAB (q.v.) to catch sparks.

FOO-FOO JOINT or FOO-FOO VALVE: n., penis. [foo-foo (Caribb.) is also a dumpling made from plantain (or 'Adam's fig') E.R.]

FRIGHTENED: verbal adj., surprised; 'I shouldn't be frightened if . . .' , 'I shouldn't be surprised if . . .'

GALLIWO: n., freak; used of hermaphrodite or sexually imperfect livestock but extended to anyone considered odd.

GARM: vb., howl; cats are said to 'garm' before they die.

GEEVE: vb., exude dampness or stickiness, e.g. of condensation on a wall. (Geevor Mine - the mine with the sweating walls?) Hence GEEVY, adj. Sometimes pronounced as 'give'.

GRAMMASO: n., wood-louse; rhymes to 'cow'.

GRASS-STONE: n., granite of poor quality.

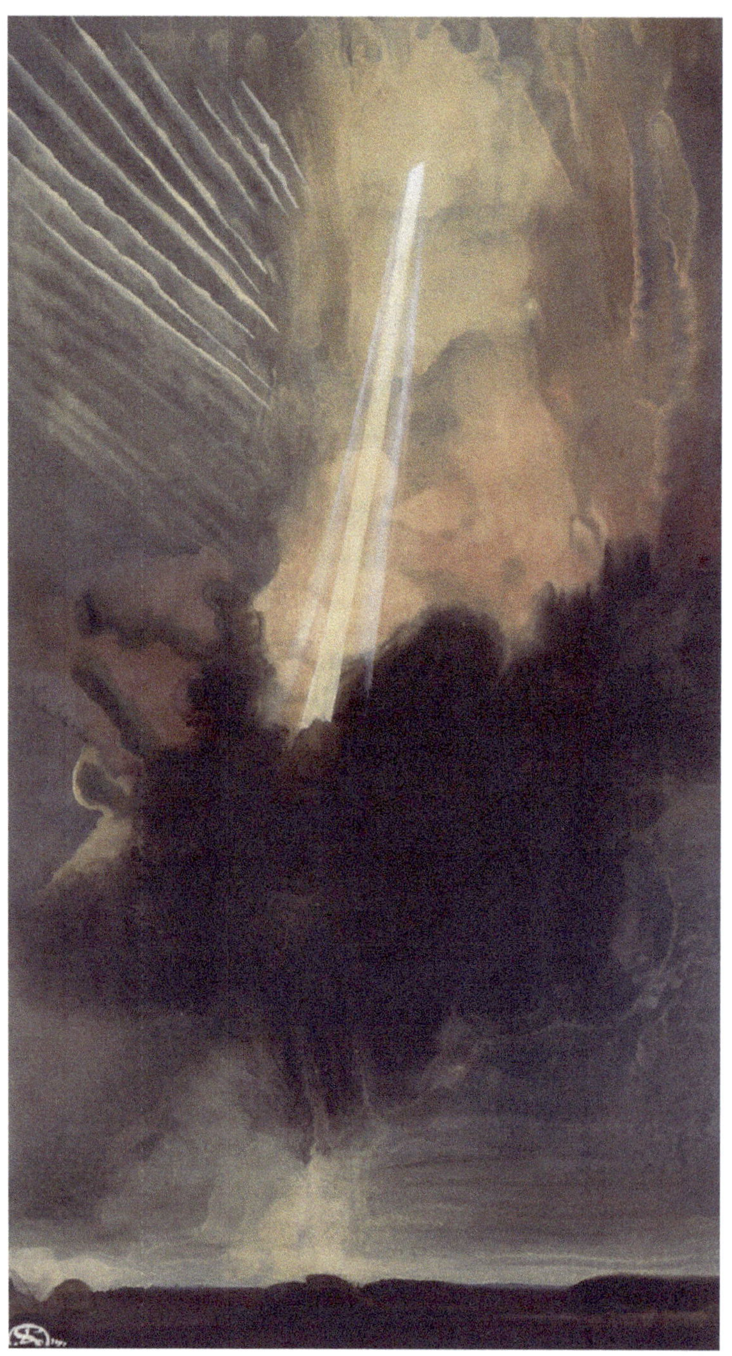

82. *L'Ascension* (1974, mixed media on paper laid down on board, 41¾ x 23½ in., 106 x 60 cm)

GREN: n., snare, wire-trap; hence, to go GRENNING (vb.) for rabbits.

HEBBA: n., loud shouting, cognate with 'hubbub' ? Huers are said to have raised a HEBBA when they sighted a shoal of fish. See HUER.

HEDGE: n., bank of earth and stones, sometimes topped with vegetation used as a boundary. See FENCE.

HOVES: n.pl., rain-drippings from a roof (old houses were built without a gutter.) Pronounced as two syllables. See LAUNDER.

HOW? : prep., Why? How don't you leave it? 'Why don't you leave it?'

HOYIT: n., snipe (*Gallinago caelistis*); onamatopoeic, from bird's cry.

HUER: n., a sentinel posted in former times on a headland above the sea to watch for incoming shoals of pilchards &c. When these were sighted, the HUER would shout loudly to warn the fishermen of the neighbourhood. Cognate with 'Hue and cry' ? See HEBBA.

HUME: vb., used passively, to be dug up, to be brought up (from the ground); used in a derogatory sense. Cognate with 'humus'?

JAFFLE: vb., gobble, eat ravenously.

JEALOUS: adj., suspicious, I'm jealous that he tore my fishing-net, 'I suspect that', &c.

JOUSTER: n., travelling fish-salesman, in former times with a horse-drawn cart. Vowel sound as in 'cow'.

KEET: n., described as a pale grey flattish insect, something like a wood-louse (see GRAMMASOW) but longer and with a pointed tail which emits a bad smell. (I cannot identify this creature.)

KELLAS: n., stone chipped from Blue Elvan rock.

KILTER: n., mess, confusion; in a kilter, 'in a state of chassis'.

KING-CROWNER: n., the name of a large butterfly said to be plentiful in Penwith some fifty years ago - perhaps the Monarch butterfly (*Anosia Plexippus*) or possibly one of the larger Fritillaries, described as red-brown and black with white spots and much larger than a Red Admiral. It flew by day. (The incidence of the Monarch butterfly varies much from year to year and from one locality to the other, but was it ever plentiful?)

KISKEY: n., kex.

KITTY-BAGS: n.pl. leggings for farm-workers which used to be improvised from flour-bags.

KYTIE: adj., dotty, 'touched' ; Newlyn people say Mousehole people are kytie. See DOOLALLEY TAPS and *not quite exactly*.

LAG: vb., cover, usu. with mud or anything dirty ; same word as to 'lag' water-pipes.

LAUNDER: n., gutter on a building. See HOVES.

LEAK: vb., drip; often used of laundry. Also 'sweating-leaking'.

LEW: adj., sheltered ; cognate with 'leeward', 'leward'.

LURGY: adj., lazy, layabout; hard 'g'.

MAKE-ON: vb., attack.

MAUN: n., large basket; rhymes to 'dawn'.

MAY: n., sycamore-tree (*Acer Pseudo-Platanus*) - not the hawthorn; 'to bring in the may' (or mays) on May-day refers to the flowering branches of sycamore, &c. Hawthorn (*Cratoegus oxyacantha*) would not be in blossom on May 1st.

MONEY-QUIBBER: n., one who 'quibbles' over money, haggler.

MORES: n.pl., roots.

MOW: n., corn-stack; rhymes to 'cow'. Hence MOWIE, n., stack-yard.

MULK: n., fool; vowel-sound as in 'bull'.

MURRIAN: n., ant.

OISEY: adj., hoarse, wheezy, onamatopoeic, cognate with 'groise', a gob of phlegm?

ORGAN : n., pennyroyal (Metha pulegium).

ORGANS: n.pl., haws, hawthorn-berries, fruit of *Cratoegus oxyacantha.*

PEETH :n., well; the Cornish *pyth.*

PENNY-CAKES: n.pl., navelwort (*Cotyledon umbilicus*) - the names refer to the shape of the leaves.

PINEY: n., pine-cone.

PLANCHEON: n., wooden ceiling which is the floor of the room above, cognate with Fr. *plancher.*

PLUM: adj., stupid, unenterprising; soft as a ripe plum? Or perhaps cognate with 'plummet' in the sense of obstructive weight?

PROUD: adj., showy, stand-offish, always used pejoratively - by others in the neighbourhood. Mousehole people are said to be 'stinkin' proud'.

PURVINS (PURVIINGS ?): n.pl., cuttings of cloth left over from sewing. It was usual for a sewing-woman to visit outlying farms by the day. See TIFFLINS.

PUT-GOING: vb., used passively, put down, killed - chiefly of domestic animals.

PYKE: n., two-pronged fork for lifting hay &c.

QUAIL: vb., used passively, wither, wilt; usually referring to greenstuff – 'the lettuces are quailed'.

RATTLE-CAN-STAVE: n., hoyden.

RUBBIDULLYAN or RUBBIDULGEY (soft 'G'): n., confusion; all in a rubbidullyan, 'all at sixes and sevens', very untidy. Mr. Giles's association is with a Zulu word meaning a wild dance accompanied by the noise of drums. Onamatopoeic, it would seem to date from the Zulu wars?

SCRAW: n., scratch, graze.

SHOTE: n., chute (of water).

SHOWL: n., shovel, usu. with a long handle; vowel sound as in 'cow'.

SILVERFINCH: n., chaffinch (?)

SKAT: vb., break; cognate with 'shatter'.

SKETTY: adj., poor, thin; used of skimmed milk.

SLAB: n., old-fashioned kitchen-range, coal-burning and often surrounded by decorative cast-iron and polished brass. Most have now been replaced by modern cookers. See FLAG-STONE.

SLAG: n., drizzle, whence SLAGGY, adj., drizzling.

SLIGH : adj., ill, sickly.

SLOAK: vb., draw away, drain away.

SLON : n., sloe, fruit of blackthorn (*Prunus spinoza*); see BULLAUN.

SMEECH: n., sooty smoke.

SPALL: n., granite stone chipped from the block so irregularly as to be unsuitable for building , and only used in hedges. Rhymes to 'Mall'.

SPLAT: n., patch of ground without herbage; cognate with Fr. *plât*?

SQUIDDLES: n.pl., nervous restlessness, 'the fidgets'; she's got the squiddles and goes on like a hoyit, 'She's too nervy to settle to anything but darts from one place to another like the zig-zag flight of a snipe'.

STANK: vb., go, go about.

STREAM: vb., rinse; used by laundry.

STRIVE DOWN: vb., hector, overbear.

STROATHER: n., hurry; also as vb., 'to stroather along'.

SY: n., scythe.

TAP: vb., sole (a shoe); hence TAP, n., from the cobbler's tapping of nails during repair?

TEAKL: n., kettle; 'tea-kettle'?

TEASY: adj., irritable, snappish.

TEEL: vb., plant, plant out.

THWART: adj., cross-eyed, squinting.

TIE: n., mattress, usually a feather-bed.

TIFFLINS (or TIVLINGS ?): n.pl., ends of cotton thread. See PURVINS.

TIZ-WHIZ: n., toy windmill; onamatopoeic.

TOMMY-HOOK: n., tool for hedging; a SHOWL (q.v.) with a spike or hook at the back.

TOWEELY: n., a name for several small wading birds, often the ringed plover (*Aegialitis hiaticula*); onamatopoeic from the birds' cries.

TUBBAN or TUPPEN: n., clod or tuft of earth and grass.

TUBBLE: n., tool for cutting turf as fuel; this was piece-work, the average output being 1000 turves per day. Cognate with TUBBAN?

UGLY: adj., angry, violent.

UP : prep., on; I had my new dress up, 'I had my new dress on'.

URGE: vb., retch.

VINNY: adj., with black hairs in the outer layers of an animal's coat; in cows, perhaps caused by a Jersey strain in the breed. Farmers used to like at least one vinny cow in a herd as they were considered good milkers.

VOR: n., furrow or a line between rows of plants; a ploughed field consists of alternate VOR and COMB, or furrow and crest. See COMB.

WET-LEAKING: adj., very wet; see LEAK.

WIDDEN: n., smallest pig of a litter; equivalent to 'cadydwen', 'barling', 'blacktopper' &c in other dialects.

WISHT: adj., pale, pinched; cognate with 'washed-out' ?

Folk-beliefs

BLACKBERRIES should not be eaten later than Paul Feast (the Sunday nearest to Oct. 10th; after that, the Piskeys make water on them. A variant says that it is the keets who do this. (See KEET.) The date also varies: beyond the parish of Paul, it is given as Sept. 29th (St. Michael being a frequent surrogate for the Sun-god.)

BULLANS, i.e. sloes, should be picked when ripe and covered with sugar in an airtight jar. Opened at Christmas, they will have made a wine 'which can be used to check diarrhoea'. (True.)

A CAT frisking warns of 'a gale o'wind coming'.

CHAMOMILE (*Matricaria chamomilia*) flowers, dried and infused as a tisane are good for colds.

COAL is lucky; if you find a piece lying in the road, dance three times round it for good luck. This belief is interesting in that it must have developed recently, coal not being generally available in Cornwall until last [19th] century, when only the better-off people could afford it - others were lucky to find it by chance.

DAVIDSON'S HUT is a small shed-like building a few steps up a lane nearly opposite the Penlee lifeboat-station. It commemorates the almost forgotten poet John Davidson (1857-1909) who drowned himself off these shores. When the body was found it was dressed in women's clothes. According to a recent folk tradition it rested here for some hours before being taken to Penzance.

THE DEAD are 'all around us'; they are felt to participate in a life diffused into the atmosphere of the place where they lived and died. When people recount, for instance, the drolleries of John Stone, he is near and enjoying them too. But there is little faith in a personal immortality – 'we shall never see them again' is said of one's departed relations. A depersonalised continuance is envisaged - we have lived on earth before and will do so again. These intimations - they are scarcely convictions - derive from a stratum of consciousness deeper than the Nonconformist or Low-Anglican Christianity which is usually professed (if anything is) at a conscious level.

THE DEVIL'S DRINKING TROUGH is a piece of granite about eighteen inches long hollowed out to form a trough, which lies near the entrance to an old farm on the way to Tregadgwith. The Devil is said to drink from this each evening at dusk, and the air about the entrance-gate to be always cold. The Devil seems to be imagined almost as a domestic animal.

ELDER (*Sambucus nigra*) is the piskey's tree. It is lucky to have one growing in your garden. An infusion of dried elder leaves is good for chest-complaints. (True.)

THE GHOST at the cross-road known as 'The Ring and Thimble' (between Paul and Newlyn) is that of a man who was cruel to his hounds and now haunts the spot himself in the form of a huge hound, at midnight and at the full of the Hunter's Moon. More than one person has told me that they have seen a black creature, not quite a dog but more the size of a donkey, in the hedgerows nearby. There is a valley at the back-end of Lamorna where, according to a Mousehole fisherman, 'you will meet your ancestors'.

GREEN is the fairies' colour and so it is (or was) considered unlucky to wear it except in special circumstances. (See PAIN.) Shopkeepers in Penzance used to find it difficult to sell a green dress.

GUISE-DANCING and GUISERS - pronounced 'geezers' (hard 'g'). Half a century ago, around Christmas and New Year, guise-dancing was still spontaneously practised by youngsters, who blackened their faces and dressed up in any fantastic rags they could lay hands on. Often there was no pretence of performing a 'St.George and the Dragon' play; the guisers just pranced and shouted, the occasion being taken as a time of license when destructive fooling was allowed (or at least endured). The wilder gangs used to terrify their neighbourhood, damaging gardens, gates, and windows, even smashing the contents of a house if they could gain entry, their disguise making identification difficult. (Compare the custom of 'the Lord of Misrule'.) Others less violent would go from house to house begging for sweets or pennies. To-day, the custom, its rougher elements suppressed, survives as mumming when fostered by Old Cornwall Societies.

HORSE-SHOES are lucky; if you find one, fasten it to your door with the ends upward.

MAGPIES bring bad luck; if you see one you should spit. If you see two, spit twice.

'MAY-MONDAY' is an unlucky day on which to begin anything, especially something difficult or tricky. May 1st falling on a Monday would mark the congruence of a Sun-date, i.e. Beltane (cross-quarter day between the Spring Equinox and the Summer Solstice) with the weekly day of the Moon.

THE MONUMENT MEADOW. On Nov. 26th, 1793, a Mousehole man named William Trewawas murdered a neighbour of his, Mrs. Martha Bluett, as she was going home after dark from Paul Churchtown. He waylaid the elderly widow and robbed her in a meadow on the east side of the road linking the two places - at that date probably no more than a track. Some say she was returning from a tour of inland vilages where she sold salt for curing, as the custom then was. As he ran down the hill with the money she called out that she had recognised him, whereupon he turned back and cut her throat. Some children at Paul claimed to have seen what happened, so the landlord of the King's Arms brought them to an identification parade of the local men. When it came to his turn, Trewawas tried to bluff his way out, saying to a little girl, 'I suppose you'll say I'm guilty, my dear ?' and she replied, 'yes, you are.' Trewawas was arrested and the next year was hanged at Launceston gaol. Thc then Lord St. Levan, who owned the land bordering the lane, set up a monument consisting of a granite cross of the 'Latin' type but with the ends of the arms and the head rounded, and a plaque at their junction inscribed with a warning about 'Thou shalt do no murder.' Next day the lettering was all but obliterated, probably by relations of Trewawas who wanted the incident forgotten. People still living remember as children listening at the cross 'to hear Martha Bluett scream'; and many were nervous of passing the monument at night. Finally in the early Twenties of this [20th] century the R.D.C. decided to demolish it, covering the place where it stood with large blocks of granite. It is said that nothing will grow over these, and in fact there is far less vegetation here than elsewhere in the hedge. Though the fact seems to be that Mrs. Bluett was a Mousehole woman, being related to the celebrated Dolly Pentreath, there is another story that she lived alone in a little house next to the hedge of what is still called 'the Monument Meadow' though now a school playing-field. The remains of a small building at the spot became easily visible since clearing the undergrowth in 1971.

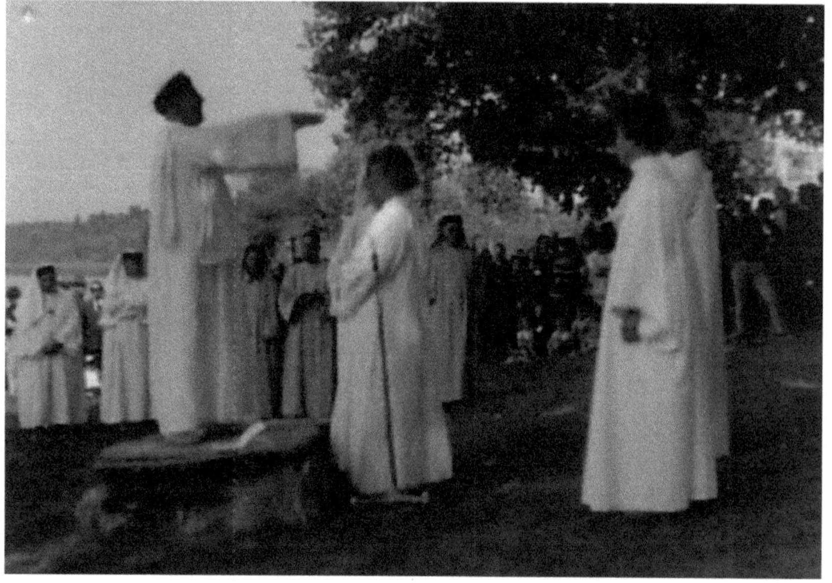

83. Ithell at Breton Gorsedd, Paimpont, summer 1964, being received by the Grand Druid

Appendix IIA

Artwork

Dimensions in the following lists follow standard practice of height preceding width. Any automatic techniques mentioned such as décalcomania, fumage, stillomancy, entoptic graphomania, parsemage &c are described in the 'Mantic Stain' and 'Children of the Mantic Stain' (see Appendix IIC : Bibliography). The Newlyn and Orion galleries in Newlyn and in Penzance, respectively, came under shared management for a period, and were known as the Newlyn Orion Galleries. The artist's 1973 exhibition of flower paintings was in Penzance, but her larger 1976 retrospective exhibition referred to as 'Penzance, Newlyn Orion Gallery' was in the gallery at Newlyn. '1990 listing' refers to an inventory taken in that year of Ithell Colquhoun's works stored with the National Trust, Cornwall, to whom she bequeathed them. The symbol (s) refers to dimensions seen of a work within its surround or frame and is restricted to details in the 1990 listing. Selected inscriptions on the reverse are given in quotations. Public holding sites are given where known. AD = auction data. It is not always possible to determine whether AD titles are given or known; these should be interpreted with caution where appearing in the 'known' title list.

DATED : KNOWN TITLES

1921

1. ***Flowers*** : c.1921, watercolour, 21.8 x 16.8 cm. 'Margaret Colquhoun, age 15'. 1990 listing.

2. ***Nature*** : c.1921, watercolour, 17.4 x 15.8 cm. 'Margaret Colquhoun, age 15'. 1990 listing. Depicts finches at their nest.

3. ***Washing Day*** : c.1921, ink, 14.5 x 21.5 cm. Illustration study 'Peggy Colquhoun, age 15'. 1990 listing.

4. ***A Windy Day*** : c.1921, ink, 19 x 18.5 cm. Illustration study 'Margaret Colquhoun, age 15'. 1990 listing.

1925

1. ***Mount Errigal from Cashelnagor*** : c.1925, pencil, 22.9 x 14 cm. 1990 listing.

1929

1. ***The Four Elements*** : c.1929, oil on board, 28 x 22 in., 71 x 56 cm.

2. ***Judith Showing the Head of Holofernes*** : oil on canvas. University College, London. Shown at the Royal Academy Exhibition of 1931.

1930

1. ***The Judgement of Paris*** : c.1930, oil on canvas, 24½ x 29½ in., 62 x 75 cm. Hove Museum and Art Gallery. Exhib. 1936, Cheltenham, Municipal Art Gallery; 1976, Penzance, Newlyn Orion Gallery; 1977, London, Parkin Gallery. See also the Merz collage of 1966 on the same subject.

2. ***Self-Portrait*** : oil on canvas, 20 x 14 in. Exhib. 1974, London, Leva Gallery; 1977, London, Parkin Gallery. Probably one of the three oil paintings designated as Portrait at the 1936 Cheltenham exhibition.

3. ***Sketch of Flowers*** : oil on canvas, 14 x 10 in. Exhib. 1973, Penzance, Orion Gallery; 1975, Bath, The Little Gallery; 1977, London, Parkin Gallery. 1990 listing gives 1929 and 35.8 x 25.8 cm.

4. ***Study of Shells***. Royal Cornwall Museum, Truro, on loan.

5. ***Susanna and the Elders*** : oil on canvas, 30 x 21 in. Exhib. 1932, London, New English Art Club; c. late 1970s, Woodbridge, The Simon Carter Gallery (also illus. in b/w in a

magazine advertisement for this exhibition); 1976, Penzance, Newlyn Orion Gallery; 1977, London, Parkin Gallery.

1931

1. ***Cartoon for a Painting of a Nude*** : indian ink and charcoal, 23¼ x 12¼ in. Exhib. 1974, London, Leva Gallery; 1977, London, Parkin Gallery. (Illus. in b/w catalogue front cover, Parkin Gallery.)

2. ***Clothes on a Chair :*** indian ink and pastel, 12½ x 8½ in. Exhib. 1936, Cheltenham, Municipal Art Gallery (as *Armchair with Clothes*); 1977, London, Parkin Gallery.

3. ***Clothes on a Divan*** : oil on board, 25.3 x 35.4 cm. 1990 listing.

4. ***Death of Lucretia*** : oil on canvas. Exhib. 1936, Cheltenham, Municipal Art Gallery; 1976, Penzance, Newlyn Orion Gallery.

5. ***Death of the Virgin*** : oil on canvas, 77 x 51½ in. Exhib. 1933, London, New English Art Club; 1935, London, Whitechapel Art Gallery; 1936, Cheltenham, Municipal Art Gallery; 1977, London, Parkin Gallery.

6. ***Head*** : oil on canvas, 8 x 6 in. Exhib. 1974, London, Leva Gallery; 1977, London, Parkin Gallery.

7. ***Jocelyn Chewett*** (Mrs Stephen Gilbert) : ink, 22.2 x 35.8 cm. 1990 listing.

8. ***Marlowe's Faust*** : oil on canvas, 48 x 36 in., 121 x 90 cm. Government Art Collection. Exhib. 1931, London, New English Art Club; 1935, London, Whitechapel Art Gallery; 1936, Cheltenham, Municipal Art Gallery; 1977, London, Parkin Gallery. More accurately 'A Scene from Marlowe's Doctor Faustus'.

1932

1. ***Cactus*** : ink and watercolour. Exhib. 1936, Cheltenham,

Municipal Art Gallery; 1973, Penzance, Orion Gallery. AD 13.6.2002 gives 1933, watercolour, 18.8 x 21.3 cm.

2. ***Cartoon for Feroze Mehta*** : charcoal and ink. Exhib. 1977, London, Parkin Gallery.

3. ***Cartoon for a Portrait of Mrs Gray*** : indian ink and charcoal, 22 x 15 in. Exhib. 1974, London, Leva Gallery; 1977, London, Parkin Gallery.

4. ***Chrysanthemums*** : pencil and watercolour, 7½ x 10 in. Exhib. 1936, Cheltenham, Municipal Art Gallery; 1973, Penzance, Orion Gallery (as 1933); 1977, London, Parkin Gallery.

5. ***Conrad Veidt*** : c.1932, ink and wash, 25.4 x 19.3 cm. 1990 listing.

6. ***Conrad Veidt*** : c.1932, crayon, 25.5 x 19.4 cm. 1990 listing.

7. ***Convolvulus*** : ink and watercolour. Exhib. 1936, Cheltenham, Municipal Art Gallery; 1973, Penzance, Orion Gallery.

8. ***Feroze Mehta*** : oil on canvas, 22 x 16 in. Exhib. 1936, Cheltenham, Municipal Art Gallery (as Phirozsha Mehta, presumed same painting) ; 1974, London, Leva Gallery; 1977, London, Parkin Gallery.

9. ***Greek Woman*** : pencil and watercolour. Exhib. 1977, London, Parkin Gallery.

10. ***Madame Primmer*** : oil on canvas, 29 x 21½ in. Exhib. 1936, Cheltenham, Municipal Art Gallery; 1974, London, Leva Art Gallery; 1977, London, Parkin Gallery.

11. ***Pomegranate Flowers*** : watercolour and pencil. Exhib. 1936, Cheltenham, Municipal Art Gallery; 1973, Penzance, Orion Gallery.

1933

1. ***Amaryllis*** : ink and watercolour. Exhib. 1973, Penzance, Orion Gallery.

2. ***Anemones*** : coloured ink. Exhib. 1973, Penzance, Orion Gallery. 1990 listing gives ink and wash, dimensions 18.7 x 11.1 cm.

3. ***Bed (II) (Greece)*** : watercolour and pencil, 25.4 x 41.1 cm. 1990 listing. Probably the same as Bed, shown in 1936 at Cheltenham.

4. ***Bird*** : indian ink. Exhib. 1977, London, Parkin Gallery.

5. ***The Castalian Spring (Delphi)*** : watercolour, 25.2 x 40.3 cm. (s). 1990 listing.

6. ***Cave, Delphi*** : watercolour and pencil, 40.5 x 25.4 cm. (s).1990 listing.

7. ***Chrysanthemums*** : watercolour and pencil. Exhib. 1973, Penzance, Orion Gallery. Possibly also ink wash, 35.1 x 43.3 cm.(s). Exhib. 1936, Cheltenham, Municipal Art Gallery. 1990 listing.

8. ***Elektra Mangoletsi (Ikon)*** : watercolour and pencil, 25.5 x 19.3 cm. 1990 listing.

9. ***Eliah Mangoletsi (Ikon)*** : watercolour and pencil, 25.5 x 19.3 cm. 1990 listing.

10. ***Hibiscus Plant*** : ink and gouache, 13¾ x 7½ in. Exhib. 1936, Cheltenham, Municipal Art Gallery (as watercolour); 1973 , Penzance, Orion Gallery; 1977, London, Parkin Gallery. AD 3.6.1999, watercolour, 34.5 x 18 cm.

11. ***India-Rubber Plant*** : ink and gouache, 11¾ x 6¼ in. Exhib. 1936, Cheltenham, Municipal Art Gallery (as

watercolour, Rubber Plant); 1973, Penzance, Orion Gallery; 1977, London, Parkin Gallery.

12. ***Kyria Kázou*** : watercolour and ink, 28 x 21.5 cm. 1990 listing (as Kuria Kazou).

13. ***Lily Leaves and Tomatoes*** : pencil and watercolour. Exhib. 1936, Cheltenham, Municipal Art Gallery; 1973, Penzance, Orion Gallery.

14. ***Madeleine in her Coffin*** : ink, 34.3 x 18.5 cm. Exhib. 1936, Cheltenham, Municipal Art Gallery. 1990 listing.

15. ***Morning Glory* (I)** : pencil and watercolour. Exhib. 1936, Cheltenham, Municipal Art Gallery; 1973, Penzance, Orion Gallery.

16. ***Morning Glory* (II) :** pencil and watercolour. Exhib. 1936, Cheltenham, Municipal Art Gallery; 1973, Penzance, Orion Gallery.

17. ***Nasturtiums*** : sepia ink and watercolour, 13½ x 10¼ in. Exhib. 1936, Cheltenham, Municipal Art Gallery; 1973, Penzance, Orion Gallery; 1977, London, Parkin Gallery.

18. ***Roderick Usher*** : ink, 34.3 x 18.4 cm. Exhib. 1936, Cheltenham, Municipal Art Gallery. 1990 listing.

19. ***Sister Eudoxia*** : oil on canvas, 24 x 15 in. Exhib. 1936, Cheltenham, Municipal Art Gallery; 1977, London, Parkin Gallery.

20. ***The Song of Songs*** : oil on canvas. Exhib. 1936, Cheltenham, Municipal Art Gallery; 1976, Penzance, Newlyn Orion Gallery.

1934

1. ***Cartoon for 'The Man in the Doorway': Portrait of Humfry Payne, the Archeologist*** : ink, pencil and watercolour on

tracing paper, 26 x 12¼ in. National Portrait Gallery, London, NPG 5269, as Humfry Gilbert Garth Payne. Exhib. 1974, London, Leva Gallery(as *The Man in the Doorway*, study for painting of Humphrey Payne, the Archaeologist); 1977, London, Parkin Gallery.

2. ***Cartoon for Portrait of Miss Dittman*** : c.1934, charcoal and ink. Exhib. 1977, London, Parkin Gallery.

3. ***Gloxinias*** : c.1934, indian ink and watercolour. Exhib. 1936, Che1tenham, Municipal Art Gallery; 1977, London, Parkin Gallery.

4. ***Hyacinth and Cyclamen*** : pencil and watercolour. Exhib. 1973, Penzance, Orion Gallery.

5. ***Kyria Kázou*** : oil on canvas, 22 x 15½ in. Exhib. 1935, London, Royal Society of British Artists; 1936, Cheltenham, Municipal Art Gallery; 1974, London, Leva Gallery; 1977, London, Parkin Gallery.

6. ***Madonna Lily*** : pencil and watercolour. Exhib. 1973, Penzance, Orion Gallery.

7. ***Miss Dittmer*** : oil on canvas, 20½ x 22 in. Exhib. 1977, London, Parkin Gallery.

8. ***Painting* (II)** : c.1934, oil on canvas, 27 x 41 cm. 1990 listing.

9. ***Water-Lilies*** : gouache. Exhib. 1973, Penzance, Orion Gallery. (possibly 1936, London, Fine Art Society, title only stated.)

10-12. ***The Woman of Andros*** : watercolour, ink and pencil, 50.3 x 40.5 cm. Three drawings for illustrations to *The Woman of Andros* by Thornton Wilder (1. 'Chrysis moved slowly down . . .'; 2. 'The beautiful woman leaning against the parapet. . .'; 3. 'Then raising herself on one elbow . . .'). Exhib. 1936, Cheltenham Municipal Art Gallery. 1990 listing.

13. ***Zetta Heidenstamme*** : pencil and gouache. Exhib. 1977, London, Parkin Gallery. Possibly *Zetta* (as watercolour), 1936, Cheltenham, Municipal Art Gallery.

1935

1. ***Cartoon for 'Self-Portrait'*** : c.1935, ink and watercolour. Exhib. 1977, London, Parkin Gallery.

2. ***Clematis*** : oil on board, 16 x 13 in. Exhib. 1936, London, Fine Art Society; 1973, Penzance, Orion Gallery.

3. ***Crane-Flowers*** : oil on canvas, 17½ x 14 in., 44.4 x 35.5 cm. Exhib. 1936, London, Fine Art Society.

4. ***Flowers in a Greenhouse*** : oil on canvas, 24 x 18 in. Exhib. 1936, Cheltenham, Municipal Art Gallery; 1936, London, Fine Art Society; 1973, Penzance, Orion Gallery.

5. ***Flowers in a Yellow Vase*** : oil on canvas, 32 x 14 in. Exhib. 1973, Penzance, Orion Gallery. Similar title, 1962 work.

6 ***Lily*** : oil on board, 51.0 x 38.0 cm. Exhib. 1936, Cheltenham, Municipal Art Gallery; 1936, London, Fine Art Society; 1972, Exeter, City of Exeter Art Gallery; 1973, Penzance, Orion Gallery.

7. ***The Man in the Doorway***: National Portrait Gallery, London, NPG 6230 (as *Humfry Gilbert Garth Payne*), oil on canvas, 27 x 14 in., 68.5 x 35.5 cm. Exhib. 1936, Cheltenham, Municipal Art Gallery.

1936

1. ***Anthurium*** : oil on canvas, 32 x 20 in. Exhib. 1973, Penzance, Orion Gallery.

2. ***Arcade, Nice*** : watercolour, 47 x 39.5 cm. All AD 26.5.1994.

3. ***Arums and Amaryllis*** : oil on canvas, 24 x 20 in. Exhib. 1936, London, Fine Art Society; 1973, Penzance, Orion Gallery.

4. ***Canna*** : oil on canvas. Cheltenham, Municipal Art Gallery. Exhib. 1936, the same gallery.

5. ***Catleya*** : oil on canvas, 23½ x 23½ in. Exhib. 1937, London, Heal's Gallery; 1938, London, Everyman's Theatre Foyer; 1973, Penzance, Orion Gallery; 1977, London, Parkin Gallery (which also reports shown in 1936, Fine Art Society, but not seen in catalogue).

6. ***Cradle Orchid*** : watercolour and ink, 21.9 x 17 cm.(s). 1990 listing. If on silk is the one shown at 1936 Fine Arts Exhibition in London.

7. ***Datura*** : oil on panel, 24 x 18½ in. Exhib. 1936, London, Fine Art Society. AD 26.11.1995 gives 61 x 47 cm.

8. ***Doorway, Corsica*** : watercolour and pencil, 31.4 x 33 cm.(s). 1990 listing.

9. ***Gateway, Corsica*** : watercolour and crayon, 31.8 x 39 cm.(s). 1990 listing.

10. ***Ground Floor Façade, Tenerife*** : watercolour and pencil, 33.7 x 46.5 cm.(s). 1990 listing.

11. ***Lifeboat, Corsica*** : watercolour and body colour over pencil, 17 x 15 in., 43.5 x 39 cm.

12. ***Madagascar Aroid*** : oil on canvas. Exhib. 1936, London, Fine Art Society.

13. ***Pitcher Plant***: watercolour and pencil, 18.8 x 12 cm.(s). 1990 listing.

14. ***Rails*** : oil on board, 18 x 15 in., 45.5 x 37.5 cm. Exhib. 1939, London Gallery; 1971, London, Hamet Gallery; 1974, London, Leva Gallery; 1976, Penzance, Newlyn Orion Gallery; 1977, London, Parkin Gallery; 1985, London, Blond Fine Art.

15. ***Small Anthurium*** : watercolour and pencil, 18.7 x 12 cm.(s). Exhib. 1936, London, Fine Art Society. 1990 listing.

16. ***Small Yellow Lily*** : watercolour and pencil. 1990 listing.

17. ***Spotted Lilies*** : oil on canvas, 24 x 24 in. Exhib. 1936, London, Fine Art Society; 1973, Penzance, Orion Gallery.

18. ***Sun-Flower*** : oil on canvas, 22 x 18 in., 56.0 x 46.0 cm. Exhib. 1936, London, Fine Art Society; 1972, City of Exeter Art Gallery (as *Sunflower*); 1973, Penzance, Orion Gallery; 1977, London, Parkin Gallery (as *Sunflowers*).

19. ***Water-Lilies*** : oil on board. Exhib. 1936, London, Fine Art Society.

1937

1. ***Agave, Corsica*** : watercolour, crayon and pencil, 55 x 44 cm. 1990 listing.

2. ***Corner*** : oil on board, 28 x 15½ in. Exhib. 1939, London Gallery; 1939, London, Peter Jones Gallery; 1972, Harvane Gallery; 1974, London, Leva Gallery; 1977, London, Parkin Gallery; 1986, London, Mayor Gallery.

3. ***Corsican Boy*** : charcoal and watercolour. Exhib. 1977, London, Parkin Gallery.

4. ***Fruit in a Bowl* (I)** : tempera on paper. Exhib. 1977, London, Parkin Gallery.

5. ***Fruit in a Bowl* (II)** : tempera on paper. Exhib. 1977, London, Parkin Gallery.

6. ***Head of an Italian Girl*** : Conté pencil, 16 x 15 in. Exhib. 1974, London, Leva Gallery; 1977, London, Parkin Gallery.

7. ***Lucy Cornford*** : Conté pencil, 15¾ x 17½ in. Exhib. 1974, London, Leva Gallery (as *Portrait Study of Lucy Cornford*); 1977, London, Parkin Gallery.

8. ***Pears*** : oil on board. Tate Gallery Archives (TGA 929) photostat.

9. ***Tulips*** : pencil and watercolour. Exhib. 1977, London, Parkin Gallery.

10. ***Village Lane, Corsica*** : watercolour and crayon, 40 x 32.8 cm. 1990 listing.

1938

1. ***Alchemical Figure*** : gouache and pencil, 16 x 12.7 cm. 1990 listing.

2. ***Aloe, Corsica*** : watercolour and crayon (mounted on canvas), 55.3 x 44.7 cm. 1990 listing.

3. ***Aloe (detail)*** : watercolour and crayon, 48 x 33.8 cm. 1990 listing.

4. ***Beach-Boy*** : Conté pencil and watercolour, 12½ x 16½ in. Exhib. 1974, London, Leva Gallery; 1977, London, Parkin Gallery.

5. ***Cartoon for 'Scylla'*** : charcoal and chalk. Exhib. 1977, London, Parkin Gallery.

6. ***Death's Head and Foot*** : object (carved chalk decorated with tempera). Exhib. 1939, London, Mayor Gallery.

7. ***Desert Growth*** : c.1938, oil on board, 33 x 22.8 cm, 13 x 9 in. See also same title, 1949.

8. ***Drowned Sailor*** : sepia ink, 14 x 17½ in. Exhib. 1974, London, Leva Gallery; 1977, London, Parkin Gallery.

9. ***Fruit Peelings*** : tempera on board, 7½ x 7½ in., 19 x 19 cm. Exhib. 1939, London Gallery; 1941, London, Whitechapel Art Gallery; 1942, Bournemouth Art Gallery; 1971, Hamet Gallery; 1974, London, Leva Gallery; 1977, London, Parkin Gallery. 1990 listing.

10. ***Head of Corsican Boy*** : Conté pencil and watercolour, 17½ x 15¾ in. Exhib. 1974, London, Leva Gallery.

11. ***Heart*** : object (carved chalk decorated with tempera). Exhib. 1939, London, Mayor Gallery.

12. ***Interior with Staircase*** : pencil and watercolour, 40 x 56 cm. (all AD.)

13. ***José Asleep*** : Conté pencil, 17½ x 15¾ in. Exhib. 1974, London, Leva Gallery; 1975, Newlyn, Newlyn Art Gallery; 1977, London, Parkin Gallery.

14. ***Mediterranean Buildings*** : watercolour, 39 x 49.5 cm. All AD 13.3.1988.

15. ***Mediterranean Terraces*** : 41.5 x 36.5 cm. All AD 13.3.1998.

16. ***Orchids*** : watercolour and crayon, 32.8 x 25.4 cm. 1990 listing.

17. ***Scylla (Méditerranée)*** : oil on board, 36 x 24 in., 91.4 x 61.0 cm. Purchased by Tate Gallery, 1977, accession TO2140. Exhib. 1939, London, Mayor Gallery; 1939, London Gallery; 1961, Newlyn Gallery; 1971, Hamet Gallery; 1974, London, Leva Gallery; 1976, Penzance, Newlyn Orion Gallery; 1977, London, Parkin Gallery; touring exhibition Sept.1986-April 1987, Swansea, Bath, Newcastle, Llandudno.

18. ***View of Houses*** : watercolour, 38.5 x 49 cm. All AD 17.7.2001.

19. ***Water-Flower*** : oil on canvas, 41 x 30 in. Exhib. 1973, Penzance, Orion Gallery.

1939

1. ***L'Ancre (Méditerranée)*** : oil on canvas, 22 x 22 in. Exhib. 1939, London, Mayor Gallery; 1939, London Gallery; 1939, Northampton Gallery; 1939, Oxford, The Ashmolean Museum; 1940, London, Leicester Galleries; 1941, Harrogate Gallery; 1971, London, Hamet Gallery; 1974, London, Leva Gallery; 1976, Penzance, Newlyn Orion Gallery; 1977, London, Parkin Gallery.

2. ***Beau Gosse (Méditerranée)*** : oil on board, 35 x 21¼ in., 89 x 52 cm. Exhib. 1941, Harrogate.

3. ***Cartoon for Gouffres Amers*** : indian ink. Exhib. 1977, London, Parkin Gallery.

4. ***Cartoon for Painting, Le Phare*** : ink, 13¾ x 17½ in. Exhib. 1974, London, Leva Gallery; 1977, London, Parkin Gallery.

5. ***Cucumber*** : tempera on board, 15½ x 12 in. Exhib. 1939, London Gallery; 1974, London, Leva Gallery; 1977, London, Parkin Gallery; 1985, London, Blond Fine Art (as tempera on panel, 12¼ x 5½ in., 31 x 14.3 cm.). A Tate Gallery print is endorsed 'tempera on panel' and the height/width ratio appears about 2:1. There is conflict in the dimensions.

6. ***Gouffres Amers (Méditerranée)*** : oil on canvas, 28½ x 36 in., 71.2 x 91.3 cm. Hunterian Art Gallery, Glasgow. Exhib. 1939, London, Mayor Gallery; 1940, R.S.B.A. Int. Ex.; 1941, Bagshaw Gallery; 1941, Batley Gallery; 1941, Harrogate Gallery; 1961, Newlyn Gallery; 1971, London, Hamet Gallery.

7. ***L'Hélice (Méditerranée)*** : oil on canvas, 22 x 22 in., 56 x 56 cm. Exhib. 1939, London Gallery; 1939, Northampton Art Gallery; 1941, Harrogate Gallery; 1941, Batley Gallery; 1974,

London, Leva Gallery; 1976, Penzance, Newlyn Orion Gallery; 1977, London, Parkin Gallery.

8. ***Interior*** : oil on board, 36 x 24 in., 91.4 x 60.9 cm. Hove Museum and Art Gallery. Exhib. 1939, London Gallery; 1939, Oxford, The Ashmolean Museum; 1940, London, Leicester Galleries; 1941, Harrogate Gallery; 1941, Batley Gallery; 1961, Newlyn, Newlyn Gallery; 1974, London, Leva Gallery (illus. b/w front cover catalogue but ascribed to 1938 in text); 1976, Penzance, Newlyn Orion Gallery; 1977, London, Parkin Gallery; 1978, London, Parkin Gallery; 1979-80, London, Hayward Gallery.

9. ***Le Phare (Méditerranée)*** : oil on panel, 27 x 35 in. Exhib. 1939, London, Mayor Gallery; 1939, Northampton Art Gallery; 1971, London, Hamet Gallery.

10. ***Rivières Tièdes (Méditerranée)*** : oil on wood, 36 x 24 in., 91.1 x 61.2 cm. Southampton City Art Gallery. Exhib. 1939, London, Mayor Gallery; 1939, London Gallery; 1939, Northampton Art Gallery; 1941. Harrogate Gallery; 1961, Newlyn, Newlyn Art Gallery; 1971, London, Hamet Gallery; 1974, London, Leva Gallery; 1976, Penzance, Newlyn Orion Gallery; 1977, London, Parkin Gallery; 1985, Scottish Arts Council, touring ex.; 1986, Leeds City Art Gallery.

1940

1. ***Alchemical Figure*** : watercolour, 36.4 x 25.4 cm. 1990 listing.

2. ***Alchemical Figure 1940*** : watercolour and pencil, 34 x 17.6 cm. 1990 listing.

3. ***The Bird or the Egg*** : c.1940, watercolour, 25.8 x 16.3 cm. 1990 listing.

4. ***Bronze Figure in the Desert*** : watercolour and crayon, 45.5 x 40.5 cm. 1990 listing.

5. ***Cake 1940*** : watercolour and pencil, 17.6 x 11.2 cm. 1990 listing.

6. ***Cardinal Points*** : oil on canvas, 14 x 20 in. Illus. Witt Library.

7. ***The Comet*** : watercolour, 13 x 8.4 cm. 1990 listing.

8. ***The Concealed Mouth*** : watercolour, 13 x 8.4 cm. 1990 listing.

9. ***Conservatory*** : watercolour and crayon, 45 x 40.3 cm. 1990 listing.

10. ***Conservatory*** : watercolour and crayon, 45 x 40.5 cm. 1990 listing.

11. ***Conservatory*** : watercolour, pencil and ink, 79 x 57.5 cm. 1990 listing.

12. ***Dance of the Nine Maidens*** : watercolour and pencil, 45 x 29 cm. 1990 listing.

13-18. ***Dance of the Nine Maidens*** : watercolour and ink. 45 x 29 cm. (one 29 x 45 cm.) Six studies. 1990 listing.

19-20. ***From the Dance of the Nine Maidens*** : ink and crayon, 32 x 22 cm. Another 29 x 45 cm. 1990 listing.

21. ***Diagrams of Love*** : watercolour, 8.4 x 13 cm. 1990 listing. See also 1941, same title.

22. ***The Dunes*** : c.1940, oil on canvas, 18 x 36 in., 45.7 x 91.4 cm. Illus. Witt Library.

23. ***Earth Process*** : c.1940, watercolour, 35 x 35 cm. 1990 listing.

24. ***Heart of Corn*** : watercolour, 13 x 8.4 cm. 1990 listing.

25. ***The Heart's Directions*** : watercolour, 23 x 18.2 cm. 1990 listing.

26. ***The Homunculus* (I)** : watercolour, 30.3 x 24 cm. 1990 listing.

27. ***The Homunculus*) (II)** : watercolour, 30.3 x 24 cm. 1990 listing.

28. ***Hypnagogic Image*** : watercolour, 28.4 x 42 cm. 1990 listing.

29. ***Hypnagogic Image*** : watercolour, 30.2 x 21.8 cm. 1990 listing.

30. ***Middle East*** : watercolour and crayon, 26.6 x 40.5 cm. 1990 listing.

31. ***The Opal* (I)** : watercolour, 21 x 28.8 cm. 1990 listing.

32. ***Snow Maiden*** : watercolour, 39 x 29.2 cm. 1990 listing.

33. ***Tenth Taro*** : London Museum, 1942.

34. ***The Thirteen Streams of Magnificent Oil*** : c.1940, watercolour and pencil, 32.7 x 20.7 cm. 1990 listing.

35. ***Three Elements*** : c.1940, watercolour, 35 x 25 cm.(s). 1990 listing.

36. ***Tidal Wave and Volcano*** : watercolour, 17.8 x 27.3 cm. 1990 listing.

1941

1. ***Alchemical Figure*** : ***Androgyne 1941*** : watercolour, ink and crayon, 37.3 x 23.3 cm. 1990 listing.

2. ***Circulation of the Blood*** : watercolour, 35.5 x 25.5 cm. 1990 listing.

3. ***Communicating Vessels*** : watercolour, 41.2 x 31.6 cm. 1990 listing.

4. ***Dance of the Nine Opals*** : watercolour, ink and pencil, 25.5 x 35.3 cm. 1990 listing.

5. ***Diagrams of Love*** : watercolour, 25.8 x 18 cm. 1990 listing.

6. ***King and Centre*** : watercolour, 35.5 x 25.4 cm. 1990 listing.

7. ***The Pine Family*** : oil on canvas, 18 x 20 in., 45.7 x 50.8 cm. Israel Museum, Jerusalem. Exhib. 1942, London, International Arts Centre; 1972, City of Exeter Art Gallery; 1976, Penzance, Newlyn Orion Gallery; 1977, London, Parkin Gallery; 1982, Paris, Galerie 1900-2000 ('Peinture Surrealiste en Angleterre'); 1985, Colchester, The Minories; 1985, London, Blond Fine Art; 1985, Hull, Ferens Art Gallery. Illus. cover *Osmazone*. Some galleries quote 1940.

8. ***Sentiment of Eruption*** : c.1941, watercolour, 35.5 x 25.5 cm. 1990 listing.

9. ***The Tree of Veins* (II*)*** : c.1941, watercolour, 23.1 x 18.2 cm. 1990 listing.

10. ***The Trees*** : watercolour, 36.7 x 30.2 cm. 1990 listing.

11. ***Volcanic Landscape***. Exhib. 1942, London Museum.

1942

1. ***The Bride Carried a Bunch of Tethered Flies*** : oil.

2. ***Bride of the Pavement*** : oil on canvas, 30 x 24 in., 76 x 61 cm. Exhib. 1947 (March), London, Mayor Gallery; 1953, Cambridge, Heffer Gallery; 1976, Penzance, Newlyn Orion Gallery.

3. ***Dance of the Nine Opals*** : oil on canvas, 22½ x 28 in., 51 x 69 cm. Exhib. 1942, London Museum; 1945, Derby Art Gallery; 1974, London, Leva Gallery; 1976, Penzance, Newlyn Orion Gallery; 1985, London, Blond Fine Art. AD 22.5.1996 gives 57 x 71 cm.

4. ***Philosopher's Stone*** : mixed media on board, 36 x 24 cm. All AD 16.5.1996.

5. ***The Three Inner Preoccupations of Surrealism: Excrement, Blood, Penetration*** : c.1942, watercolour, 25.7 x 18 cm. 1990 listing.

6. ***Tree Anatomy*** : oil on board, 22¼ x 11¼ in., 56.9 x 29.0 cm. Exhib. 1942, London, Leicester Galleries; 1948, Bradford, Cartwright Hall Gallery; 1972, City of Exeter Art Gallery; 1974, London, Leva Gallery; 1976, Penzance, Newlyn Orion Gallery; 1977, London, Parkin Gallery; 1985, London, Blond Fine Art.

1943

1. ***Empedocles*** : oil on canvas, 22 x 15 in., 56 x 38.1 cm. Exhib. 1946, Bradford, Cartwright Hall Art Gallery; 1961, Newlyn, Newlyn Gallery; 1974, London, Leva Gallery (as 23 x 17 in.). AD 6.3.98, 60.5 x 42.5 cm.

2. ***'Pénil des Menhirs'*** : Exhib. 1947 (March), London, Mayor Gallery.

1944

1. ***Ages of Man*** : oil on panel, 115/8 x 71/8 in. Exhib. 1947 (March), London, Mayor Gallery; 1974, London, Leva Gallery. 29.4 x 18.2 cm in 1990 listing.

2. ***An Eclipse*** : oil on panel, 66.7 x 38.4 cm. Exhib. 1947 (March), London, Mayor Gallery. 1990 listing.

3. ***Sea-Star* (I)** : oil on board, 14 x 10½ in., 35.5 x 26.7 cm. Exhib. 1947 (March), London, Mayor Gallery; 1974, London, Leva Gallery; 1976, Penzance, Newlyn Orion Gallery. See 1962 for *Sea-Star* (II).

4. ***Tendrils of Sleep* (I)** : oil on board, 56.0 x 30.0 cm. Exhib. 1947 (March), London, Mayor Gallery; 1961, Newlyn Gallery;

1972, City of Exeter Art Gallery. AD 18.10.1990 gives 57.1 x 29.2 cm.

1945

1. ***Dreaming Leaps : in Homage to Sonia Araquistain*** : oil on paper, 31 x 21½ in., 80.0 x 55.0 cm. Exhib. 1947 (March), London, Mayor Gallery; 1972, City of Exeter Art Gallery; 1976, Penzance, Newlyn Orion Gallery; 1986, Leeds City Art Gallery.

2. ***E.L.A.S.*** : oil on panel, 19.5 x 14.5 cm. 1990 listing.

3. ***Garden of Adonis*** : oil and ink on board, 20 x 24.7 cm. 1990 listing.

4. ***Landscape of Nightmare*** : oil on panel, 8¾ x 11½ in., 22 x 29.2 cm. Exhib. 1947 (March), London, Mayor Gallery; 1985, Colchester, The Minories.

5. ***A Visitation* (I)** : oil on canvas, décalcomania, 24 x 20 in., 61.5 x 51 cm. Exhib. 1946, London, Redfern Gallery; 1972, City of Exeter Art Gallery; 1974, London, Leva Gallery; 1976, Penzance, Newlyn Orion Gallery; 1985, London, Blond Fine Art; 1986, Leeds City Art Gallery (illus. in colour in catalogue). A Visitation (II) was exhibited at the Mayor Gallery in 1947 (March).

6. ***A Visitation* (II)** : Exhib. 1947 (March), London, Mayor Gallery. Might be the preceding work.

1946

1. ***Alcove*** : Exhib. 1947 (March), London, Mayor Gallery. (See 1948/1 for *Alcove* (II).

2. ***Arbour*** : Exhib. 1947 (March), London, Mayor Gallery.

3. ***Arethusa*** : Exhib. 1947 (March), London, Mayor Gallery.

4. ***Elemental*** : c.1946, ink, 24.8 x 24.6 cm.(s). Exhib. 1947 (Dec.), London, Mayor Gallery. 1990 listing.

5. ***Genius Loci*** : oil on board, 28½ x 25½ in., 73.8 x 65.8 cm. Exhib. 1947 (March), London, Mayor Gallery; 1950, Bradford, Cartwright Hall Art Gallery; 1972, City of Exeter Art Gallery (as 1947 work); 1974, London, Leva Gallery. AD 1.10.1997 gives 72.5 x 65 cm.

6. ***Gorgon*** : oil on board, 22¾ x 22¾ in. Exhib. 1947 (March), London, Mayor Gallery; 1952, Bradford, Cartwright Hall Art Gallery; 1976, Penzance, Newlyn Orion Gallery.

7. ***Guardian Angel*** : tempera, 12½ x 14½ in., 32 x 36.5 cm. Exhib. 1947 (March), London, Mayor Gallery.

8. ***Linked Senses*** : c.1946, ink and watercolour, décalcomania, 47.5 x 66 cm.(s). Exhib. 1947 (Dec.), London, Mayor Gallery; 1976, Penzance, Newlyn Orion Gallery (as ink and gouache). 1990 listing.

9. ***The Long Journey***. : oil on board, 8½ x 13¼ in. Exhib. 1947 (March), London, Mayor Gallery; 1989, London, Blond Fine Art.

10. ***Self-Portrait*** : ink and gouache, fumage. Exhib. 1976, Penzance, Newlyn Orion Gallery. Same title exhib. as drawing 1947 (Dec.), London, Mayor Gallery.

11. ***The Winnowers*** : Exhib. 1947 (March), London, Mayor Gallery.

1947

1. ***Attributes of the Moon*** : oil on board, 86.5 x 34.2 cm. Exhib. 1947 (March), London , Mayor Gallery; 1947, London, Redfern Gallery; 1972, City of Exeter Art Gallery; 1976, Penzance, Newlyn Orion Gallery.

2. ***Butterflies on Carrion*** : ink and gouache, superautomatism. Exhib. 1976, Penzance, Newlyn Orion Gallery.

3. ***Depression*** : c.1947, ink and wash, 44.2 x 31 cm.(s). Exhib. 1947 (Dec.), London, Mayor Gallery (drawings); c.1974, Newlyn Art Gallery; 1977, London, Parkin Gallery. 1990 listing.

4. ***Interior Landscape*** : ink drawing, superautomatism, 41.5 x 31.5 cm.(s). Royal Cornwall Museum, Truro, on loan. Exhib. 1976, Penzance, Newlyn Orion Gallery. 1990 listing.

5. ***Linked Islands* (I)** : c.1947, watercolour and ink, 44.5 x 31.7 cm. (s).1990 listing.

6. ***Linked Islands* (II) :** ink and gouache, décalcomania, 12¼ x 17½ in. Possibly (as *Linked Islands*) exhib. 1976, Penzance, Newlyn Orion Gallery.

7. ***Rock Pool*** : ink drawing, entoptic graphomania, 44.3 x 31 cm.(s). Exhib. 1947 (Dec.), London, Mayor Gallery; 1976, Penzance, Newlyn Orion Gallery. Perhaps reproduced in *Grimoire of the Entangled Thicket*, p.11 as *Rock-Pool, Lamorna.* 1990 listing (as c.1948).

8. ***Roman Sun*** : oil on board, 30¾ x 19¾ in., 78.0 x 50.5 cm. Exhib. 1947 (March), London, Mayor Gallery; 1950, Bradford, Cartwright Hall Art Gallery; 1972, City of Exeter Art Gallery; 1974, London, Leva Gallery.

9. ***St. Elmo*** : c.1947, pen, black ink, gouache. Cartwright Hall, Bradford. Exhib. 1948, Bradford, Cartwright Hall Art Gallery.

10. ***Saltimbanco*** **:** Exhib. 1947 (March), London, Mayor Gallery.

11. ***Santa Warna's Wishing Well*** : c.1947, ink and watercolour, décalcomania, 45 x 32 cm.(s). Exhib. 1947 (Dec.) London, Mayor Gallery; 1976, Penzance, Newlyn Orion Gallery. 1990 listing.

12. ***Still Water*** : oil on board, décalcomania, 15 x 18 in., 38.8 x 46.0 cm. Exhib. 1947(March), London, Mayor Gallery; 1972, City of Exeter Art Gallery; 1974, London, Leva Gallery; 1985, Colchester, The Minories. Hampstead Heath pond.

13. ***The Three Wands*** : c.1947, ink and gouache, fumage. Exhib. 1976, Penzance, Newlyn Orion Gallery.

14. ***Torn Veil*** : ink drawing, stillomancy, 44.5 x 31 cm. Exhib. 1947 (Dec.), London, Mayor Gallery ; 1976, Penzance, Newlyn Orion Gallery (as entoptic graphomania). 1990 listing.

15. ***Toy*** : indian ink and watercolour, superautomatism, 17 x 12¼ in., 42 x 31.5 cm. Exhib. 1948, Dublin, National College of Art; 1948, London, A.I.A. exhibition; 1976, Penzance, Newlyn Orion Gallery; 1977, London, Parkin Gallery (as 1946). 1990 listing.

1948

1. ***Alcove* (II)** : oil on board, 9 x 13½ in. See 1946/1 for *Alcove*

2. ***Fantasia on Fruit*** : c.1948, ink and watercolour, 29.7 x 26.6 cm.(s). 1990 listing.

3. ***Foam Flower*** : c.1948 (possibly 1947), watercolour and ink, 30.3 x 42.2 cm.(s). 1990 listing. See also same title exhib. 1947 (Dec.), Mayor Gallery (drawings).

4. ***Marine*** : c.1948 (possibly 1947), watercolour, pencil and crayon, 26.5 x 19 cm.(s). 1990 listing. See also same title exhib.1947 (Dec.), Mayor Gallery (drawings).

5. ***Moment of Death*** : ink and watercolour on paper, 13½ x 12½ in., 34.3 x 31.8 cm. Exhib. 1985, Colchester, The Minories.

1949

1. ***Autumnal Equinox*** : oil on canvas, 81 x 32 in., 205.0 x 82.0 cm. Exhib. 1953, Bradford, Cartwright Hall Art Gallery; 1972,

City of Exeter Art Gallery; 1976, Penzance, Newlyn Orion Gallery.

2. ***Desert Growth* (I)** : oil on board, 12½ x 10 1/8 in., 31.8 x 25.5 cm. AD 14.7.98 gives *Desert Growth*, tempera and oil on board 29.0 x 25.5 cm. See also same title, c.1938.

3. ***Dingle Bay*** : oil on board, 10 x 14 in. Exhib. 1974, London, Leva Gallery; 1985, London, Blond Fine Art.

4. ***Kerry Landscape*** : oil on board, 12 x 16 in., 30.0 x 40.0 cm. Exhib. 1974, London, Leva Gallery; 1985, London, Blond Fine Art.

5. ***Oil on the Beach*** : c.1949, ink and gouache, parsemage. Exhib. 1976, Penzance, Newlyn Orion Gallery.

6. ***On the Beach*** : ink and watercolour , 22.6 x 22.6 cm.(s). 1990 listing. Same title was exhib. 1947 (Dec.), by the Mayor Gallery, perhaps a preliminary drawing.

1950

1. ***Crater's Edge*** : c.1950, oil on board, convulsive landscape. Exhib. 1976, Penzance, Newlyn Orion Gallery.

2. ***Creation du Monde*** : oil on board, convulsive landscape, 10¼ x 12 in., 26.0 x 31.0 cm. Exhib. 1976, Penzance, Newlyn Orion Gallery.

3. ***Giantesses Undressing to Bathe*** : oil on canvas, 141.0 x 130.0 cm. Exhib. 1972, City of Exeter Art Gallery; 1976, Penzance, Newlyn Orion Gallery.

4. ***Knockbrack*** : oil on board, 10 x 12 in., 25.0 x 30.0 cm. Exhib. 1974, London, Leva Gallery; 1985, London, Blond Fine Art.

5. ***Sea Mother*** : c.1950, ink and wash, parsemage. Exhib. 1976, Penzance, Newlyn Orion Gallery. 1990 listing.

6. ***Woman of Beare*** : oil on canvas. Exhib. 1976, Penzance, Newlyn Orion Gallery.

1951

1. ***Dervish*** : indian ink, 17 x 12¼ in., 44 x 31.25 cm. Exhib. c.1973, Newlyn Art Gallery; 1977, London, Parkin Gallery. 1990 listing includes similar title and size but c.1952.

1952

1. ***Atomic Psychosis*** : oil on paper, convulsive landscape, 58 x 31 in., 147.5 x 79.5 cm. Exhib. 1972, City of Exeter Art Gallery ; 1976, Penzance, Newlyn Orion Gallery ; 1985, London, Blond Fine Art (as oil on board). Also, year unknown, Bradford, Cartwright Hall Art Gallery.

2. ***La Cathédrale Engloutie*** : oil on canvas, 51½ x 77 in., 131.0 x 195.0 cm. Israel Museum, Jerusalem. Exhib. 1952, Bradford, Cartwright Hall Art Gallery; 1952, London, Royal Academy; 1953, London, Women's International Art Club; 1972, City of Exeter Art Gallery; 1976, Penzance, Newlyn Orion Gallery.

3. ***Fertile Cloud*** : c.1952, watercolour and ink, 24 x 19 cm.(s).1990 listing.

4. ***Flesh Flowers*** : watercolour and pencil, 25.5 x 19.8 cm.(s).1990listing.

5. ***Grotto of the Sun and Moon*** : oil on canvas, 122.0 x 91.5 cm. Exhib. 1963, Ostend, Cultural Centre; 1972, City of Exeter Art Gallery.

6. ***Polarity*** : c.1952, ink and wash, frottage, 42.2 x 30.2 cm.(s). Exhib. 1976, Penzance, Newlyn Orion Gallery.

1953

1. ***Leave Uncombed Your Darling Hair*** : c.1953, ink drawing, superautomatism, 44.4 x 31.2 cm. (s). Exhib. 1976, Penzance,

Newlyn Orion Gallery. Illus. front cover of catalogue. 1990 listing.

2. ***Life of the Pine* (II)** : c.1953, ink and wash, 24.7 x 36.8 cm.(s). 1990 listing.

1954

1. ***Andante*** : c.1954, ink wash, 30.5 x 22.8 cm.(s). 1990 listing.

2. ***Crucifixion*** : c.1954, oil on panel, 225 x 121 cm. Composition included in mural designs for Maze Hill. 1990 listing.

3. ***L'Incendie*** : c.1954, ink, 26.8 x 20.3 cm.(s). 1990 listing.

1955

1. ***Landscape with Antiquities, Lamorna***: oil on canvas, 92 x 61 cm. Royal Cornwall Museum, Truro, on loan. Exhib. 1976, Penzance, Newlyn Orion Gallery. 1990.

1956

1. ***Morrab Magnolia*** : oil on canvas, 24 x 24 in. Exhib. 1973, Penzance, Orion Gallery.

1960

1. ***Alchemy up-to-date*** : collage, tinted with coloured inks, 18.0 x 21.0 cm. Exhib. 1972, City of Exeter Art Gallery; 1976, Penzance, Newlyn Orion Gallery.

2. ***Death of a Vampire*** : c.1960, décalcomania, ink and wash, 37.5 x 26 cm.. Royal Cornwall Museum, Truro, on loan. Exhib. 1976, Penzance, Newlyn Orion Gallery (as *Death of the Vampire*, ink and gouache). Note: an ink and gouache work *Death of the Vampire in a Magic Mirror* was exhibited at Derby Art Gallery in their 1945 'Exhibition of Contemporary Art' and was possibly an early study of the subject, of unknown date.

3. ***World Moth*** : ink and ready-made. Exhib. 1976, Penzance, Newlyn Orion Gallery.

1962

1. ***Blaze*** : oil on board, 35.2 x 30.4 cm. Exhib. 1976, Penzance, Newlyn Orion Gallery. 1990 listing.

2. ***Blizzard*** : mixed media, 27.9 x 30.5 cm. All AD 2.6.1994.

3. ***Flowers in a Yellow Vase*** : oil on board, 13 x 9 in. Exhib. 1973, Penzance, Orion Gallery.

4. ***Insignia of Penzance*** : cardboard sculpture. Exhib. 1976, Penzance, Newlyn Orion Gallery.

5. ***Oranges and Grapes*** : ink wash, 23.3 x 26.4 cm. (s). 1990 listing.

6. ***Sea- Star* (II)** : mixed media on board, 38 x 27 cm. All AD 16.5.1996. See 1944 for *Sea-Star* (I).

7. ***Stalactite*** : oil on board, 58 x 14 in., 147.2 x 35.0 cm. Exhib. 1963, London, F.B.A. Galleries, Women's International Art Club; 1972, City of Exeter Art Gallery (as oil on canvas); 1985, London, Blond Fine Art .

8. ***Still Life*** : oil on canvas, 40.5 x 76.5 cm. 1990 listing.

9. ***Temptation of St. Anthony*** : oil on board, 57.0 x 89.5 cm. Exhib. 1963, London, Royal Watercolour Society Galleries; 1972, City of Exeter Art Gallery; 1976, Penzance, Newlyn Orion Gallery. 1990 listing.

1963

1. ***Bird of Passage*** : collage, 22.5 x 14.0 cm. Exhib. 1972, City of Exeter Art Gallery; 1976, Penzance, Newlyn Orion Gallery.

2. ***Cucumber in Paper*** : oil on panel, 17.5 x 14 cm. 1990 listing.

3. ***Day Star* (I)** : mixed media on aluminium foil, laid on card, 15¾ x 14 in., 40 x 35.5 cm. Perhaps the same as 1964/8.

4. ***Grapefruit and Lemons*** : oil on canvas, 25.4 x 35.4 cm. 1990 listing.

5. ***Our Lady of Gracious Living*** : collage, 21.0 x 21.0 cm. Exhib. 1972, City of Exeter Art Gallery; 1976, Penzance, Newlyn Orion Gallery.

6. ***Potentate* (I)** : oil on board, collage, 76.0 x 40.0 cm. Exhib. 1963, London, Royal Watercolour Society Galleries; 1972, City of Exeter Art Gallery; 1976, Penzance, Newlyn Orion Gallery.

7. ***Roses in a Vase*** : oil on panel, 28 x 16.5 cm. 1990 listing.

8. ***The Seasons*** : oil on canvas, 87.0 x 120.0 cm. Exhib. 1963, London, Royal Watercolour Society Galleries; 1972, City of Exeter Art Gallery.

1964

1. ***Aircraft Trace* (I)** : ?enamel on board, 40.5 x 30.3 cm. 1990 listing.

2. ***Byzantine Cross*** : Merz collage, 91.5 x 75.0 cm. Exhib. 1972, City of Exeter Art Gallery.

3. ***Day Star*** : oil on paper. Exhib. 1976, Penzance, Newlyn Orion Gallery.

4. ***Nativity*** : oil on board, 16 x 20 in., 41 x 51 cm.

5. ***Oil-and-Water-Nymph*** : oil on canvas, 108.0 x 73.0 cm. Exhib. 1967, Newlyn, Newlyn Gallery; 1972, City of Exeter Art Gallery.

6. ***Room with a View*** : Merz collage. Exhib. 1976, Penzance, Newlyn Orion Gallery.

7. ***St. Patrick's Breast-Plate*** : Merz collage. Exhib. 1976, Penzance, Newlyn Orion Gallery.

8. ***Star Painting*** : oil on foil. Exhib. 1976, Penzance, Newlyn Orion Gallery.

9. ***Steering Wheel for a Sky Pilot*** : Merz collage. Exhib. 1976, Penzance, Newlyn Orion Gallery.

10. ***Unidentified Flying Object*** : 40.5 x 30.4 cm. 1990 listing. See also same title and size to 1 mm. for 1968/2.

1965

1. ***Embryo Fetish*** : Merz collage. Exhib. 1976, Penzance, Newlyn Orion Gallery. AD 20.9.1995 gives mixed media on board, 46 x 36 cm.

2. ***Gate of Ivory and Gate of Horn*** : c.1965, ink and gouache, stillomancy, 29 x 45 cm.(s). Exhib. 1976, Penzance, Newlyn Orion Gallery. 1991 listing.

3. ***Harbour Illuminations* (I)** : black and coloured chalks, 47 x 61.5 cm.

4. ***Harbour Illuminations* (II*)*** : coloured chalks, 47 x 61.5 cm.

5. ***Harbour Illuminations* (III)** : coloured chalks, 47 x 61.5 cm.

6. ***Petits Fours*** : c.1965, ink and wash, 17.3 x 23.6 cm. 1990 listing.

7. ***Totem*** : Merz collage. Exhib. 1976, Penzance, Newlyn Orion Gallery.

8. ***World-Moth*** : collage, 20.5 x 28.0 cm. Exhib. 1972, City of Exeter Art Gallery.

1966

1. ***Celtic Cross*** : Merz collage, 90.0 x 60.0 cm. Exhib. 1972, City of Exeter Art Gallery.

2. ***Judgement of Paris*** : Merz collage. Exhib. 1976, Penzance, Newlyn Orion Gallery.

3. ***Khamsin*** : Merz collage. Exhib. 1976, Penzance, Newlyn Orion Gallery. AD 2.6.1994 gives 45.7 x 45.7 cm.

4. ***Marsh-Spectre*** : oil on paper, 72.0 x 110.0 cm. Exhib. 1972, City of Exeter Art Gallery.

5. ***Nuclear Explosion 'Bikini'*** : gouache109 x 70.cm. All AD 6.2.1981.

6 ***Primordial Slime*** : oil on paper, convulsive landscape, 70.0 x 83.0 cm. Exhib. 1972, City of Exeter Art Gallery; 1976, Penzance, Newlyn Orion Gallery.

7. ***Serpent of Genesis*** : oil on paper, 88.5 x 59.5 cm. Exhib. 1967, Czechoslovakia, touring with Fantasmagie group; 1968, Newlyn, Society of Artists; 1972, City of Exeter Art Gallery.

8. ***Shells on a Seashore*** : Merz collage. Exhib. 1976, Penzance, Newlyn Orion Gallery.

9. ***Twin God*** : Merz collage. Exhib. 1976, Penzance, Newlyn Orion Gallery.

10. ***Woodland Ride*** : oil with collage on board, 46.0 x 45.5 cm. Exhib. 1972, City of Exeter Art Gallery.

1967

1. ***Batman and Robin* (I)** : collage, 10.3 x 20.5 cm. Exhib. 1972, City of Exeter Art Gallery.

2. ***Batman and Robin* (II)** : collage. Exhib. 1976, Penzance, Newlyn Orion Gallery.

3. ***Cave*** : ink and ready-made, collage. Exhib. 1976, Penzance, Newlyn Orion Gallery.

4. ***Family Group*** : Merz collage, 81.0 x 100.7 cm. Exhib. 1972, City of Exeter Art Gallery.

5. ***Succulent*** : Merz collage. Exhib. 1976, Penzance, Newlyn Orion Gallery.

6. ***Thunderbolt*** : oil on carboard, 91.5 x 61 cm. All AD 20.9.1995.

1968

1. ***Temple Entrance*** : Merz collage (cardboard, polystyrene, paper, mixed media), 10 x 14 in. (25.5 x 35.5 cm.) Exhib. 1976, Penzance, Newlyn Orion Gallery.

2. ***Unidentified Flying Object*** : ink, 40.4 x 30.5, 1990 listing.

1969

1. ***Brass Plaque in the Vestibule of Franciscan Church, Valetta*** : ink, 14.2 x 13.7 cm. 1990 listing also gives rough sketch, *Brass Plaque*, ink, 20.2 x 11.5 cm.

2. ***Break-up of a Space Rocket*** : oil on paper, convulsive landscape, 71.0 x 109.5 cm. Exhib. 1969, West Berlin, Fantasmagie International Exhibition; 1972, City of Exeter Art Gallery; 1976, Penzance, Newlyn Orion Gallery.

3. ***Clay Statuette, 'The Maltese Venus'*** : ink and crayon, 25 x 18 cm. 1990 listing also gives rough sketch, *Maltese Venus*, crayon, 25.3 x 20 cm.

4. ***Colours of the Sea*** : oil on paper, 70.5 x 109.5 cm. Exhib. 1972, City of Exeter Art Gallery.

5. ***Computer Stains*** : ink and ready-made, collage, 20.5 x 12.6 cm. Exhib. 1972, City of Exeter Art Gallery (dated 1970); 1976, Penzance, Newlyn Orion Gallery.

6. ***De Profundis*** : enamel on board, 29.7 x 31.5 cm. Exhib. 1972, City of Exeter Art Gallery.

7. ***Depths of the Sea*** : watercolour, ink and pencil, 29.3 x 19.5 cm. 1990 listing.

8. ***Dust-Devil*** : enamel on board, 119 x 82.5 cm. 1990 listing.

9. ***Madonna*** : ink and wash, 25.5 x 28.8 cm., drawing for painting. 1990 listing.

10. ***Madonna*** : oil on board. Exhib. 1976, Penzance, Newlyn Orion Gallery.

11. ***Neolithic Temple at Mnarja, Malta*** : ink and crayon, 19.3 x 20.8 cm. 1990 listing.

12. ***Neolithic Type, Malta*** : ink and crayon, 23 x 18.5 cm. 1990 listing also gives rough sketch, *Neolithic Type*, crayon, 20.2 x 11.5 cm.

13. ***Night Storm at Sea*** : enamel on board, 61.0 x 122.0 cm. Exhib. 1972, City of Exeter Art Gallery.

14. ***Permutation* (I)** : collage, 23.8 x 9.0 cm. Exhib. 1972, City of Exeter Art Gallery.

15. ***Permutation* (III)** : collage, 22.5 x 15.0 cm. Exhib. 1972, City of Exeter Art Gallery.

16. ***Prehistoric 'Disk Idol', Valetta Museum . . .*** : ink, 17.9 x 16.3 cm. 1990 listing also gives rough sketch, *Pre-Historic Disk-Idol*, ink and crayon, 20.2 x 11.5 cm.

17. ***Rocky Island*** : oil on board, 27½ x 42 in., 70 x 107 cm.

18. ***Rocky Island*** : oil on paper, 80.5 x 107.0 cm. Exhib. 1969, West Berlin, Fantasmagie International Exhibition; 1971, Newlyn Gallery (as *Rock Island*); 1972, City of Exeter Art Gallery; 1985, London, Blond Fine Art (as 31½ x 46 in., 80 x 116 cm.).

19. ***Rose of the Palace of Fire*** : mixed media on paper laid down on board, 27¾ x 38¾ in., 70.5 x 99.0 cm,. Exhib. 1969, West Berlin, Fantasmagie International Exhibition; 1972, City of Exeter Art Gallery. Witt library gives oil and watercolour on paper, laid down on board, 83.7 x 110.5 cm, 33 x 43½ in. AD gives watercolour 84 x 110.5 cm.

20. ***Sea-Pool in Limestone, Malta*** : ink and crayon, 16.6 x 15 cm. 1990 listing.

21. ***Street in Rabat, Decorated . . .*** : ink and wash, 18.7 x 16.2 cm. 1990 listing also gives rough sketch, *Street in Rabat*, ink, 11.5 x 20.2 cm.

22. ***Tarzan*** : collage. Exhib. 1976, Penzance, Newlyn Orion Gallery.

23. ***Thunderbolt*** : Merz collage. Exhib. 1976, Penzance, Newlyn Orion Gallery.

24. ***Volcanic Landscape*** : enamel on board, convulsive landscape, 76.5 x 101.8 cm. Exhib. 1972, City of Exeter Art Gallery; 1976, Penzance, Newlyn Orion Gallery.

1970

1. ***Haunted Hedge*** : enamel on board, convulsive landscape, 61.0 x 106.8 cm. Exhib. 1971, Newlyn, Newlyn Gallery; 1972, City of Exeter Art Gallery; 1976, Penzance, Newlyn Orion Gallery.

2. ***Holed Stone, Carnac*** : ink, 25 x 15.9 cm. 1990 listing.

3. ***Mound of Tumiac, Ile de Rhuys*** : ink and crayon, 17 x 25.6 cm. 1990 listing.

4. ***Pools in Sand*** : ink and crayon, 18 x 25.6 cm. 1990 listing.

5. ***Portrait of a Dignitary*** : Merz collage, 69.5 x 100.4 cm. Exhib.

1972, City of Exeter Art Gallery; 1976, Penzance, Newlyn Orion Gallery.

6. ***Sun-Child*** : Merz collage, 60.5 x 60.5 cm. Exhib. 1972, City of Exeter Art Gallery.

7. ***Three-Dimensional Object*** : ready-made sculpture. Exhib. 1976, Penzance, Newlyn Orion Gallery.

1971

1. ***Altar to Pan*** : ink and gouache, stillomancy. Exhib. 1976, Penzance, Newlyn Orion Gallery.

2. ***Cornish Landscape*** : collage. Exhib. 1976, Penzance, Newlyn Orion Gallery.

3. ***Cornish Landscape*** : oil on board, 60.5 x 40.0 cm. Exhib. 1972, City of Exeter Art Gallery.

4. ***Dryad: Silver Fir*** : drawing, 20.0 x 22.0 cm. Exhib. 1972, City of Exeter Art Gallery.

5. ***Dryad: Vine*** : watercolour, 20.3 x 21.3 cm. All AD 14.2.02.

6. ***Dryad: Willow*** : drawing, 20.0 x 22.0 cm. Exhib. 1972, City of Exeter Art Gallery.

7. ***Elemental*** : oil on paper, stillomancy, 15.0 x 23.0 cm. Exhib. 1972, City of Exeter Art Gallery; 1976, Penzance, Newlyn Orion Gallery. Mayor Gallery (Dec. 1947) showed a drawing of that name.

8. ***Eye of Horus*** : Merz collage. Exhib. 1976, Penzance, Newlyn Orion Gallery.

9. ***Fading Ghost*** : ink and newspaper, collage. Exhib. 1976, Penzance, Newlyn Orion Gallery.

10. ***Flowers in a Vase*** : oil on board. 28 x 16.7 cm. Exhib. 1973, Penzance, Orion Gallery (as 8 x 6 in.) 1990 listing.

11. ***Geometric*** : collage of coloured paper, 29.6 x 34 cm. 1990 listing.

12. ***Graphomania: Black*** : drawing, 25.5 x 19.0 cm. Exhib. 1972, City of Exeter Art Gallery.

13. ***Graphomania: Blue*** : drawing, 20.8 x 29.5 cm. Exhib. 1972, City of Exeter Art Gallery.

14. ***Graphomania: Blue-Black*** : drawing, 20.5 x 29.8 cm. Exhib. 1972, City of Exeter Art Gallery.

15. ***Graphomania: Mixed Colours, Green and Blue*** : pen and coloured ink and paper collage 8 x 12 in., 20 x 30.5 cm. Undated but assumed contemporary with series.

16. ***Graphomania: Pencil* (I)** : drawing, 34.0 x 34.0 cm. Exhib. 1972, City of Exeter Art Gallery.

17. ***Hill Forest*** : collage, 22.7 x 20.5 cm. Exhib. 1972, City of Exeter Art Gallery.

18 . ***Marsh Spirit*** : ink and gouache, stillomancy, 20.5 x 22.0 cm. Exhib. 1972, City of Exeter Art Gallery; 1976, Penzance, Newlyn Orion Gallery.

19. ***Middle Eastern Landscape*** : Merz collage, 91.0 x 91.0 cm. Exhib. 1972, City of Exeter Art Gallery; 1976, Penzance, Newlyn Orion Gallery.

20. ***Open Entrance*** : Merz collage, 23.0 x 16.0 cm. Exhib. 1972, City of Exeter Art Gallery; 1976, Penzance, Newlyn Orion Gallery. 1990 listing gives collage of plastic pegs, coloured paper and foil.

21. ***Ripples*** : Merz collage, 37.5 x 68.5 cm. Exhib. 1972, City of

Exeter Art Gallery; 1976, Penzance, Newlyn Orion Gallery. AD 27.11.2001 gives sculpture, 39 x 68 cm.

22. ***Serapis*** : ink and gouache, stillomancy, 19.0 x 22.0 cm. Exhib. 1972, City of Exeter Art Gallery; 1976, Penzance, Newlyn Orion Gallery.

23. ***Shaman*** : mixed media cardboard collage with perforated plastic, 17½ x 18½ in., 44.5 x 47 cm.

24. ***Spine of Osiris*** : Merz collage. Exhib. 1976, Penzance, Newlyn Orion Gallery.

25. ***Volcano Spirit*** : ink and gouache, stillomancy, 20.5 x 22.0 cm. Exhib. 1972, City of Exeter Art Gallery; 1976, Penzance, Newlyn Orion Gallery.

26. ***Winter Sunset*** : oil on board, 38.8 x 59.3 cm. Exhib. 1971, Newlyn, Newlyn Gallery; 1972, City of Exeter Art Gallery.

1972

1. ***Delius' Irmelin*** : oil or enamel on board, 91.5 x 76.2 cm. Exhib. 1972 , Newlyn, Newlyn Gallery; 1972, City of Exeter Art Gallery (as enamel); 1976, Penzance, Newlyn Orion Gallery (as oil).

2. ***Orange Lilies*** : oil on paper, 8 x 6 in. Exhib. 1973, Penzance, Orion Gallery.

3. ***Past and Future*** : collage, 16.7 x 17.0 cm. Exhib. 1972, City of Exeter Art Gallery.

4. ***Rising Sap*** : ?oil on panel, 50.2 x 67 cm. 1990 listing.

5. ***Summer Flowers*** : oil on board, 6 x 5 in. Exhib. 1973, Penzance, Orion Gallery.

6. ***Volcano*** : oil on paper, convulsive landscape, 69.0 x 102.0

cm. Exhib. 1972, City of Exeter Art Gallery; 1976, Penzance, Newlyn Orion Gallery.

1974

1. ***A la Claire Fontaine*** : enamel on board, 34 x 42 cm

2. ***L'Ascension*** : mixed media on paper laid down on board, 41¾ x 23½ in., 106 x 60 cm. Exhib. 1976, Penzance, Newlyn Orion Gallery as *Messiaen's L'Ascension*, 1973, oil on board.

3. ***Cherry Blossom in a Vase*** : pastel, 36 x 23.5 cm. (s).1990 listing.

4. ***Child of a Sea Monster*** : mixed media on board, 15 x 46 cm. All AD 16.5.1996.

5. ***Dawn Clouds*** : mixed media, 11.2 x 34 cm. All AD 2.6.1994.

6. ***Flowers in a Blue Glass*** : pastel, 36 x 23.4 cm.(s). 1990 listing.

7. ***Lily in a Blue Glass*** : 30.8 x 23.4 cm.(s). 1990 listing.

8. ***Roses in a Blue Glass*** : pastel, 36 x 23.2 cm.(s). 1990 listing.

1976

1. ***Begonias with Fatsia Leaves*** : oil on canvas, 21 x 25 in., 53.3 x 63.5 cm.

2. ***Mirror Overflowing*** : enamel and gold on board, 28.7 x 24 cm. 1990 listing.

3. ***Notre Dame - La Cathédrale Façade*** : oil on board, 36 x 30¾ in., 91.5 x 75.5 cm. AD Illus. Christie's catalogue 3.6.1999. AD 14.11.2000, mixed media.

4. ***Stockhausen's Poles*** : oil on board. Exhib. 1976, Penzance, Newlyn Orion Gallery.

5. ***Sunrise through Bushes*** : enamel on panel, 30.3 x 20.6 cm. 1990 listing.

6. ***Winter Sunset*** : oil on canvas, 51 x 61 cm. 1990 listing.

1977

1. ***Cucumber in Tissue*** : ?enamel on board, 23.8 x 14 cm. 1990 listing.

2. ***Moon-Bird*** : watercolour and ink, 28 x 22.3 cm. 1990 listing.

3. ***Mountain Valley at Sunset*** : watercolour, 23 x 32.4 cm. 1990 listing.

4. ***Pools Undersea*** : oil and enamel on board, 11.9 x 30.3 cm. 1990 listing.

5. ***Rock Pool*** : ink and enamel on board, 19.3 x 24.2 cm. 1990 listing.

6. ***Seashore at Night*** : watercolour and ink, 20.3 x 27.8 cm. 1990 listing.

7. ***Spangly Gloom*** : ?enamel on board, 30.3 x 25.2 cm. 1990 listing.

8. ***Stream-Bed*** : enamel on board, 10.1 x 47.6 cm. 1990 listing.

9-13. ***Tarot Pack*** : enamel on board, five framed paintings of tarot cards, each 12 x 9 in. Exhib. 1977, Newlyn.

14. ***Winter Tree*** : enamel on board, 30.3 x 25.3 cm. 1990 listing.

15. ***Woodland Valley*** : watercolour and ink, 22.8 x 30.4 cm. 1990 listing.

1978

1. ***Cloud-Portent*** : enamel on paper, 23 x 32.5 cm. 1990 listing.

2. ***Dusk on the Shelly River* (I)** : oil on canvas, 68.5 x 51 cm. 1990 listing.

3. ***Exotic Flower*** : c.1978 , enamel on board, 16.4 x 16 cm. 1990 listing.

4. ***Fire and Water*** : enamel on paper, 32.5 x 23 cm. 1990 listing.

5. ***Flowering Tree in a Storm*** : enamel on paper, 32.5 x 23 cm. 1990 listing.

6. ***Germination*** : enamel on paper, 37.8 x 28 cm. 1990 listing.

7. ***The Gyre*** : enamel on paper, 45.8 x 32.5 cm. 1990 listing.

8. ***High Rise*** : c.1978 , collage of coloured paper, 20.3 x 20.9 cm. 1990 listing.

9. ***Idea of a Rose*** : enamel on paper, 32.5 x 23 cm. 1990 listing.

10. ***In the Alembic*** : enamel on paper, 23 x 32.5 cm. 1990 listing.

11. ***Misty Sunrise*** : enamel on paper, 23 x 32.5 cm. 1990 listing.

12. ***Moonlight through Mist*** : enamel on paper, 23 x 32.5 cm. 1990 listing.

13. ***Night Pools*** : enamel on paper, 32.5 x 45.8 cm. 1990 listing.

14. ***Primal Fire*** : enamel on paper, 32.5 x 23 cm. 1990 listing.

15. ***Sea Depths*** : enamel on paper, 32.5 x 45.8 cm. 1990 listing.

16. ***Sea-Swell*** : enamel on paper, 23 x 32.5 cm. 1990 listing.

17. ***Seething*** : enamel on paper, 11.5 x 16.3 cm. 1990 listing.

18. ***Sunlight on Rock-Pool*** : enamel on paper, 23 x 32.5 cm. 1990 listing.

19. ***Towards the Tessaract*** : watercolour and ink, 17.3 x 16.2 cm. 1990 listing.

20. ***Train-Face*** : enamel on paper, 34.1 x 19.3 cm. 1990 listing.

21. ***Vice-Regent of the Sun*** : c.1978, Merz collage (gold and oil + plastic form on panel), 25.2 x 19.7 cm. 1990 listing.

22. ***Volcanic Flare*** : enamel on paper, 32.5 x 23 cm. 1990 listing.

1979

1. ***Arum*** : chalk and watercolour, 29 x 19.6 cm.(s). 1990 listing.

2. ***Coral Formation*** : enamel on paper, 16.2 x 23 cm. 1990 listing.

3. ***Deep Water*** : enamel on paper, 16.2 x 23 cm. 1990 listing.

4. ***Earth Bubbles*** : enamel on paper, 23 x 32.5 cm. 1990 listing.

5. ***Eruption*** : enamel on paper, 16.2 x 23 cm. 1990 listing.

6. ***Fatima*** : enamel on paper, 16.2 x 23 cm. 1990 listing.

7. ***Growth in Water*** : oil and pencil on board, 20.2 x 30.5 cm. 1990 listing.

8. ***Growth Undersea*** : oil on board, 19 x 30.3 cm. 1990 listing.

9. ***Icy Sunrise*** : enamel on paper, 16.2 x 23 cm. 1990 listing.

10. ***Lake in a Desert Place*** : enamel on paper, 23 x 32.5 cm. 1990 listing.

11. ***Libran Angel*** : enamel on panel, 61 x 32.3 cm. 1990 listing.

12. ***Memories of Mount Etna* (II)** : enamel on paper, 16.2 x 23 cm. 1990 listing.

13. ***Once in a Green Moon*** : enamel on paper, 16.2 x 23 cm. 1990 listing.

14. ***The Third Eye*** : Merz collage, paint, wood, bottle top, 25.8 x 13.2 cm. 1990 listing.

15. ***Veined Petals*** : enamel on paper, 23 x 32.5 cm. 1990 listing.

16. ***Volcanic Fires*** : enamel on paper, 23 x 32.5 cm. 1990 listing.

17. ***Winter Seascape*** : watercolour wash and crayon, 19.6 x 29.6 cm. 1990 listing.

18. ***Woodland Fungus*** : enamel on paper, 16.2 x 23 cm. 1990 listing.

1980

1. ***Agonised Head*** : watercolour and ink, 29.5 x 19.6 cm. 1990 listing.

2. ***Angel with a Gold Collar*** : collage, oil and corrugated card, 76 x 106 cm. 1990 listing.

3. ***Buddleia with Roses in a Jar*** : ? felt-pen, 18.2 x 18.8 cm.(s). 1990 listing.

4. ***La Chapelle Etrange*** : collage, three postcards and paint on card, 16.7 x 29.9 cm. 1990 listing.

5. ***Circles*** : watercolour and acrylic, 16.1 x 20.9 cm. 1990 listing.

6. ***Dark Fire*** : enamel on board, 24.5 x 31.8 cm. 1990 listing.

7. ***Godetia Flower*** : ink, acrylic and pencil, 21.8 x 28.8 cm.(s). 1990 listing.

8. ***Le Manoir Etrange*** : collage, three postcards and paint on card, 17.9 x 47.5 cm. 1990 listing.

9. ***A Rose is a Rose is a Rose*** : acrylic on board, 25.4 x 19.7 cm. 1990 listing.

10. ***Roses and Rosewood* (II)** : ink and watercolour, 21.9 x 29.1 cm. 1990 listing.

11. ***Roses in a Red Vase*** : ink and ?felt-pen, 28.8 x 18.4 cm. 1990 listing.

12. ***Summer Flowers* (II)** : oil on board, 15 x 15.9 cm.(s). 1990 listing.

1981

1. ***Klingsor's Castle*** : collage, colour photographs on silver card, 29.6 x 19 cm. 1990 listing.

2. ***Poppy*** : c.1981, acrylic, 24.6 x 19 cm. (Monographed as 1981, dated on back as 1980.) 1990 listing.

3. ***Torso*** : enamel on board, 26.7 x 25.3 cm. 1990 listing.

1983

1. ***House*** : collage, 31.5 x 29 cm. All AD 14.2.2002.

UNDATED : KNOWN TITLES

Excluding Work First Shown in Cheltenham, Municipal Art Gallery and at London, Fine Art Society, 1936.

Ace of Cups : watercolour and ink, 19.2 x 19 cm. This and the three below probably shown in 1977 at the Newlyn Gallery. 1990 listing.

Ace of Discs : watercolour, 19.3 x 19 cm. 1990 listing.

Ace of Swords : watercolour, 19.2 x19 cm. 1990 listing.

Ace of Wands : watercolour, 19 x 19.2 cm, 1990 listing.

Adam : ?oil on panel, 33 x 22.7 cm. 1990 listing.

Arum Lilies : oil on canvas, 66 x 61 cm. All AD 3.6.2003.

Bait : Exhib. 1947 (Dec.), Mayor Gallery (drawings)

Bloodstone : ink and wash, 7.7 x 12.3 cm.(s). 1990 listing.

The Call of the World 1701-1927 : watercolour and ink, 60.5 x 50.6 cm. Rough for a poster for Birthday Pageant of the SPG (Society for Propagation of the Gospel ?). 1990 listing.

Cathedral Interior (I) : ink and wash, 23 x 32.4 cm. 1990 listing.

Cathedral Interior (II) : ink wash, 32.5 x 23 cm. 1990 listing.

Christian Marriage (I) : possibly c.1942, watercolour, 23 x 18.2 cm. 1990 listing.

Christian Marriage (II) : possibly c.1942, watercolour and pencil, 27.2 x 17.7 cm. 1990 listing.

Cornish Dawn : oil on panel, 13.2 x 20.1 cm. 1990 listing.

Cottage and Prucklish Mountain : c.mid-1920s, watercolour and pencil, 19.2 x 25.2 cm. 1990 listing.

Dancing Pony (possibly given title) : watercolour and crayon, 74 x 38 cm. 1990 listing. Costume design.

Death of the Vampire in a Magic Mirror : gouache and ink. Exhib. 1945, Derby Museum and Art Gallery. Note: *Death of the Vampire* (c.1960) was shown in 1976 at the Newlyn Orion Gallery; now on loan in the Royal Cornwall Museum, it may be another study of the same subject.

Décalcomania : gouache, five such titled works of various sizes (two of 32.5 x 45.8 cm., two of 51 x 31.5 cm., one of 32.5 x 45.7 cm.) 1990 listing.

Donegal Mountains : oil on board, 26.5 x 37.5 cm. 1990 listing.

Dorset Downs : watercolour, 13.9 x 22.9 cm. 1990 listing.

Elemental : drawing. Exhib. 1947 (Dec.) Mayor Gallery. Possibly the same as 1971 work.

Embers : watercolour and ink, 44.5 x 31.5 cm. 1990 listing.

Ephesian Diana : 61.5 x 42 cm. All AD 27.11.2001, as sculpture.

Errigal from Gortahork : watercolour, 23.1 x 14 cm. 1990 listing.

Exposed on the Mountains of the Heart : oil on card, 25.8 x 38.3 cm.(s). 1990 listing. AD c.2003 gives oil on board.

The Eye. Exhib. 1958, Kingston upon Hull, Ferens Art Gallery.

Fire Opal : watercolour, 17.7 x 13.7 cm.(s). 1990 listing.

Floats. Exhib. 1947 (Dec.), Mayor Gallery (drawings).

Flying Fish : ink and paint on panel, 16.5 x 22 cm. 1990 listing.

Foam-Flower. Exhib. 1947 (Dec.), Mayor Gallery (drawings).

Forms of Pleasure. Exhib. 1941, Harrogate.

Fruit : watercolour and ink, 18.2 x 23 cm. 1990 listing.

Fungi. Exhib. 1947 (Dec.), Mayor Gallery (drawings).

Gateway : watercolour and crayon (collaged), 50.5 x 44.6 cm. 1990 listing.

The Glenna, Gortahork : c.mid-1920s, pencil sketch, 22.6 x 14 cm. 1990 listing. The Glenna river, Gortahork, N.W. Donegal.

Goblin Market : watercolour and ink. Five drawings for illustrations plus cover decoration: (Goblin with apples, 23.3 x 30.6 cm. (cover); Goblins carrying apples, 23 x 28.7 cm.; Girl with fruit and goblins, 23 x 28.7 cm.; Girls hiding among rocks, 23 x 28.7 cm.; Iris by a river, 23.28.7 cm.; Thorny Tree, 23 x 28.7 cm.) 1990 listing.

Happy Birthday : watercolour and pencil, 12 x 7.8 cm.(s). 1990 listing.

Harbour : ink, 44.7 x 31.3 cm. 1990 listing.

Heads of Angels : watercolour, gouache and gold ink, 30.5 x 60.5 cm. 1990 listing.

The Heart of Corn : watercolour, 25 x 17.5 cm.(s). Exhib. 1941, Harrogate. 1990 listing.

L'Homme Approximatif : watercolour and ink, 41.3 x 31.6 cm. 1990 listing.

Horus : ink and wash, 25 x 26 cm.(s). 1990 listing.

Hour-Glass. Exhib. 1947 (Dec.), Mayor Gallery (drawings).

Initiation : watercolour, 18.5 x 37.3 cm. 1990 listing.

Interior. Exhib. 1947 (Dec.), Mayor Gallery (drawings).

Interior, Corsica : watercolour and crayon (collaged), 56 x 40.5 cm. 1990 listing.

Larval Images : watercolour, 25.2 x 17.4 cm. Exhib. 1941, Harrogate. 1990 listing.

Lavenders Blue : watercolour and ink, 27.4 x 15.5 cm. Drawing for illustration. 1990 listing.

The Light of the Magistry : watercolour and pencil, 30.6 x 23.2 cm. 1990 listing.

Low Tide : ink, 35.5 x 26 cm.(s). Exhib. 1947 (Dec.), Mayor Gallery (drawings). 1990 listing.

Machine for Conjuration : watercolour, 27.9 x 20.2 cm. 1990 listing.

Marine. Exhib. 1947 (Dec.), Mayor Gallery (drawings).

Mars Opposition Saturn : watercolour and ink, 34.3 x 30.7 cm. 1990 listing.

Mask and Wig for the Dark-haired Girl (Bird of Hermes) : watercolour and pencil, 37.6 x 25.2 cm. 1990 listing. Costume design.

Mask and Wig for the Fair-haired Girl (Bird of Hermes) : watercolour and pencil, 37.5 x 25.2 cm. 1990 listing. Costume design.

Mask for the Phoenix (Bird of Hermes): watercolour and pencil, 40.4 x 25.1 cm. 1990 listing. Costume design.

Mausoleum : watercolour and ink, 30.1 x 21.7 cm. 1990 listing.

Mephistopheles and Faust : oil on board, 25.4 x 30.4 cm. 1990 listing.

Monogamy : watercolour and ink, 31 x 21.5 cm. 'Diagram I' on back; another, same medium and size. 'Diagram II' on back. 1990 listing.

Morphological Study : ink, diameter 31.3 cm.(s). 1990 listing.

Mystical Scene : oil on board, 18¾ x 23¼ in., 50.5 x 59 cm. Perhaps a given title for auction sale.

Nativity : oil on canvas, 41 x 51 cm. All AD 27.10.1994.

Nest among Leaves. Exhib. 1947 (Dec.), Mayor Gallery (drawings).

On the Beach. Exhib. 1947 (Dec.), Mayor Gallery (drawings).

Onions : ink wash, 31.4 x 35.8 cm. 1990 listing.

Oriental Dancer : ?oil on board, 72.5 x 55 cm. 1990 listing.

Orpheus and Eurydice : watercolour and pencil, 29.9 x 24.8 cm. 1990 listing.

Pears : pencil, 13.5 x 8 cm. 1990 listing. (See 1937 for oil painting.)

Perspective Study : gouache, 47 x 40.3 cm. (on reverse 'Rome Scholarship in Mural Painting'). 1990 listing.

Petit Ménage : watercolour and pencil, 36.2 x 20.6 cm. 1990 listing.

Pine Mother : watercolour and ink, 22.7 x 18 cm. 1990 listing.

Pisces. Exhib. 1947 (Dec.), Mayor Gallery (drawings).

Poe's 'Red Death' : gouache, 38.5 x 56 cm.(s). 1990 listing.

Portrait of an Artist : oil on board, 12 x 10 in., 30.5 x 25 cm. Exhib. 1985, London, Blond Fine Art. Possibly Portrait also shown at Cheltenham.

Puzzle : ink, 35.2 x 26.5 cm. Exhib. 1947 (Dec.), Mayor Gallery (drawings). 1990 listing.

Pygmalion and Galatea : watercolour and collage, 51 x 34 cm. 1990 listing.

Ring-Master (possibly given title) : watercolour and crayon, 74.5 x 51 cm. 1990 listing. Costume design.

Rock Pool. Exhib. 1947 (Dec.), Mayor Gallery (drawings).

Room with a View : mixed media, 45 x 42.5 cm. All AD 8.6.1999.

Santa Warna Lands. Exhib. 1947 (Dec.), Mayor Gallery (drawings).

Sardine and Eggs : watercolour, 22.3 x 17.3 cm.(s). 1990 listing.

Scarecrow. Exhib. 1947 (Dec.), Mayor Gallery (drawings).

The Seasons : oil on canvas, 87 x 119.5 cm. 1990 listing.

Second Adam : watercolour and pencil, 45.7 x 32.4 cm. 1990 listing.

Secret Wells : watercolour and ink, 27.8 x 20.2 cm. 1990 listing.

Self-portraits (ink and wash) owned by the National Portrait Gallery (Nos. 6485, 6486).

Shell Fish : watercolour and ink, 22.3 x 18 cm.(s). 1990 listing.

Shoreside : oil on board, 22 x 25 in., 55.9 x 63.5 cm. AD 4.3.1998 adds 'Still Life'.

Sun in Hawthorn. Exhib. 1947 (Dec.), Mayor Gallery (drawings).

The Sunset Birth : oil on canvas, 15½ x 28 in., 39.3 x 71.2 cm. Depiction of the Men-an-Tol ringstone and megalithic alignment.

Sunspot : watercolour and ink, 66 x 44 cm. Exhib. 1947 (Dec.), Mayor Gallery (drawings). 1990 listing.

Tekke Um-Haram : ink and wash, 44.5 x 31.2 cm. 1990 listing. See Notes on Appendix IIA.

Tekke of Um-Haram (II) : ink and wash, 44.6 x 31 cm. 1990 listing. See Notes on Appendix IIA

The Tenth Tarot. Exhib. 1941, Harrogate; 1942, London, London Museum.

The Tree of Veins (I) : watercolour, 25.7 x 18 cm. 1990 listing. Probably c.1941, same period as *The Tree of Veins* (II).

Triton : watercolour and pencil, 22.9 x 30.4 cm. 1990 listing.

Les Vases Communicants : oil on canvas, 13 x 16 in., 33 x 41 cm.

Water : watercolour, 44.5 x 31.2 cm.(s). 1990 listing.

Zephyr and Aurora : watercolour, 41.1 x 31.6 cm. 1990 listing.

Undated Artwork First Shown at Cheltenham, Municipal Art Gallery (C); and London, Fine Art Society (L), 1936

Aaron Meeting Moses in the Desert. Oil (C).

Banana-Flower. ?Oil (L).

Bedroom Window. Watercolour (C).

Begonias. Oil (CL).

Begonias and Leaves. ?Oil (L).

The Bhikku Ananda. Watercolour (C).

Bird-of-Paradise Flowers. Oil (CL).

By the Sea. Watercolour (C).

Cactus and Palm. ?Oil (L).

Cactus Screen. Oil on silk (L).

Canna. Oil (C).

*Chrysanthemums.*Watercolour, ink wash, 35.1 x 43.3 cm.(s). (C). 1990 listing. Possibly 1933 work.

Convent of the Annunciata. Oil (C).

La Conversation Pertinente. Watercolour and ink, 48.8 x 36.7 cm. (C). 1990 listing.

Convolvulus and Nasturtium. Watercolour (C).

Courgette. Oil (CL).

Cradle Orchid. Watercolour on silk (L).

Cymbidium Orchid. ?Oil (L).

'Cynara'. Watercolour. Illus. to Ernest Dowson's poem. (C). Publication not ascertained.

Design for Mosaic. Another, same title. Medium unknown (C).

Double Coco-Nut. Watercolour on silk (L). Exhib. 1939, London Gallery.

The Drawing Room. Ink (C).

Dust Sheet. Medium unknown (C).

Dying Gloxinia. Oil (C).

'Elle'. Watercolour (C).

'Elle caresse un petit garçon'. Ink (C).

'Elle joue aux cartes'. Ink (C).

'Elle regarde le plafond'. Ink (C).

'Elle se coiffe'. Ink (C).

The Fool. Distemper (C).

Foot. Pastel (C).

Fungi. Watercolour on silk (L).

The Future Eve. Gouache, design for painting on silk (C).

Gipsy. Oil (C).

Gloxinias. ?Oil (L).

Gold-Fish. Watercolour (C).

The Grave-Circle at Mycenae. Watercolour (C).

House in Athens. Oil (C).

Jam Jar. Ink (C).

Japanese Water-Flower. Pastel (C).

The Juggler. Distemper (C).

Libation for the Argo. Oil (C).

Love Birds. Medium unknown (C).

Magnolia. Watercolour (C).

Milledge. Ink (C).

Mountain at Delphi. Oil (C).

Myconos. Watercolour (C).

Plants in a Window. Medium unknown (C).

Portrait (three paintings). Oil (C).

Reflection (I). Watercolour (C).

Reflection (II). Watercolour (C).

Rose of Jericho. Watercolour (C).

The Serpent Power. Gouache, design for painting on silk (C).

The Sofa. Watercolour (C).

Solanium. ?Oil (L).

Still Life. Distemper (C).

Still Life. Watercolour (four paintings) (C).

Studies of Gloxinia. Watercolour (C). Possibly 1934, Gloxinias, watercolour and ink, as exhib. 1973, Penzance, Orion Gallery.

Sunflower and Dahlias. Oil (C).

Water-Lilies. ?Oil (L). See also 1934, gouache painting, as exhib. 1973, Penzance. Orion Gallery.

Wenduyne. Oil (C).

Zadkine's Garden. Ink (C).

Zetta. Watercolour (C).

DATED OR APPROXIMATELY DATED : TITLES NOT PROVIDED BY ARTIST, IN 1990 LISTING

c.1920s. Study of a church, pencil, 40.5 x 25.1 cm.

?1922. Drawing for illustration, watercolour and ink, 23 x 17.2 cm. Shipwreck, goblin head.

Mid-1920s. Studies of insects and a cottage, pencil, 25.5 x 19.5 cm.

Mid-1920s. Study of sea and rocks, pencil, 22.8 x 14 cm.

Mid-1920s. Study of water and rocks, pencil, 22.8 x 14 cm. On back 'The Glenna, Gortahork'.

Mid-1920s. Wave study, pencil, 14 x 22.8 cm.

1926. Architectural study, gabled house in garden, watercolour and pencil, 38 x 35.3 cm.

1926 (Dec.). Architectural study, figures in a green and orange garden, watercolour and pencil, 38 x 50.7 cm.

1927 (Feb.). Architectural study, columned and stepped interior, watercolour and pencil, 28.3 x 43.2 cm.

1927 (Feb.). Architectural study, lorry on village green, watercolour and pencil, 19 x 34.3 cm.

Late 1920s. Nude study, woman in a necklace, ink and wash, 56.1 x 38.2 cm.

Late 1920s. Portrait study, girl with plaits round her ears, pencil, 28 x 38.2 cm.

Late 1920s. Standing nude, pencil, 38.2 x 14 cm.

c.1930. Two drawings for a mural, café, Lord's cricket ground, watercolour and gouache, 45 x 61 cm., 45.5 x 62 cm.

c.1930s. Shell studies, watercolour and pencil, 25.4 x 35.5 cm.

1931. Chinese flower in a glass jug, ink and chalk on brown paper, 27.7 x 21 cm.

1931. Seaweed in a glass, watercolour, 15.7 x 12 cm.(s).

1931. Study of a foot, ink and chalk, 22.5 x 21.3 cm. Maybe exhib. 1936, Cheltenham, Municipal Art Gallery, as pastel.

1931. Study of a goldfish bowl, watercolour and pencil, 15.6 x 16.4 cm. Maybe exhib. 1936, Cheltenham, Municipal Art Gallery as *Gold-Fish*.

1931. Chinese flower in a glass jug, ink and chalk on brown paper, 27.7 x 21 cm.

1932. Goldfish tank and fruit, watercolour and ink, 11.8 x 14.9 cm.

1932. Marrows, watercolour and ink, 12.6 x 22.8 cm. Probably exhib. 1936, Cheltenham Municipal Art Gallery as *Marrows*.

1932. Sketch for a restaurant decoration, Rue de la Grand Chaumière, watercolour and ink, 10.7 x 20 cm.

1932. Study of fruit and pots, watercolour and ink, 9.3 x 8.4 ?inches.

1933. Study of mountains, ink, 19.3 x 25.5 cm.

1933. Woman in a dressing gown, watercolour and pencil, dimensions missing.

1936. Mushrooms and fungi, ?watercolour on silk, 50.9 x 34 cm. Maybe exhib. 1936, London, Fine Art Society as *Fungi.*

1937. Italian building, gouache, 40 x 48.1 cm.

c.1940s. Cover illustration for *Grimoire of the Entangled Thicket*, watercolour and pencil, 16.5 x 25.3 cm. Must be drawing subsequently intended for book in 1973. ('Sea Anemone' was used.)

1941. Composition : three growing forms, watercolour and ink, 32.4 x 43.5 cm.

1941. Hogarth's house at Chiswick, watercolour and pencil, 35 x 45 cm. Another, 45 x 35 cm.

1942. Christian Marriage figure, watercolour, 17.5 x 16 cm.

1942. Three-eyed figure, ink, chalk and watercolour, 47 x 38.3 cm.

c.1945. Figure study, crayon, 45 x 58.2 cm.

c.1946. Rough for *Ideal Home* cover of June 1946, watercolour and gouache, 34.5 x 35.7 cm.

c.1946.Painting for *Ideal Home* cover of June 1946, oil on canvas, 50.8 x 50.8 cm.

c.1946. Proof pull of above cover, 38 x 30.6 cm.

c.1948. Rough on an architect's drawing for mural for NCR factory, Dundee, 1948, watercolour and ink, 69 x 82 cm.

c.1948. Rock pool.

c.1948. Four designs for murals on four quarters of a sheet printed for the Mural Painters Exhibition, 1948, ink and gouache. 1. Bar in a cruising liner, 23.8 x 27.7 cm.; 2. Corridor in a junior school, 23.7 x 32 cm.; 3. Church in a new town, 32.2 x 35.6 cm.; 4. Town hall, 28.5 x 32.2 cm.

c. 1952. Material for murals at Maze Hill (Trevor Dannatt, architect) 1952. 1. Sheet of photographs of 3 drawings plus scale model of building and murals, 40.5 x 51 cm.; 2. Rough sketch of mural on architect's drawing, watercolour and ink with gold and silver, 34 x 64.5 cm.; 3. Rough for mural composed of geometric heads, watercolour and ink with gold and silver (collaged), 17.8 x 30.5 cm.; 4. Rough for mural composed of geometric heads, watercolour and ink with gold and silver (collaged), 17.7 x 30.5 cm.; 5. Rough sketch of mural on architect's drawing, watercolour and ink with gold and silver, 39.5 x 67.3 cm.

c.1955-6. Five drawings for illustrations for *Goose of Hermogenes* [not used by publisher], each watercolour and ink. 1. *Corolla's pinions*, 37.5 x 26.7 cm.; 2. *The traditional Sakti group*, 26 x 18.3 cm.; 3. *Corolla's pinions*, 23.5 x 18 cm.; 4. *It is called the bed of Empedocles*, 26 x 18.4 cm.; 5. *The King of the Fishes*, 27.3 x 21 cm.

1975. Abstract (?lightning), ?oil and enamel on board, 12.7 x 46 cm.

1975. Abstract, long horizontal, pink and green, ?acrylic on board, 15.1 x 91.5 cm.

1976. Architect's blueprint of a drawing for RIBA competition: design for a monument to Queen Elizabeth II, 59.5 x 84 cm.

1977. Flowering landscape, watercolour and ink. Two, 39.2 x 32.4 cm. and 45.8 x 32.4 cm.

1977. House front (?Tenerife), oil on board, 41 x 31.9 cm.

1977. Plant forms, oil on board, 30.4 x 20.2 cm.

1978-9. Ten abstract compositions bound in a book, enamel on paper, each 26 x 16.4 cm. (1978 two, 1979 eight).

1980. Study of flowers in a jug, ink and acrylic, 18.7 x 28.8 cm.(s).

1980. Village and waterfall, collage of two postcards and paint on card, 20.1 x 24 cm.

1981. Abstract, green with pink and silver, enamel and acrylic on paper, 40.8 x 28 cm.

1982. Abstract, rock or shell form, oil on panel, 22 x 19 cm.

c.1983. Drawing for a book-jacket, 'Ozmazone' by IC, ink, 22.9 x 16.2 cm.

EXTRA ITEMS. UNDATED

The preceding lists indicate the artist's prodigious industry. A selection of items which do not fit previous lists are given below. Where known, the 1990 listing references are given.

Book-jacket, folded as cover, *The Clothes of God*, by Alice Buck and Claude Palmer, 22.3 x 17.9 cm. D/561.

Book-jackets, folded as covers, *The Living Stones : Cornwall* and *The Crying of the Wind : Ireland*, by Ithell Colquhoun. Each 22.3 x 17.2cm. D/562,563. Also rough for book-jackets, folded as cover, *The Crying of the Wind*, ink and gouache (collaged), 22.5 x 18 cm. D/566; same title, watercolour, 22.2 x 17.8 cm. D/568.

Drawing for a book-jacket, 'Pauline' by Jacques Chardonne, gouache, 19.7 x 15.6 cm. Another, folded as cover, 19.3 x 15.4 cm. D/259/1-2.

Drawing for magazine cover, Carrow Works Magazine, gouache and pencil, 31.7 x 27.1 cm. D/586. [This was Colman's of Norwich.]

Drawing for mural, 'Benedict YAE' decoration for a children's waiting room in a hospital, gouache and pencil, 39.7 x 68.5 cm. D/581. Another, showing design *in situ,* 19 x 30.3 cm. D/584.

Four roughs for a book-jacket, *Reminiscences of an Epicure* by Francis Cunynghame, three ink and gouache,one ink, various sizes;plus one folded as cover, 22.3 x 16.8 cm. D/565/1-5.

Murals for extension to District Hospital, Moreton-in-the-Marsh. (See ch.3, note 12.)

Rough for a book-jacket, *Writings of Edith Stein*, edited and translated by Hilda Graef, watercolour and ink, 23 x 15.2 cm.; another, folded as cover, 22.2 x 16.8 cm. D/560/1-2.

Rough for a book-jacket, 'The Twelve Pins, Roundstone, Galway'. Watercolour and ink (collaged), 25.5 x 38.4 cm. D/567.

UNDATED : TITLES NOT PROVIDED BY THE ARTIST

These items are in abundance in the 1990 listing, when many titles/descriptions of undated items were provided by Elizabeth Knowles. They have not been included. Book-jackets were exceptions, since they were descriptively specific and noteworthy. It was not ascertained whether they were commissioned or accepted by a publisher.

Appendix IIB

List of Exhibitions

1930. London, Goupil Gallery. 'Decorative Work and Stage and other Designs'.

1931. London, New English Art Club.

1931. London, Royal Academy.

1932. London, New English Art Club.

1935. Dublin, Royal Hibernian Academy of Arts.

1935. London, The Royal Society of British Artists. 183rd Exhibition.

1935. London, Whitechapel Art Gallery. 'Mural Decorative Paintings'.

1936. Cheltenham, Municipal Art Gallery. 'Decorations, Paintings and Drawings'.

1936. London, Fine Art Society. 'Exotic Plant Decorations'.

1937. London, Heal's Mansard Gallery.

1937. London, The London Group. 36th Exhibition.

1938. London, Whiteley's, Everyman's Theatre Foyer.

1939. London, Artists' International Association Exhibition.

1939. London, London Gallery. 'Living Art in England'.

1939. London, London Gallery. Title NK.

1939. London, Mayor Gallery. 'Ithell Colquhoun and Roland Penrose'.

1939. London, Peter Jones Gallery. 'Towards the Abstract'.

1939. London, Tate Gallery. 'Mural Painting in Great Britain 1919-1939. An Exhibition of Photographs'.

1939. Northampton, Borough Art Gallery. 'British Surrealist and Abstract Paintings'.

1939. Oxford, The Ashmolean Museum. 'Younger British Painters'.

1940. London. The Leicester Galleries. Title NK.

1940. R.S.B.A. Artists International Exhibition.

1941. Bagshaw Gallery. Title NK.

1941. Batley Gallery. Title NK.

1941. Harrogate Gallery. Title NK.

1941. London, Whitechapel Art Gallery, Artists' International Association Exhibition.

1942. Bournemouth Gallery. Title NK.

1942. London, Redfern Gallery. Title NK.

1942. Leicester, City Museum. 'New Movements in Art'.

1942. London, International Arts Centre. 'Surrealist Exhibition'.

1942. London, The Leicester Galleries. 'Artists of Fame and Promise'.

1942. London, London Museum. 'New Movements in Art'.

1945. Derby, Derby Museum and Art Gallery. 'Exhibition of Contemporary Art'.

1946. Bradford, Cartwright Hall.

1946. London, Hampstead Arts Council. 'Hampstead Artists Past and Present'.

1947. London, Mayor Gallery, March 5th-28th. (Paintings).

1947. London, Mayor Gallery, Dec. 3rd-24th. (Drawings).

1947. Paris, Les Surindépendents. 40th Exhibition.

1947. London, Redfern Gallery. Title NK.

1948. Bradford, Cartwright Hall, Spring Exhibition.

1948. Dublin, National College of Art. 'Irish Exhibition of Living Art'.

1948. London, Artists' International Association Exhibition.

1949. London, Whitechapel Art Gallery. 'Pictures for Schools'.

1950. Arts Council Travelling Exhibition. 'Society of Mural Painters'.

1950. Bradford, Cartwright Hall, Spring Exhibition.

1952. Bradford, City Art Gallery Jubilee Exhibition.

1952. London, Royal Academy.

1953. London, Women's International Art Club.

1953. Cambridge, Heffer Gallery. Represented as solo exhibition by I.C. but possibly included a minor showing by another artist.

195? Scottish Arts Council. 'The Scottish Scene'.

1957. Gallery I. Title NK.

1958. Kingston upon Hull, Ferens Art Gallery. 'Some Contemporary Women Painters'.

1960. London, Hampstead Town Hall. 'Hampstead Artists 1900-1960'.

1961. Newlyn Gallery. 'Ithell Colquhoun: Retrospective Exhibition of Oil Paintings'.

1962. Liege, Galerie d'Art Jean Dols. 'Exposition Internationale Fantasmagie'.

1963. London, Royal Watercolour Society Galleries. 'Cornish Experiment'.

1963. Ostend, Cultural Centre. 'Artists from Newlyn'.

1963. London, F.B.A. Galleries, Women's International Art Club.

1967. Newlyn Gallery. 'Constructions and Collages'.

1967-8. Czechoslovakia (touring), Poesie-Fantasmagie exhibition. Paintings and collages.

1968. Newlyn, Society of Artists.

1969. West Berlin, Fantasmagie International Exhibition. Paintings.

1969. West Berlin, Kunstamt Wilmersdorf. Paintings.

1969. Hamburg, Galerie für Zeitgenössiche Kunst. Constructions and Collages.

1969. Apeldoorn, Holland, Fantasmagie International Exhibition. Paintings.

1970. Bristol Art Centre. Paintings, Constructions, Collages.

1971. Newlyn Gallery. Gouaches, Montages, Collages.

1971. London, Hamet Gallery. 'Britain's Contribution to Surrealism in the 30s and 40s'.

1972. London, Gallery Edward Harvane. 'On the Edge of Dreams. (Aspects of Surrealism in British Art, 1932-1971.)'

1972. Exeter, City of Exeter Art Gallery. 'Ithell Colquhoun. Paintings, Collages and Drawings'.

1973. Penzance, Orion Gallery. 'Flower and Plant Paintings'.

197? Woodbridge, The Simon Carter Gallery. 'Exhibition of British Paintings and Watercolours 1900-1935'. Year NK.

1974. London, Drian Galleries. 'The Feminine Eye'.

1974. London, Leva Gallery. 'Ithell Colquhoun: an Exhibition of Surrealist Paintings and Drawings from 1930-1950'.

1974-75. London, Camden Arts Centre. 'Hampstead in the Thirties: A Committed Decade'. Paintings and photographs.

1975. Plymouth Art Centre. Title NK.

1975. Bath, The Little Gallery. Title NK.

1975. Newlyn Gallery. Title NK.

1976. Penzance, Newlyn Orion Galleries. 'Ithell Colquhoun: Surrealism : Paintings, Drawings, Collages 1936-1976'.

1977. Newlyn Gallery (side gallery). 'The Taro as Colour'.

1977. London, Parkin Gallery. 'Ithell Colquhoun: Paintings and Drawings 1930-1940'.

1977. London, Sloane Street, New Art Centre. 'Cornwall, 1945-1955'. Drawings.

1978. London, Hayward Gallery. 'Dada and Surrealism Reviewed'. Paintings and tropical butterflies.

1978. London, Parkin Gallery. 'Summer Exhibition'.

1979-80. London, Hayward Gallery. 'Thirties'.

1982. Paris, Galerie 1900-2000. 'La Peinture Surrealiste Anglaise 1939-1960'.

1985. Colchester, The Minories, 6th April - 5th May; London, Blond Fine Art, 22nd May - 22nd June; Hull, Ferens Art Gallery, 6th July - 4th August. 'A Salute to British Surrealism 1930-1950'.

1985. London, Blond Fine Art, 16th October - 16th November. 'British Women Surrealists'.

1985. Scottish Arts Council. 26th February - 16th November. Touring Glasgow, Perth, Ayr, Edinburgh. 'One City a Patron. British Art of the 20th Century from the Collections of Southampton Art Gallery'.

1986. Leeds. Leeds City Art Gallery. 'Angels of Anarchy and Machines for Making Clouds. Surrealism in Britain in the Thirties'. Included extracts from *Goose of Hermogenes.*

1986 (Sept.)-1987 (April). Touring exhibition Swansea (Glynn Vivian Art Gallery), Bath (Victoria Art Gallery), Newcastle (Polytechnic Gallery), Llandudno (Mostyn Art Gallery). 'Contrariwise: Surrealism and Britain 1930-1986'.

1988. London, Mayor Gallery. 'British Surrealism 50 Years on'. Included photograph of the artist and copy of `The Moths' from the *London Bulletin.*

1989. London, Blond Fine Art, 4th - 18th June. Title NK.

1991. University of California. Details not confirmed.

1999. Leeds, City Art Gallery. 'Surrealism in Britain'.

1999. London, Tate Gallery. 'Portraits of the Artist'.

Appendix IIC

Bibliography

Published Items, Ithell Colquhoun

c.1927-1930. 'The Prose of Alchemy', *The Quest*, London.

1938/1939. 'The Double Village', *London Bulletin*, No.7, Dec.-Jan., p.23.

1939. 'The Moths', *London Bulletin*, No.10, Feb., p.11.

1939. 'What do I Need to Paint a Picture?', *London Bulletin* No.17, June, p.13.

1939. 'The Volcano', *London Bulletin* No.17, June, pp.15 and 17.

1939. 'The Echoing Bruise', *London Bulletin* No.17, June, pp.17-18.

c.1941-2. One drawing. *In* Cunard, N. and Banting, J. (eds), Salvo for Russia.

1944. 'Everything Found on Land is Found in the Sea'; Extracts from 'Goose of Hermogenes' draft; 'The Water Stone of the Wise'. *In* Comfort, A. and Bayliss, J. (eds), *New Road 1943*, pp.196-199.

1944. 'Aged Six', *View*, ser.4, No.2, p.52.

1946. Response to questionnaire. In *Le Savoir Vivre*, Le Miroire Infidèle, Brussels.

1949. 'The Mantic Stain', *Enquiry*, Vol.2, No.4, pp.15-21.

1952. 'Children of the Mantic Stain', *Athene*, No.2, pp.29-35.

1954 onwards, book reviews for *Ore*, various issues (on authors A.Alvarez, Geoffrey Ashe, Richard Burns, John Creasey, David Jones,

Gertrud Kolmar, John Michell, Brian Louis Pearce, John Cowper Powys, Eric Ratcliffe, J.J. Williamson.)

1955. *The Crying of the Wind : Ireland*, Peter Owen, London.

1957. The *Living Stones : Cornwall*, Peter Owen, London.

1961. *Goose of Hermogenes*, Peter Owen, London.

1962. 'L'Isle de la Fleur Nocturne' ('Night Blossom Island'), Prose poem review, *Fantasmagie*, No.9, pp.16-17.

1963. 'La Goelette Etoile de Mer' ('The Schooner Hesperus'), *Soleils*, Paris.

1970. 'The Interlace', *Quest*, No.1, March, p.12.

1970. 'The Openings of the Body', *Quest*, No.4, Dec., pp.26-27.

1971. 'Bergie and Zan', *Prediction*, Jan., pp.24-26.

1971. 'Kurt Schwitters en Angleterre', *Fantasmagie*, No.29, Feb.

1971. 'Cornish Earth', *The Cornish Review*, No.18, Sept.

1971. 'Aperçu sur l'origine du Collage', *Fantasmagie*, No.31, Dec.

1971. 'Extracts from *Goose of Hermogenes*', *Transformaction*, No.4, pp.16-18.

1971. 'Incantations', *Transformaction*, No.4, pp.20-21.

c.1971 'Frontiers of Belief', *Man, Myth and Magic*, No.80, pp.2257-2258.

1973. *Grimoire of the Entangled Thicket*, Chariot Poets, No.4, Ore Publications, Stevenage.

1973. 'The Chain Poem', *Transformaction*, No.5, pp.22-23.

1975. *Sword of Wisdom : MacGregor Mathers and 'The Golden Dawn'*, Neville Spearman, London; Putnam, New York.

1977. 'The Taro as Colour'. Article issued on occasion of exhibition at Newlyn, 1977 showing designs for a Tarot pack, accompanying five sets of drawings.

1979. 'The Zodiac and the Flashing Colours', *Hermetic Journal*, No.4, pp.5-7.

1979. 'Colour and the Two Sigils', *Hermetic Journal*, No.4, pp.8-9.

1979. 'Memoir of E.J.L. Garstin', *Hermetic Journal*, No.6, pp.11-14.

1979. 'Notes on the Colouring of the Homer's Golden Chain Diagram', *Hermetic Journal*, No.6, pp.15-17.

1981. 'Women in Art'. Letters, *Oxford Art Journal*, p.65. Comment on Dawn Ades' article.

c.1981. 'Notes on Automatism'. In *Melmoth*, No.?

c.1982. *Osmazone*, Dunganon, Örkeljunga, Sweden.

1982. 'Coronach for Iona', *The New Celtic Review*, Aug.-Oct., p.5.

1983. 'A Dream', *Wood and Water*, Vol.2, No.6.

1985. Foreword to *Rosiecrucian Secrets of Dr.John Dee* (edited with Preface, Introduction and explanatory notes by E.J. Langford Garstin), Aquarian Press. Taken from single MS in BL and attributed to Dee.

Selected Unpublished (or Publication Unknown) MSS Ithell Colquhoun

Titles from the Tate Gallery archive records TGA 929 uncatalogued box list. These are very approximate divisions. Known titles of poems are in Notes to her poetry. (TES 'essays and short stories', TSP 'stories and poetry', T other boxes); Caduceus Books holdings 2003, some with included artwork described, about 80 items. Selection only (CB). It will be appreciated that Ithell Colquhoun's wide interests involved a kaleidoscope of manuscripts, some unfinished, some fully finished, some in the form of notes. The author considered that future researchers should have as much information as possible pending a completed catalogue but they should be aware that at this stage the Tate archives bears no responsibility for any inaccuracies in the boxed uncatalogued titles or the presence or otherwise of stated items. Their listing is a guide only. h = assumed or known handwritten copy, i.e. not TS.

Alchemical Dictionary (T)

Appearance (TES)

The Applicant (TES)

Aspects of Graal-Symbolism (TES)

Atlantis (CBh)

Bed of Spikes (TES)

Behold the Wood of the Cross (CB). Artwork, watercolour and pencil, plus text

Bird of Hermes - a Dance Play in one Act (TSP)

Blue Anubis (T)

Canvas in the Wind (T)

Clever Woman (TES)

Comedy in a Café (TES)

Concerning the Interior Stars (CB). Essay

The Connection between Mysticism and Blasphemy (TES)

Converts (TES)

Correspondence with Mary Burrow (CB)

Counterparts in Mallorca (TES)

Crowley in Time, Overture (CB). Account of interests in Crowley

The Daily River (TES)

Dance of the Nine Opals (TES) [see painting 1942]

Death of the Elegy (TES)

Development of the Cross (CB). The development of the Latin cross from the cube. Artwork. Five images, watercolour, pen, metallic paint on graph paper (2.5 x 2.5, 3 x 4, 5 x 4, 5 x 3, 5.5 x 4 inches)

Development of the Double Cube (CB). The development of the Cross from the double cube with reference to the sephiroth. Artwork. Five images, watercolour, pen, metallic paint on paper (3 x 2, 6 x 5, 7 x 6, 7 x 5.5, 8 x 6 inches)

Dimensional Interrelation : a Meditation on the Platonic Solids (T)

The Divine Marquis and the Myth of Liberty (TES)

Erotics of Ballet (TSP)

Essay on Genesis (TES)

Experiments in Numerology (T)

Explanation for Painting on Silk (TES)

Geomancy (T)

The Golden Fleece (T)

Harbour and Promontory (TES)

The Importance of *A Vision* by W.B. Yeats (T)

The Infernal Worlds of the Qabalah (T)

Karl Germer. Correspondence to Ithell Colquhoun (CB)

Key to 'Moonchild' by Aleister Crowley (CB)

Letter from Behind an Iron Curtain (TES)

Lights in the Air (TSP)

Little Anthology of Inadvertent Surrealism (T)

Medea's Charms (TES)

Memorandum on W.B. Crow's Order of Hidden Masters (CB)

A Meditation on the Platonic Solids (CB)

Note on the Colouring of the Homer's Golden Chain Diagram – Tarot System – based on an early morning dream in July 1918 (T)

Notes on 'The Assassins' (T)

Notes on 'Magic' by Kenneth Grant (T)

Notes on 'The Magician : his training and work' by W.E. Butler (T)

Notes on Traditional Techniques in Painting (T)

Notes on Stirling's Canon (T)

The Old Black Rocks (TES)

The Order of Melchisidek (TES)

The Order of the Sun and Moon, Nicaragua (TES)

The Other Echidna (TES)

An Outline of a Preliminary Ceremony Connected with the Banishing Ritual of the Pentagram (CBh). May 8th, 1964

Paganism (T)

Pied Beauty (TES)

The Pilgrimage (T, CBh). One-act play

The Positive Virtues (TES)

The Process of Art (T)

The Quest of the Divine (TES)

Recollection of Kurt Schwitters (T) [probably finalised as the article in *Fantasmagie* No.29 of 1971]

The Schooner Hesperus (TES)

Saga of the Count (CBh). Meeting of I.C. with Crowley's son

Sketches of different types of cross (T)

The Stream of St Bride (TES)

Surrealism and Hermetic Poetry (T)

Tamara Bourkhoun. Correspondence to Ithell Colquhoun 1959-1975 (CBh)

Taro Meditations (CBh)

Thinking Pictures (TES)

Three Paintings by Paule Vézelay : Salon des Surindépendants, Paris, November 1932 (T)

The Torso Laughs (CB). Background of Pat McAlpine, mother of Ataturk Crowley. Account of Penwith coven.

The Tree Alphabet and the Tree of Life (T)

Until Twelve (T)

Waters of Life (TES)

Sources referring to Ithell Colquhoun, Published Items

Acquisitions 1976-8: 1978, London, Tate Gallery, pp.41-2.

ADDISON, N and BURGESS, L. (eds) (2000). *Learning to Teach Art and Design in the Secondary School*, Routledge Falmer, London.

ADES, DAWN. (1980). 'Notes on Two Women Surrealist Painters: Eileen Agar and Ithell Colquhoun', *Oxford Art Journal*, Vol.3, No.1, April, pp.36-42.

BATTERSBY, CHRISTINE (1988,1990,1992). In *Women's Art Magazine*, Nos. 23,33, 49, resp.

BRADLEY, FIONA (1997). *Surrealism*, Tate Gallery Publishing.

BUCK, LOUISA (1988). *The Surrealist Spirit in Britain,* Whitford and Hughes, London, Number 13.

BUCK, LOUISA (1992). 'Faceless Femmes Fatales', *Women's Art Journal*, No.49, 16-17.

CHADWICK, WHITNEY (1985). *Women Artists and the Surrealist Movement*, Thames and Hudson.

Exhibition Catalogues: 1948, London, Mayor Gallery; 1972, Exeter City Art Gallery; 1976, Penzance, Newlyn Orion Galleries; 1977, London, Parkin Gallery; 1978, London, Hayward Gallery; 1986,

Leeds City Art Galleries; 1987, Lausanne, Musée Cantonal des Beaux-Arts.

GALE, MATTHEW. Tate Gallery web site, October 1997.

GAZE, DELIA. (ed.) (1997). *Dictionary of Women Artists*, pp.411-13, Fitzroy Dearborn, London and Chicago.

GORDON, JAN (1939). 'Art and Artists', *The Observer*, June 18th.

HEDLEY, G. (1988). 'Let her Paint : Ten Women Painters in Southampton City Art Gallery', pp.24-5, Southampton City Art Gallery.

KACZYNSKI, R. (2002) *Perdurabo : The Life of Aleister Crowley*, New Falcon Publications.

LIBMANN, BRIGITTE (1994). 'British Women Surrealists: Deviants from Deviance'. In *This Working Day World : Social, Political and Cultural History of Women's Lives, 1914-45*, Taylor and Francis, London, pp.156-8.

Obituaries : *The Independent*, April 26th, 1988; *The Times*, April 14th, 1988, *The Guardian*, April - , 1988.

RATCLIFFE, ERIC (2003). 'Ithell Colquhoun (1906-88): A Background to the Artist'. In *Goose of Hermogenes* (paperback edition, Peter Owen), pp.2-6.

RATCLIFFE, ERIC (2004). 'Ithell Colquhoun: The Versatile Surrealist'. *Wormwood*, No.2. Spring, pp.17-22.

RAY, P.C. (1971). *The Surrealist Movement in England*, Cornell University Press, Ithaca.

REMY, MICHEL (1978). *Towards a Dictionary of Surrealism in England*, Groupes Editions Marges.

REMY, MICHEL (1999). *Surrealism in Britain*, Ashgate.

RHONE, CHRISTINE. 'The Nun and the Alchemist of Lamorna Cove', *The Fountain* [no further details available, but probably post-1965].

ROSEMONT, P. (1998). *Surrealist Women*, University of Texas Press, Austin.

STANFORD, DEREK (1977). *Inside the Forties*, Sidgwick and Jackson.

STITCH, P. (1970). *Anxious Visions*, Abbeville Press, New York.

Appendix III

The Manleys and the Sea-Fencibles

MARGARET ITHELL COLQUHOUN (MANLEY ANCESTRY)

William Manley	=	Susanna Hellings
b. ~1670 b. ~1670		
m. 1705		
d. 1754, Topsham		d. 1753, Topsham
|		
John Manley	=	Sarah Bryant
b. 1709, Topsham		b. ~ 1700, Topsham
m. 1732, Topsham		
d. 1800, Topsham		d. 1766, Topsham
William Manley	=	Frances Babbage (née Woodford)
|		
b. 1744, Topsham		b. ~ 1740
m. 1766, Topsham		
d. 1804, Topsham		d.1774, Topsham
|		
Captain John Manley	=	Martha Medland
(Cornwall & Devon Sea Fencibles)		
b.1769, Topshamb.1770, Moretonhampstead		
m. 1793, Moretonhampstead		
d.1858, Dublin		d.1848, Topsham
|		

William Nicholas Manley b. 1799	=	Elizabeth Browne b.1802, Dublin
William George Nicholas Manley VC., CB. b.1831, Dublin b.1843 m. 1869, Sheerness d.1901, Cheltenham	=	Maria Elizabeth Darton d.1913, Cheltenham
Georgia Frances Ithell Manley b. 1873, Woolwich m. 1905 d. post -1959, Cheltenham	=	Henry Archibald Colebrook Colquhoun b. ~1870 d.1942, Cheltenham
Margaret Ithell Colquhoun b. 9.10.1906, Shillong, Assam m. 10.7.1943, Brentford d. 11.4.1988, Lamorna Valley, Cornwall	=	Toni Romanov del Renzio b. ~ 1915, Russia

On her mother's side, Ithell Colquhoun was related to West Country ancestors, one of whom, Captain John Manley (1769-1858) was charged with the defence of the coasts of Devon and Cornwall. Quite a lot is known of the Manley ancestry, even back to the 17th-century. William Manley of Topsham in Devon, the grandfather of another William Manley, whose Topsham spouse was Frances Babbage. Their marriage in 1766 produced a second son John, and their first daughter was named Frances after her mother. In turn, when John married a Moretonhampstead girl, his only daughter was named Frances. Two generations later, with possibly more intervening similarly-named daughters, Ithell's Manley mother, born in 1873, was named Georgia Frances Ithell.

Topsham, the East Devon estuary town between the Exe and the Clyst, has a well-recorded maritime background, thanks to a private but accessible database, foreseeing the value of records within what used to be a busy port of international status. Records go back to the 14th century; it enjoyed considerable foreign trade in the 18th century. It is now part of Exeter, where Ithell in 1972 was represented in a comprehensive exhibition of her art, some 300 years after her Manley great-great-grandparents were in the area.

When the future Captain John Manley came of age, he became part of the Sea-Fencible organisation, which was 20,000 strong along the country's coastline where it was vulnerable to attack by the French. The Fencible scheme commenced shortly after the French Revolution. It only disbanded when the French menace ceased, although it was stood down temporarily during 1801-3 when there was an Anglo/French armistice. There was much justification in invasion defence; many freethinkers had originally welcomed the cause of the French peasantry, but the savagery following was alien and repulsive - with it came the realisation, with fear, that revolution must not happen here, and also that the country must be protected. In 1797 a French Revolutionary Army force had actually succeeded in landing at Fishguard.

The Sea-Fencibles were thus a 'Home Guard' naval defence, staffed by soldiers but managed by the Admiralty, which was well-organised to do this. The coastal towns provided ships made capable of carrying arms, and the Government issued the weapons. A captain and lieutenants commanded a group of men trained in gunnery, who were paid a shilling a day. An inducement to join the Fencibles was a guarantee of exemption from press-ganging. John Manley had a captaincy in the Cornwall and Devon Sea-Fencibles. History did not record the details of the patrol voyages, but it is intriguing to know that Ithell was to be drawn to living in the Lamorna valley and must have made many visits to coastal landmarks familiar to her ancestor. Captain John Manley died in Dublin. He may have gone there after

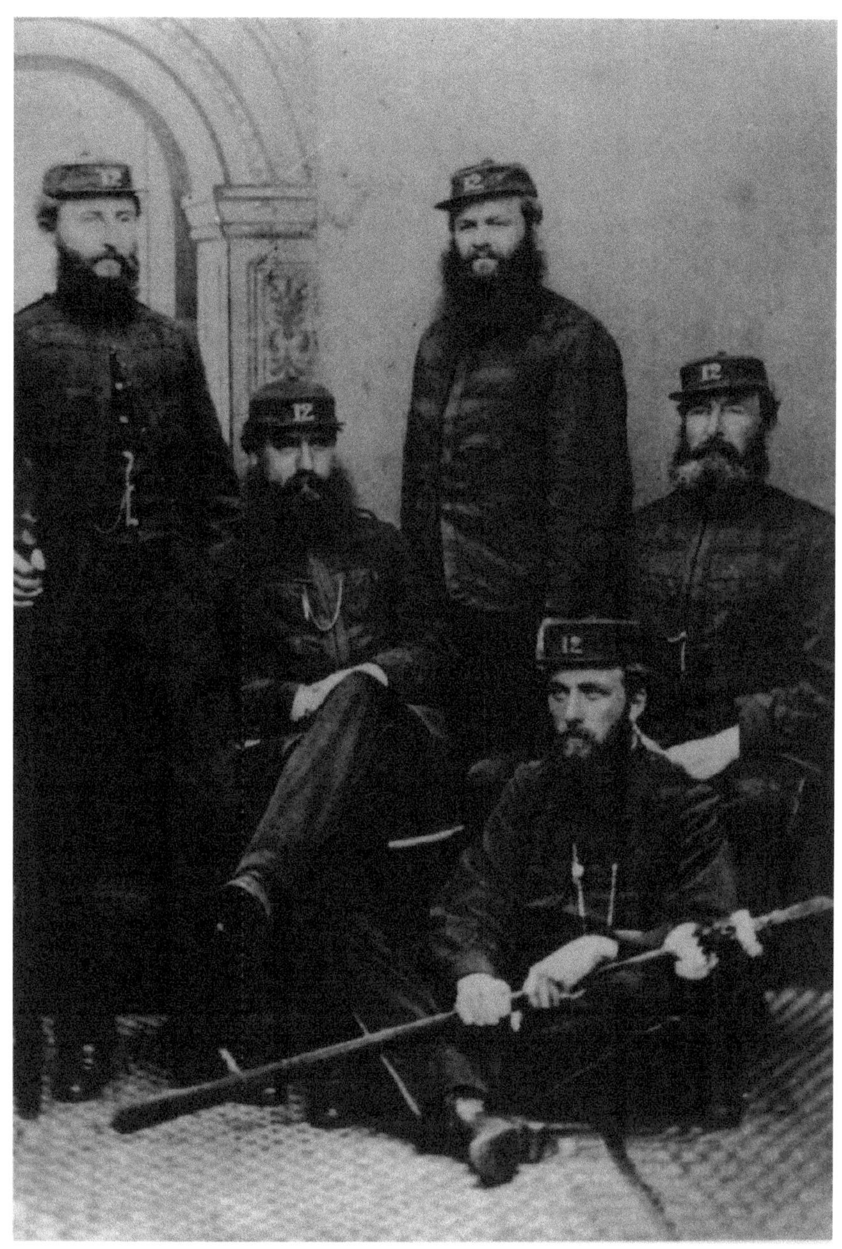

84. *Group Portrait, Officers of the 12th Regiment at Tauranga, New Zealand in 1866. Undress uniform L to R Captain O'Shaughnessy, Lt. Foster, Surgeon Manley, V.C., Lt. Triphook and Quartermaster Laver*

his wife died at Topsham. His son William married a Dublin lady, and the next Manley (William George Nicholas) was Irish-born. This Manley was awarded the Victoria Cross as described in the Notes, marrying Maria Elizabeth Darton four years later. The couple were Ithell's maternal grandparents, retiring to Cheltenham in the eighties.

Of the known children of this Manley family, Lilian Frances Georgia died in infancy, her younger sister (Ithell's mother) being born the year after. There were at least two sons. One, W.G.H. Manley, made a career in the Royal Artillery as lieutenant-colonel; the other, George E.D. Manley, died in 1901 at Chin-Kiang when 25, during the Boxer Rebellion. He was a captain in the Marine Light Infantry attached to H.M.S. Dido - a post curiously similar in rank and service to his Sea-Fencible ancestor Captain John Manley, of Topsham and Dublin.

On a lighter note, The Military Historical Society Bulletin records a letter from Georgia to *The Morning Post* telling of an appendix removal in the Franco-Prussian war by her father, whose instruments included the blade of a shoe-horn and a button-hook, all before the days of antiseptics. The patient recovered.

'Battledown Priors', the large Cheltenham Victorian detached house which Henry, Georgia, Ithell and her brother occupied in 1925, seems an appropriate title for the home of this family, ancestrally rich in military connections, sited in a prestigious estate in which many other military veterans and prominent citizens of the town lived and were to live.

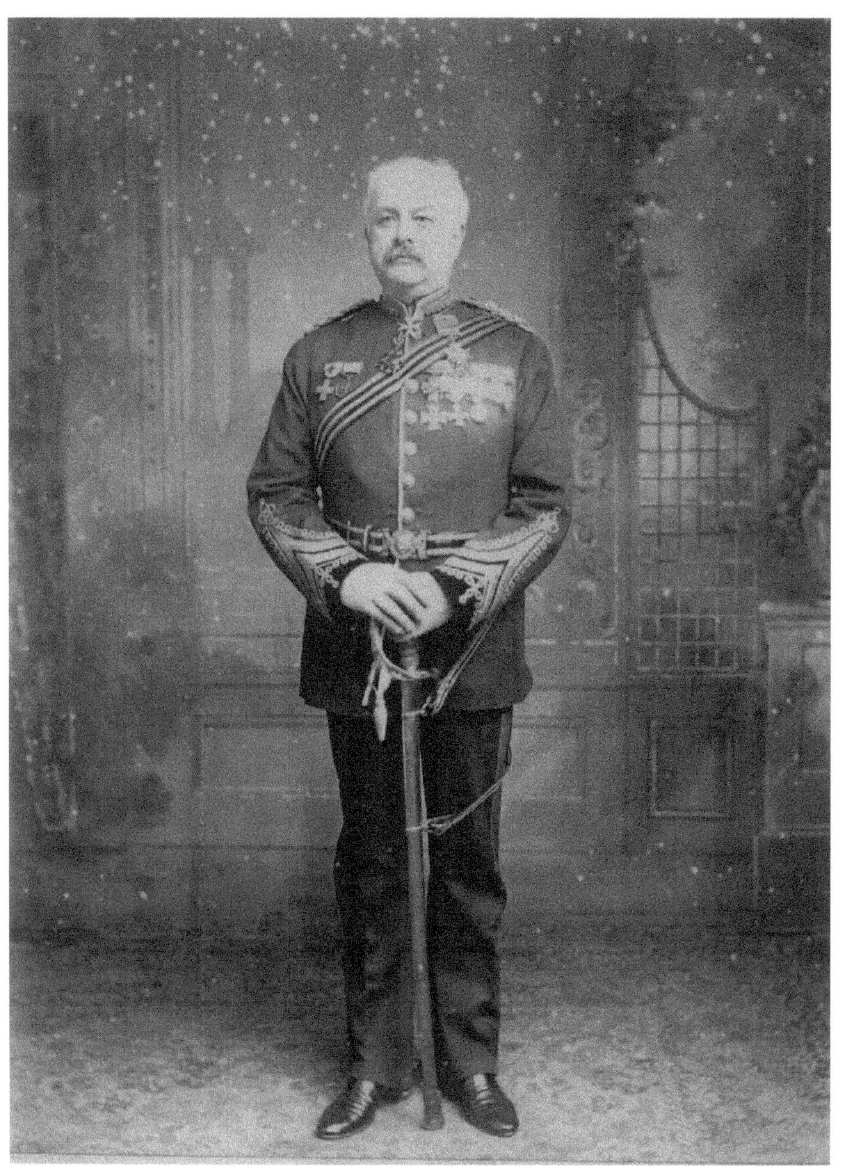

85. *William George Nicholas Manley, V.C., C.B.*

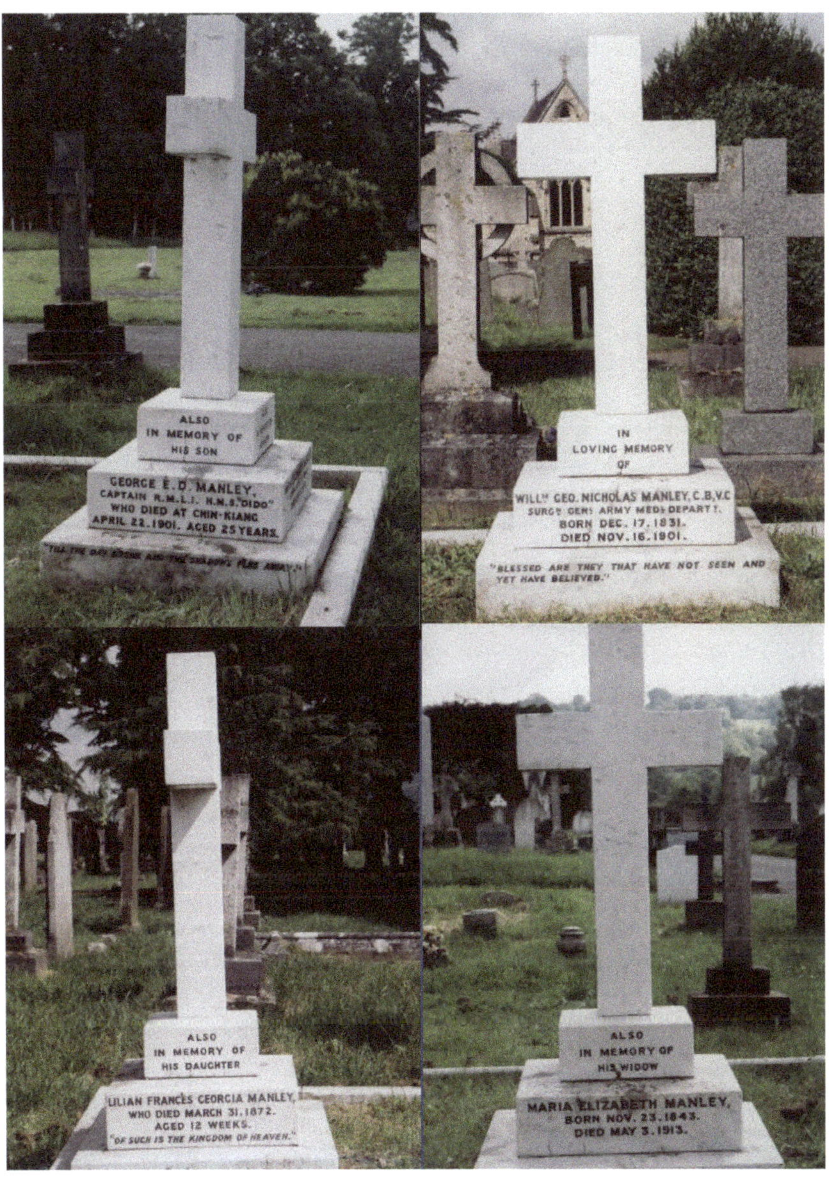

86. The Manley Memorial, Cheltenham Cemetery

Notes

Introduction

1. Ithell Colquhoun (1973) *Grimoire of the Entangled Thicket*, Stevenage, Ore Publications. Sea anemone on front cover.

2. Whitney Chadwick (1985, reprints 1995, 1997) *Women Artists and the Surrealist Movement*, London, Thames and Hudson.

3. Michel Remy (1999) *Surrealism in Britain*, Aldershot, Hampshire, Ashgate Publishing.

4. *The Crying of the Wind : Ireland*, London, Peter Owen (1955); *The Living Stones : Cornwall*, Peter Owen (1957); *Goose of Hermogenes*, Peter Owen (1961); *Sword of Wisdom : MacGregor Mathers and 'The Golden Dawn'*, London, Neville Spearman (1975).

5. See 1 above and also *Osmazone*, Örkeljunga, Sweden, Dunganon (1983). Examples of uncollected poems are in *Melmoth*, *Ore*, *Quest*, *Wood and Water*. Posthumously reprinted poems are in *Veins of Gold : Ore 1954-1995*, Austria, University of Salzburg (1997). See Chapter 10 notes for a list of more poems, quite a number presumed unpublished.

6. Ross Nichols and James Kirkup (1946) *The Cosmic Shape*, The Forge Press, London.

7. Tate Gallery archives (TGA929), London, 11pp. typescript, from Paul, Penzance, undated.

8. Nadia Choucha (1991) *Surrealism and the Occult*, Mandrake, Oxford.

1. The Formative Years

1. *India Office List*, 1937, p.605. Henry was educated at Wellington College, joining at age 13 in 1886, leaving in 1891 for Merton College Oxford, obtaining a B.A. Wellington College was granted a Royal Charter a year after the Duke of Wellington's death as a memorial to him. See also *Wellington College Register* (11th edn, 1859-1996, Old Wellingtonian Soc., 1997.) Details courtesy of the Old Wellingtonian Society.

2. Anthony Thomas (1996) *Rhodes*, BBC Books.

3. This was at Tauranga, New Zealand, April 29th, 1864, when as Assistant Surgeon with the Royal Artillery, he volunteered to accompany a storming party, and rescued many men at great danger to himself. He was later made a C.B. Previously he had served with the British Ambulance in the Franco-Prussian War, receiving the Prussian Iron Cross and other decorations (the Bavarian Order of Merit and the Geneva Cross.) See *The Register of the Victoria Cross*, p.215, published by *This England* from Cheltenham; Richard Doherty and David Truesdale (2000), *Irish Winners of the Victoria Cross*, Dublin, Four Courts Press; and *The Military Historical Society Bulletin*, vol.XIV, No.55, Feb.1964, pp.64-5. The last-named reference gives a fuller list of decorations and large photograph in an article by Major A.F. Flatow. A group photograph of officers of the 12th (East Suffolk) Regiment of Foot in Tauranga taken two years after in 1866 shows the then Surgeon Manley V.C. See R.H. Montague, *Dress and Insignia of the British Army in Australia and New Zealand, 1770-1870. Library of Australian History*, 1981, p.114. The regiment was in New Zealand during 1860-1866.

4. Interview by Michael Williams in *The Cornishman*, Jan. 1963.

5. Tate Gallery Archives (TGA 929), London, 'Until Twelve : Notes for an Autobiography by Ithell Colquhoun.' This is typed, with adult handwritten amendments. It is obviously an attempt to faithfully reproduce childhood memories, although sometimes doctored with words like 'gamut' and 'hypnogogia'. There is no record of this having been published. It may be noted that *View*, ser.4, 2, 1944, p.52, an American surrealist magazine, published a poem she had written when six. ('Aged Six.')

6. Sue Monro, 'Profile', *Peninsula Voice*, No.10.

7. Simon Buxton, private communication, 2.8.03.

2. Early Occult Interests

1. These paintings by Moina, also a Slade graduate, included one of her husband in magical regalia, and four Egyptian figures: three canvases of deities Osiris, Nephthys, Horus the Younger - and Hawkhead. Some or

all had been hung in the ante-room to the Paris temple where Moina was High Priestess. Years later when she lived in Cornwall, Ithell received a surprise gift of Moina's painting of MacGregor Mathers from Enid, daughter of the deceased Mrs. Weir.

2. The Order had passed its apogee (R.A. Gilbert in *The Golden Dawn Scrapbook : The Rise and Fall of a Magical Order*, Samuel Weiser (1997) and his *Revelations of the Golden Dawn : The Rise and Fall of a Magical Order*, quantum (1997) are relevant repetitions in the U.S.A. and U.K. out of the vast amounts of texts). However, although by 1939 most Alpha and Omega temples were dormant, the writings of Israel Regardie externalised much Golden Dawn knowledge, and in America where some temples had been short-lived, there were later resurgences of interest which crystallised into many publications about the Golden Dawn.

3. Garstin left unpublished essays 'Alchemy and Astrology', and 'A Glossary of Alchemical Terms'. He published *Theurgy* and *The Secret Fire* in 1930 and 1932, respectively. Ithell Colquhoun commented on the Glossary in *Sword of Wisdom* (pp. 277ff).

4. Ithell Colquhoun, 'Memoir of E.J.L. Garstin', *Hermetic Journal*, No.6, 1979, pp. 11-14.

3. Into the Thirties

1. Henry and Georgia, lived together at 53 Battledown Priors from about the mid to late twenties until 1942. According to Kelly's Directory, Henry is listed as at 25 Park Place in 1926 and in 1930 at the Priors. Henry died in September 23rd, 1942 prior to Ithell's marriage to Toni in the following year, and the widowed Georgia moved elsewhere. Later, in about the mid-sixties, the old estate was rased to be replaced by a development of flats termed Battledown Priors Estate.

A 1932 O.S. map confirms the extent of the original Priors and its grounds, with entrance avenue from the Approach. The exact date of building of 'Battledown Priors' is unknown; it seems to have been named after a house in the area of the project from the beginning. Successive names were 'Abercorn', 'Mayville' and then 'Battledown Priors'. In the absence of earlier addresses, it could be assumed that Ithell, with her brother and parents, were at 25 Park Place. Henry could be there from about 1921 on retiring from the Service. The children and Georgia may have been at Weymouth first, but there is no backing proof. Later, when Ithell was studying in London, and for some time after, she would visit her parents at Battledown Priors. She married soon after the death of her father, by which time her brother Robert was out of the country, serving as a Staff-Captain in India.

2. 1930, London, 'Decorative Work and Stage and Other Designs', Goupil Gallery.

3. This and Judith were each familiar subjects. The seventeenth-century women painters Sirani and Gentileschi painted many Judiths. The attempted seduction of Susanna executed by the latter painter was also a popular theme in Italy. (See Whitney Chadwick (1996), *Women, Art, and Society*, London, Thames and Hudson, pp.100ff.) See also André Masson's surrealist work *The Death of Holofernes* (1960).

4. Surrealism, read later as encompassing painting (but not music), defined as 'pure psychic automatism by which it is intended to express either verbally or in writing, the true function of thought. Thought dictated in the absence of all control exerted by reason, and outside all aesthetic or moral preoccupations.' A random starting point in the various painting processes had to be provided, and from this for groundwork the surrealist painter explored via free-thought processes.

5. Various letters, Tate Gallery Archives (TGA 929).

6. 1931, 1933, London, New English Art Club; 1935, London, 'Mural Decorative Paintings', Whitechapel Art Gallery; 1935, London, 183rd exhib., Royal Society of British Artists; 1935, Dublin, Royal Hibernian Academy of Arts.

7. 1936, London, 'Exotic Plant Decorations', Fine Art Society; 1936, Cheltenham Art Gallery. At Cheltenham, four works were a painting recorded as an illustration to Ernest Dowson's 'Cynara' poem and three as illustrations to Thornton Wilder's *Woman of Andros*. Her work in an illustrated edition of Dowson's poems has not been confirmed, and there seem no illustrated editions of the *Woman.*

8. *Gloucestershire Echo*, Feb. 1936.

9. J.G.F. Lowson, via private communication Paul McKee, 29.8.01.

10. Michel Remy, *op. cit.*, p. 204.

.

11. 1973, Penzance, 'Flower and Plant Paintings', The Orion Gallery.

12. One mural was for the women's ward (oil on canvas, 48 x 30 in.), showing a plant, perhaps a lily, rising out of water; the other (oil on board, 80 x 67 in.) for the hospital waiting room, depicting a man and woman bathing their feet in a pool, to which the woman appears to be adding more water. (Communication 8.10.01, courtesy Christopher Bastock, Tate Gallery.) The Tate Gallery in 1939 included photographs of her work in an exhibition 'Mural Painting in Great Britain'.

13. David Gascoyne (1935), *A Short Survey of Surrealism*, London, Cobden-Sanderson.

14. For example, André Breton and Philippe Soupault (1920), *Les Champs magnétiques*; André Breton (1924), *Manifeste de surréalisme*; André Breton (1928), *Le Surréalisme et la Peinture*; André Breton and Paul Eluard (1930), *L'immaculée Conception.*

15. David Brown (1988), 'Obituaries : Ithell Colquhoun', In *The Independent*, April 26th. (Text-only notices appeared in *The Times* and *The Guardian.*)

16. Mathew Gale (1997), *Dada and Surrealism*, Phaidon Press. Her bath was also a subject of Frida Kahlo's *What the Water Gave Me* painted in the same year (see Chadwick, p.91 – 'Kahlo peoples the water with a swarm of freely associated images. . .')

17. Whitney Chadwick, *op. cit.*, p.128.

18. Michel Remy, *op. cit.*, p.204.

19. *Dictionary of Women Artists* (1997), vol.1, p.412.

20. Ithell Colquhoun. Biographical Supplement, Jan. 1976 to exhibition catalogue 'Surrealism : Paintings, Drawings, Collages, 1936-1976 - Ithell Colquhoun', Newlyn Orion Galleries, 27 Feb.-23 March, 1976.

21. 'The Double Village', *London Bulletin* 7, Dec. 1938 - Jan.1939, p.23; 'The Moths', *London Bulletin* 10, Feb. 1939, p.11; 'What Do I Need to Paint a Picture?', 'The Volcano', 'The Echoing Bruise'. *London Bulletin* 17, June 15th, 1939, pp.13, 15-16 and 17, 17-18, respectively.

4. Into the Forties

1. The new project, the British Art Centre, was looking for members. Sponsored by the affluent Peggy Guggenheim, it had been supported by Roland Penrose, and Herbert Read was intended Director. In the previous year, before he had to return to Belgium, Mesens had persuaded Penrose against involvement. The latter later helped Mesens to return to England, where he continued this argument.

2. (a) Biographical Supplement, *op. cit.*, ch.3, note 20; (b) Introduction to exhibition catalogue, Michael Parkin Fine Art Ltd., London : 'Ithell Colquhoun, Paintings and Drawings 1930-1940', Nov.9th to Dec.3rd 1977.

3. Michael Parkin, *idem.*, Introduction to exhibition catalogue.

4. See Antony Penrose's memoir *Roland Penrose : the Friendly Surrealist*, Prestel, 2001, pp.139-41, for an account of the early I.C.A. exhibitions.

5. Dawn Ades, In *Surrealism : Desire Unbound*, Tate Publishing Ltd., 2001, 'Surrealism, Male-

Female', ch.7, pp.171-201.

6. Dawn Ades, *ibid.*, from note 3, p.320. 'The greater prominence of women in surrealism's later phase has also been attributed to the eagerness of the older males to welcome young women . . . they brought new blood at the time when the young male turks of the avante-garde were founding their own alternatives to surrealism . . .'

7. J.Lemprière, *Classical Dictionary*, Routledge, London, p. 94; Henry Nettleship and J.E. Sandys (eds) (1895), *Dictionary of Classical Antiquities*, Macmillan, New York, p.85; H.E. Wedeck and Wade Baskin (1971), *Dictionary of Pagan Religions*, Peter Owen, London, p.38; Michael Grant and John Hazel (1994), *Who's Who in Classical Mythology*, Routledge, London, p.59. Also see Michel Remy, *op. cit.*, p.245, who, re Attis, states: 'he himself was born from genitalia fallen on the ground, of a hermaphrodite creature, itself born out of Zeus' seed and eventually castrated by the gods, a fact which casts light on the central issues of the painting; this is the tragedy of a doomed family.'

8. '. . . an ironic playing with the theme of Gradiva referred to by Dali and by Breton in his 1937 essay "Gradiva" as "the one who advances," an epithet originally ascribed to the the magnificent god of war Mars Gradivus as he strode into battle.' (Whitney Chadwick, *op. cit.*, p.129); and ' . . . refers to her interest in the symbolism of limping, whether mythological like Hephaistos and Wayland Smith, or literary, like the Limping Devil and Captain Ahab . . .' (Michel Remy, *op. cit.*, p.245).

9. Richard Cavendish (1992), *Mythology*, Little Brown, London, p.27.

10. Chrétien de Troyes (1180), *Le Comt du Graal.*

11. Michel Remy, *Surrealism in Britain, op. cit.*, p.226.

12. From Captain R.S. Colquhoun who referred to it in a letter dated Feb. 27th, 1944. Tate Gallery Archives (TGA 929), communication from Matthew Gale of the Tate Gallery.

5. Bedford Park

1. W.B. Yeats (1955), *Autobiographies*, Macmillan, London ; Ian Fletcher (1987), *W.B. Yeats and his Contemporaries*, The Harvester Press, Brighton.

2. Derek Stanford (1970), *Inside the Forties: Literary Memoirs*, Sidgwick & Jackson, London, pp. 72-3.

3. Derek Stanford (1988), *The Memorare Sequence*, University of Salzburg Press (now *Poetry Salzburg*). Distrib. Wolfgang Goertschacher, University of Salzburg, Dept. of English and

American Studies, Akademiestr. 24, 5020, Salzburg, Austria.

4. *New Road 1943.* Published in 1944. Edited by Alex Comfort and John Bayliss from Billericay and published by the Grey Walls Press.

5. Ithell Colquhoun, *New Road 1943*, *op. cit.*, pp. 196-9.

6. Michel Remy, *Surrealism in Britain*, *op. cit.*, p.225.

7. Tate Gallery web site, October 1997.

6. Independent Spirit

1. See Sarane Alexandrian (1970), *Surrealist Art*, trans. Gordon Clough, London, Thames and Hudson, pp. 190ff., which describes the 'Exposition Internationale du Surréalisme'.

2. Ithell Colquhoun, 'The Mantic Stain', *Enquiry*, Oct.-Nov., 2, No.4, 1949, pp. 15-21; 'Children of the Mantic Stain', *Athene*, May 1952, pp. 29-34.

3. *Hampstead & Highgate Record*, Friday, March 27th, 1953; *The Daub*, April, 1953.

4. 'Decalcomania, Fumage (or making pictures by smoke)'. Report of television programme by Martin Montrose in the *Hampstead Express*, Aug. 20th, 1948.

5. Austin O. Spare and Frederick Carter, 'Automatic Drawing', *Form*, Vol. 1, No. 1, April 1916.

6. Nadia Choucha (1991), *Surrealism and the Occult*, Mandrake, Oxford, p.57.

7. *Glasgow Bulletin*, May 14th 1949; *Cape Argus*, Capetown, June 22nd, 1949; *Cavalcade*, London, July 9th, 1949.

8. *Varsity*, April 25th, 1953; *Cambridge Daily News*, April 29th, 1953.

9. *The Times Literary Supplement*, Sept. 30th, 1955; *The Lady*, Sept. 22nd, 1955; *The Universe*, Sept. 23rd, 1955. The book was also received enthusiastically by the *Irish Times* (' . . .an intelligent piece of roving reportage on a high literary level') and in Irish literary circles.

10. Kenneth Grant, private communication, 28.5.03. Details of the Nu-Isis can be found in his *Outside the Circles of Time* (Muller, 1980) and *The Ninth Arch* (Starfire, 2002). Ithell had been a member of the O.T.O. before admission to this lodge. Appendix IIC shows the depth of her interests in Crowley's legacy in her correspondence, although there is no evidence that she ever met or wanted to meet the magician.

11. Simon Buxton, private communication, 18.8.03.

7. Cornwall (arrival)

1. Christine Rhone, 'The Nun and the Alchemist of Lamorna Cove', *The Fountain* (issue details unknown). Summary description of Monica's life and books is given in this article. *I Leap Over the Wall* was published in 1949, which dates Ithell's visit to a year or two earlier when the book was only in manuscript form. It has since become available as a series of audio tapes.

2. Peter Owen, private communication, 21.8.02.

3. Robert Hunt, 'The Fairy Fair in Germoe, Bal Lane' in *Popular Romances of the West of England*, p.97.

4. *Assisi* (Dublin), the *Canadian Register*, *Southern Cross* (S. Africa), the *Advocate* (Australia), and others.

5. Simon Buxton, private communication, 18.8.03.

8. Cornwall (activities 1959-1971)

1. *op. cit.*, ch.3, note 21.

2. *op. cit.*, ch.3, note 20.

3. *Tagesbericht/Feuilleton* (Sept.25th, 1969, Berlin).

4. Ithell Colquhoun, 'Paintings, Collages and Drawings', Exeter Museums Publication No.69.

5. 'Kurt Schwitters en Angleterre', *Fantasmagie* (Bruxelles), No.29, Feb., 1971; 'Aperçu sur l'Origine du Collage', No.31, Dec. 1971.

6. Eirenaeus Philalethes (pseudon. 1668), *Tres Tractatus de Metallorum Transmutatione* . . .

7. For example (a) Sir George Ripley's Wheel which is a mandala including twelve concentric spheres said to contain 'all the secrets of the Treatise both great and small', i.e. both the complete *Opus* and the Little Work or set of operations confined to a few stages; (b) Engraving illustrations to the Twelve Keys of Basil Valentine. Both are in Johannes Fabricius (1994), *Alchemy*, Diamond Books, London, which gives references to the original sources. Pages 199 and 234 refer, respectively. Valentine was a legendary Benedictine monk, and may not have been the author of the acompanying text. Samuel Norton also shows twelve stages, to be seen in Jung's *Psychology and Alchemy*, p.229.

8. *Alchemy*, *op. cit.*, p.165.
9. Ithell Colquhoun (1943), 'The Water Stone of the Wise' in *New Road 1943*.

10. Simon Buxton, private communication, re a correspondence, 3.9.03. Tamara, in the States, had become vitally interested in the details of

the Golden Dawn system after reading the four volumes by Israel Regardie. She graduated from personal rituals in the bedroom of her NewYork apartment to the formation of her own group operating in a room set aside as a temple. Following instructions from an entity 'Raphael' via the ouija board and later by scrying by a mediumistic member in the fashion of Dr Dee's colleague Kelley, a voluminous text of 500 pages for temple working was built up. Dissatisfied with the aridity of the American occult environment and encouraged by messages via the medium, which also included an instruction to make G.D. contacts in England, she pursued various links, among whom were Ross Nichols and Ithell, and possibly Dr. MacGregor Reid, Chief of the Druid Order. In 1963 she moved to England to operate this new Order of the Pyramid and the Sphinx from Hampstead. For a long time, until her resignation, Ithell held office in Tamara's Order, which was Enochian in character. Direct contact by this date with offshoots of long-dissolved GD temples faithful to Mathers can probably be ruled out, although dissolution itself would have created many independent operators with GD training and interests which may have been passed on; apart from which Israel Regardie's 4-volume work on the Golden Dawn (1936-40) revealing details of Inner Order workings would have added adherents internationally. It was much too late to do other than dip into this 'soup' of arcane-minded enthusiasts, many of course using the system, now virtually in the public domain. Direct remnants of the original Order would have vanished. It is not known what specific contacts were made by Tamara, bar Druid-Order and Co-Masonic sources. Perhaps the Enochian bias was its own justification. Regarding the Druid Order (subtitled the British Circle of the Universal Bond), there seems a reference to Mathers as engaged in interests of the Universal Bond at one time, in *Pendragon*, mentioned in *Sword of Wisdom* ; at one time the Order had a triple grading system as in the GD.

11. Timothy d'Arch Smith (2003) *The Times Deceas'd: the Rare Book Department of the Times Bookshop in the 1960s.* Stone Trough Books, York, pp. 85-95.

12-3. Simon Buxton, private communications, 3.9.03.

14. Her image was preserved by the Cornish painter John Opie before he achieved fame in London society. Dr. John Wolcot, alias 'Peter Pindar' the satiric poet, who discovered and sponsored Opie's talents wrote of her at Mousehole:

. . . birthplace of old Doll Pentreath,
The last who jabbered Cornish - so says Daines,

Who bat like haunted ruins, lane and heath,
With Will-o'Wisp, to brighten up his brains.
Daines Barrington was the local antiquary.

15. Tim Saunders (ed.) (1999) *The Wheel – an Anthology of Modern Poetry in Cornish, 1850-1980.* Francis Boutle, London. This includes a history of the Cornish revival.

16. Ithell Colquhoun, 'Cornish Earth', *The Cornish Review*, No.18, Sept. 1971.

17. Ithell Colquhoun, 'The Interlace', *Quest*, No.1, March 1970.

9. Cornwall (activities post-1971)

1. Letter with chart 31.3.73 from Bobbie Gray. Simon Buxton, private communication, 18.8.03. The wife of William Gray who played a valuable part in reviving western esoteric tradition, whose many books include *Ladder of Lights: a Step by Step Guide to the Tree of Life and the Four Worlds of the Qabalists, including the Angelic and Archangelic Realms*; and *Two Themes of the Western Inner Way.* His last book was *Evoking the Primal Goddess: Discovery of the Eternal Feminine Within.*

2. Ithell Colquhoun, 'Frontiers of Belief', *Man, Myth and Magic*, No.80, pp. 2257-8.

3. Ithell Colquhoun, 'Bergie and Zan', *Prediction*, Jan. 1971, pp. 24-6.

4. Sir Edward Bulwer-Lytton (1842), *Zanoni.* An occult thriller.

5. Simon Buxton, private communication, 3.9.03. The new Regardie/Wang deck was published by Stuart R. Kaplan in 1977. Wang provided a guide to be studied with the deck (*An Introduction to the Golden Dawn Tarot*, published by Samuel Weiser.)

6. Ithell Colquhoun, 'Notes on Automatism', *Melmoth*, c.1981. (After *Melmoth the Wanderer.* A gothic novel (c.1820s) by Charles Robert Maturin. Having made a pact with the Devil, Melmoth wanders the globe seeking for someone to take it on and release him to a natural death.)

7. Frederick Bligh Bond (1918), *The Gate of Remembrance*, 'On Automatism', Blackwell, Oxford, p.24.

8. Hayward Gallery (1978), 'Dada and Surrealism Reviewed'.

10. Poetry

1. Ithell Colquhoun (1973), *Grimoire of the Entangled Thicket*, The Chariot Poets, No.4, Ore Publications, Stevenage. Cover illustration, 'Sea-Anemone'. Drawings and Poems.

2. Ithell Colquhoun (1983), *Osmazone*, Dunganon, Örkeljunga, Sweden. Cover

illustration, *The Pine Family*. Poems, prose.

3. The excellence and beauty of this sequence was judged to overweigh the need in a biography of a degree of respect for personal feelings not apparently released for publication. However, it is impersonal so far as any second person remains unstated and the MS is undated. As the pages (copied from Tate Gallery Archive (TGA 929) originals) were not numbered and lacked obvious order in one or two places, the version given here was order-edited, retaining all available verse blocks. Indentation of lines was faithfully reproduced, as was verse spacing so far as could be interpreted.

4. Ithell Colquhoun, 'Incantations', *Transformaction*, No.4, 1971, pp. 20-1; 'The Chain Poem', No.5, 1973, pp. 22-3.

5. Line 10 may refer to the circumstances of the painting *The Man in the Doorway* referred to earlier in ch.3. Damiana is a professionally unproven aphrodisiac, supposedly testerogenic. The herb is found in California, the Caribbean and Namibia. This poem was eventually published in *Ozmazone.*

6. *Ore* 12, 1968; *Ore* 15, 1971, Stevenage. In 'Here' some landmarks may be perceived - the furthest 'Land's End' point, the peninsular 'breast' of Cornwall, the Scillies, 27 miles west (or 28 as some travel brochures have it).

7. See Winifred M. Letts (1932), *Saint Patrick the Travelling Man : The Story of his Life and Wanderings*, Nicholson and Watson, London. She quotes a poem in the *Book of Leinster* in her ch.VI - 'Patrick Destroys Crom Cruach'. Cromm was 'made of gold' and the twelve ringing stones were 'Four times three stone idols'. St. Patrick came striding into the circle but before his crozier touched Crom, it fell on to its side.

8. A corpse transmuted to a sword in Ithell's poem is relevant to her comments in *Sword of Wisdom* (pp. 270-1) on some writing of Gerard Heym, founder-member of the Society for the Study of Alchemy and Early Chemistry, and of his journal, *Ambix*. 'His Introduction to the French translation of Gustav Meyrink's novel, *Le Dominicain Blanc* (1963) shows his insight into the theory of Taoist alchemy, traceable to China in the sixth century B.C., with especial reference to the tradition that a Sword is found materialised in the coffin of an adept whose corpse has been transmuted by the Elixir into a Body of Light.' No doubt this is the source which inspired the poem.

9. Robert Graves (1948), *The White Goddess*, Faber, London.

10. Shirley Toulson (1993), *The Celtic Year*, Element Books, Dorset.

11. Tony Pusey was prominent in the organisation of the group 'Melmoth' and the editor of the first issue of *Melmoth*, its literary vehicle, in 1980. The magazine was influential and helped to maintain the impetus in surrealistic art and writing. Three of Ithell's poems appeared in *Melmoth* No.2: ('My Star', 'Leaf of Grace', 'Question & Answer Foursome'). And in about 1983, from Sweden, Pusey published *Ozmazone* for her. The title word had been used contextually by J.K. Huysman : '. . . le suc concret, l'osmazone de la litterature, l'huile essentielle de l'art.' The 'guts', 'meat' or essential juice of the matter is intended. Culinarily, with slightly different spelling, it is a broth extracted from meat, responsible for its typical flavour.

12. This delightful prose poem might have been published in one of the journals mentioned earlier - probably the *Scillonian*. St. Warna was also the subject for two 1947 art works by Ithell (*Santa Warna's Wishing Well*, *Santa Warna Lands.*) 'The Old Man of Gugh'is a monolith on St. Agnes, described in *Meyn Mamvro* (No.47, p.17) in an article 'Scillonian Stone Rows on Gugh: Smoke and Mirrors' as a 'thin leaning slab of granite, very elegant in side view, standing 2.4 m tall'.

13. Poems and prose-poems are given as follows, alphabetically by title (quotation marks omitted) : B = this biography, CP = Child poems, G = *Grimoire*, OR = *Ore*, OS = *Osmazone*, PP = Prose-poem, SOS = 'Songs for Oriental Settings' (none believed published), SW = *Sword of Wisdom*, V= *Veins of Gold* (*Ore* 1954-1995, Univ. Salzburg). The 'Intelligence' poems which were grouped under 'The Decad of Intelligence' are on a well-known sequence of ten magical images used for meditation and corresponding to the ten sephiroth. Some are missing. None are believed published. Of the prose-poems, some were published in periodicals already mentioned in this chapter, but specifically which is not known. The wishing-well in 'The Myth of Santa Warna' was a subject of a 1947 painting *Santa Warna's Wishing Well*, and `Gods of the Cardinal Points' can be linked with a 1940 work *Cardinal Points* (see Appendix IIA).
Acrostic; I. Admirable or Hidden Intelligence; Aged Four; Aged Five; Aged Six; Aged Seven; Aged Eight; Aged Nine; Aged Ten; Aged Eleven; Anatomy of Delight; The Archangels; Between Lives; Calling Names (OS); Cardinal Points; IV. Cohesive or Receptacular Intelligence; Confidential Service (OS); Cyrnos; Dance of the Figure Cousins (B,OS); Diagrams of Love (B); Dissolution; Duir (G,OR); During an Air-Raid Alarm (PP); Eclogue; Elegy on the Hermetic Order of the Golden Dawn (SW); Elemental Weapons; Epitaph; Fall; Fearn – alder (OR,V); Fifth or Twenty-Fifth?; First Light; Flora's Holiday; The Four Degrees; The Friendship of the Heart; Funk for a Blues Singer; Gods of the

Cardinal Points; The Golden Horn (SOS); He Reasons with Himself; The Head That is Not; Here (B,OR); Hymn to the Sun; Hypnagogic Interior (OS), I See; II. Illuminating Intelligence; Imbolc (B,G); Indian Love-Lyric (SOS); Inspiration; Jingle; Lac Virginis; The Lamia; Last Appearance (OS); Leaf of Grace; Living Boy (B,OS); The Long Strand; Lost Horus (OS); Love Charm (B,OS); May-Month; Mirror of Miracles; Moment of Inertia; Morning Star; Mortificatio (PP); Moyslaght (B,OR) ; Muin (B,G); My Star; The Myth of Santa Warna (B,PP); Nature Notes (PP); Neptune in the House of Death; Nion - ash (G); Night Blossom Island (PP); VII. Occult Intelligence; Ode to the Philosophical Mercury (OS); On the Portrait of Deo Duce Comite Ferro (B,SW) or On the Portrait of S'Rioghail Mo Dhream (OR,V); Patroness of Wreckers (B,PP); The Piskey; Psalm (SOS); Punch; IX. Pure or Clear Intelligence; Question & Answer Threesome (OS) (chain-poem - one of three poets); Question & Answer Foursome - (chain poem - one of four poets); Radha; V. Radical Intelligence; Reggae; Riddle (OS); Roads of the Moon (PP); Ruis (G,OR); Rune; St. Merri (OS); III. Sanctifying Intelligence; Sent Away (B); Serenade and Sequel (SOS); Shot from a Scientific Film; Song of the Chalice Bearer – Saille (OR); Song of Ceridwen; Song of the Drop of Blood (OS); Spring Day; Sputum Lunae; Straif (G); Stretch Out; Sulphur; Swannenbrunn (OR); Tradition (SOS); Translated from the Galvanese (OS); The Twenty-Ninth Meditation; Uath – hawthorn (OR,V); Ura (G); Villa 'Gioia dei Rossi' (destroyed in the fighting near Formia, 1944) (PP); The Visit; Warning; Winter of Yew (G); Wishing-Well (PP).

11. Epilogue

1. Ithell Colquhoun, 'Letters', *The Oxford Art Journal*, July 1981, p.65.

2. Dawn Ades, 'Notes on Two Women Surrealist Painters : Eileen Agar and Ithell Colquhoun', *The Oxford Art Journal*, April 1980, pp.36-42.

3. Jonathan Blond, Introduction to catalogue for the 'British Women Surrealists' exhibition, Oct.16th-Nov.16th, 1985, Blond Fine Art, London.

4. Jennifer Mundy, ed. (2001), *Surrealism : Desire Unbound*, Tate Publishing, London, 351 pp. This includes 296 illustrations and chapters by Jennifer Mundy, David Lomas, Julia Kelly, Katharine Conley, Vincent Gille, Dawn Ades and others.

5. 'The Zodiac and the Flashing Colours', *Hermetic Journal*, No.4, 1979, pp.5-7; 'Colour and the Two Sigils', *Hermetic Journal*, No.4, 1979, pp.8-9; 'Memoir of E.J.L. Garstin', *Hermetic Journal*, No.6, 1979, pp.11-14; 'Notes on the Colouring of the Homer's Golden

Chain Diagram', *Hermetic Journal*, No.6, pp.15-17.

6. Foreword by Ithell Colquhoun to *Rosie Crucian Secrets of John Dee* (1985), ed. E.J. Langford Garstin, Aquarian Press, Wellingborough.

7. *Meyn Mamvro* – 'Stones of our Motherland'. Ed. Cheryl Saffron. It is now past its 47th issue, and reflects Ithell's passions for ancient Cornwall, with articles on earth energies, ancient stones, sacred sites, legends and folklore.

Notes to Appendix IIA

1929. ***Judith Showing the Head of Holofernes***. The widowed Judith visited the Assyrian general Holofernes who was besieging the Israelites, pretending to be a traitor. He tried to seduce her, but she cut off his head when he was in a drunken sleep. See also note 3, ch.3.

1930. ***Judgement of Paris***. A mythological episode leading to the Trojan war, with the Trojan Prince, Paris. Troy was destroyed in about 1230-1180 BC, possibly the basis for the legend, involving the abduction of Helen, Queen of Sparta by Paris and subsequent war between the Greeks and Troy. See also Homer's *Iliad.* In 1966, Ithell Colquhoun constructed a Merz collage on the same subject.

1931. *Death of Lucretia*. Legendary subject (6th century BC) of Shakespeare's *Rape of Lucrece.* Raped by Sextus Tarquinius, Lucretia plunges a knife into her heart after making others swear to expel the Tarquins.

1931. *Marlowe's Faust*. On the Faustian theme of the best of Christopher Marlowe's plays - *Dr. Faustus*, apparently showing a stage scene. A large canvas of 4 x 3 ft.

1933. *Elektra Mangoletsi (Ikon), Eliah Mangoletsi (Ikon).* National Portrait Gallery acquisition D4409 is a 1933 pencil drawing of Ithell Colquhoun by Elektra (1908-93), who was a contemporary Slade student. It was given to the NPG by Elektra's husband on her death. The relationship of Eliah to Elektra is unknown.

1933. *Madeleine in her Coffin*. Roderick and Madeleine are brother and sister in Poe's horror story of the 'Fall of the House of Usher', suffering from a mysterious illness. Madeleine dies, and her coffin is placed in a vault within the wall of the mansion. She leaves her coffin and, vampire-like, falls upon Roderick and kills him. Ithell Colquhoun's creative art includes at least two other works with vampires as subjects.

1935. *Humfry Gilbert Garth Payne*. Director of the British Archeological School in Athens with whom Ithell Colquhoun struck up a close friendship when there studying and painting. Her *Greek Woman* and *Cartoon for Feroze Mehta*, each completed in 1932, indicate the period. But it was not until 1935 that the oil painting of Payne was done, preceded by the ink and watercolour of 1934. Each was obtained by the National Portrait

Gallery. Payne died in his mid-thirties - in 1936. He married Dilys Powell, the film critic.

1936. ***Datura.*** All species of *Datura* are leafy green plants with bright fragrant pink-to-white flowers. *D. inoxia* is known as the Devil's Weed.

1936. ***Lifeboat, Corsica.*** Reflects the period when Ithell Colquhoun was photographed topless on the beach there, illustrated later in the *London Bulletin.* Other Corsican subjects were *Doorway, Corsica* ; *Gateway,Corsica* ; *Lifeboat,Corsica* in this year; and there were others in succeeding years.

1938. ***Death's Head and Foot.*** This object was carved chalk, decorated with tempera.

1938. ***Heart.*** Also carved chalk, decorated with tempera.

1938. ***Scylla***. This painting can be seen on the Tate Gallery website.

1940. ***Bronze Figure in the Desert***. Possibly relevant to one or more visits which Ithell made to Egypt, as maybe were *Middle East* and *The Dunes* of this year.

1940. ***Dance of the Nine Maidens.*** This 'Nine Maidens' was a pre-historically important circle of stones at Boscawen, not to be confused with the 'Merry Maidens' in Buryan parish. The latter name, however, derives from the legend no doubt put about by early Christians, that the stones represented village girls who thoughtlessly danced on the Sabbath, instead of attending vespers, and were transfixed by a flash of lightning, turned to stone. The Boscawen circle was reputedly the site of one of the three *Gorsedds* of Britain in a Welsh triad. (John Michell (1974*), The Old Stones of Land's End*, Garnstone Press, London; and (1973), *The View over Atlantis*, Sphere Books, London.)

1940. ***The Thirteen Streams of Magnificent Oil.*** In 1970, Ithell Colquhoun contributed an article to *Quest*, in which she posits thirteen openings in the female body, which could be adapted to receive spiritual influence from the thirteen strands in the beard of the Macroprosopus (a well-known magical image useful for meditation). This work, though unseen, may have been based on the above concepts.

1943. ***Empedocles.*** Greek philosopher (c.490-30 B.C.) His epic poem about Nature in three books was grounded on the assumption of world formation from four unchangeable elements (the usual Fire, Earth, Air, Water) which were separated by Hate but unified by Love. Empedocles' system had some common features with that of Pythagoras. There is a story of him jumping into the crater of Mount Etna, so that his sudden disappearance might make others believe that he was a god. However, the volcanic eruptions flung up his shoes, revealing the real truth of the matter.

1945. ***Dreaming Leaps : in Homage to Sonia***

Araquistain. Compare this surrealist mode of portraying this falling body of the suicide with the not dissimilar *The Waterfall* (Arshile Gorky, c.1943) and *La Chute des Roches* (André Masson, 1950).

1946. ***Gorgon.*** There were three Gorgons in Greek mythology, with serpent hair and often wings and enormous teeth. Two were immortal, the third, Medusa, being mortal. The legend of Medusa's ability to turn to stone anyone who looked at her directly, is well known. To terrify enemies the Greeks carved Gorgon-type heads on shields, breastplates, walls and gates.

1947. ***Santa Warna's Wishing Well.*** St. Warna was the patron saint of St. Agnes and her name is associated with a well there. She presided over wrecks. See also Ithell's prose poem on Santa Warna and note 12 to ch. 11. There was also an undated drawing exhibited in 1947 at the Mayor Gallery - *Santa Warna Land.*

1947/1950. ***Linked Islands (I/II).*** The eastern area of St.Agnes in the Scillies (S.W. of St.Mary's) is linked to a companion islet of Gugh at low tide. Following Ithell's poem 'The Myth of Santa Warna', the reader will see the reference to the monolith, the 'Old Man of Gugh'.

1950. ***Giantesses Undressing to Bathe.*** This canvas is a good example of 'psychic automatism', or,more specifically as applied to surrealist painting – 'psychomorphology', the recovery of innate imagery in the unconscious mind which is sparked off by a random 'stain' in the first stage of an automatic process. In this case the recovery was via a 'found object', viz., a cracked plaster wall, following the application of tracing paper to secure the pattern. The unlikely result was this 1950 painting, which took the course of figurative processes recalled from the mind's depths. Similarly Ithell's 1949 *Autumnal Equinox* resulted from being inspired by the artificial wood-graining of a door. (See 'Children of the Mantic Stain', *Athene*, May 1952, p.30.)

1952. ***Grotto of the Sun and Moon.*** This interesting painting was the result of a dream, described in ch.6.

1952. ***Atomic Psychosis.*** This appears to relate to the atomic bombs dropped on Hiroshima and Nagasaki on Aug. 6th and 9th, 1945, respectively, although 7 years earlier.

1960. ***World Moth.*** Ithell was fascinated by moths and butterflies. The Crow-Moth and the Moon-Moth occur in the author's *Goose of Hermogenes* (pp. 16-17): the female narrator says 'I was always a little afraid of the Crow-Moth. Did it mean death? and the Moon-Moth, those insubstantial cravings after immortality?'

From the prose-poem 'Nature Notes': 'Spring butterflies are very faithful, monogamous almost; winter has cooled them. They respect a colour bar, or are at least xenophobe; in experimental mood a tortoiseshell may flirt with a peacock . . . They are in another sphere, they find huge impalpable forms, strange forces; space becomes more real than time'.

In the *Hampstead Express* report of Aug. 20th, 1948, she volunteered information about a swallow-tailed moth in her Parkhill Road house: 'It has not been here long enough' . . . 'so it has not been given a name.'

1962. *Temptation of St. Anthony.* The subject of this surrealistic watercolour, shown the following year in 'Cornish Experiment' by the Royal Watercolour Society, was a popular one for painters. The legend relates that all temptations by Satan unavailed to deter Anthony, the 3rd to 4th century desert hermit, from the ascetic holy life. There were, for example, demonaic scenes by Breughel; and Salvator Rosa's giant demon astride the saint who defends himself with the Cross. There are the usual fabulous claims, such as that on his death there fell no rain from heaven for three years. He was regarded as the patriarch of monks, to be remembered on Jan. 17th.

1966. *Khamsin.* The subject for this Merz collage, the Khamsin, is a hot, dry, southerly wind which prevails in Egypt and in the deserts of Africa, from the middle of March until the first week in May.

1971. *Serapis.* The Ptolemaic form of Apis, the Egyptian lord of the underworld. Identified with Hades by the Greeks. Also a god of healing.

1972. *Delius' Irmelin*. Danish song set to music by Frederick Delius: 'There was a king in days of old / many treasures rare he owned / he knew his daughter Irmelin / of all to be the rarest one / Irmelin rose, Irmelin sun / Irmelin loveliest of them all.'

Undated artwork excluding 1936 exhibitions at Cheltenham and London

Tekke Um Haram, Tekke of Um Haram (II). Tekke is an ancient Turkoman weave used in rugs and chair upholstery. Ramisa Um Haram was a married Bedouin woman who was the companion of Mohammed the Prophet. The titles may refer to her carpet or prayer-rug of Tekke design; or to tribal connections, or to Um Haram herself. The drawings have not been seen and therefore a definite reference cannot be posited. 'Um' means 'Mother of'.

Undated artwork in 1936 exhibition at Cheltenham

The Bhikku Ananda. Referring to Alan Bennett (1872-1923), who initially was a member of the main London temple of the Golden Dawn. Ithell Colquhoun provides a few pages of biography in *Sword of Wisdom.* He left England, settled in Burma for a time, established an international Buddhist Society. Returning to England he founded the Buddhist Lodge which became the Buddhist Society here.

Notes to Appendix IIC Unpublished MSS

'My Best Ten Books'. As listed by Ithell Colquhoun with her annotations:

1. *Liber 777* by Aleister Crowley. Indispensable 'prolegomena' to occult study.
2. *The Golden Dawn* by Israel Regardie. An account of the most genuine occult group in Europe in recent times.
3. *The Kabbalah Unveiled* by S.L.MacGregor Mathers. Translation of three important books from the Zohar. Detail of the basic teachings of 2 above.
4. *A Vision* by W.B.Yeats. Based on an automatic text by a couple trained in the Golden Dawn practices.
5. *Myths and Legends of the Celtic Race* by T.W.Rolleston. A Western Pantheon summarised with poetic feeling.
6. *The Hermetic Museum* by A.E.Waite. An anthology of Hermetic imagery.
7. *The Six Centres of the Serpent Power* by Arthur Avalon (Sir John Woodruffe). The basis of Hindoo esotericism.
8. *The Tibetan Book of the Dead* by Evans-Wentz. A text from the School of Buddhism most in accordance with basic occult tradition.
9. *Le Regine* [?] *de la Juanita* by René Guénon. A reminder that the Kali Yoga is still on course.l
10. *The Golem* and other novels by Gustav Meyrink. Each deals with a different aspect of occultism, making those of Charles Williams look cosy.
    [Re Gustav Meyrink (Austrian author 1868-1932), his other novels include *The Angel of the West Window*, *The Green Face*, *The White Dominican*, *The Opal*. E.R.]

Index

D

E

F

G

H

www.ingramcontent.com/pod-product-compliance
Ingram Content Group UK Ltd.
Pitfield, Milton Keynes, MK11 3LW, UK
UKHW050317070325
455909UK00003B/4

9 781869 928988